D0871944

DATE DUE

DEMCO 38-297

THE BOLSHEVIK PARTY IN REVOLUTION

THE BOLSHEVIK PARTY IN REVOLUTION

A Study in Organisational Change

1917–1923

ROBERT SERVICE

First published 1979 by
THE MACMILLAN PRESS LTD
London and Basingstoke
Associated companies in Delhi
Dublin Hong Kong Johannesburg Lagos
Melbourne New York Singapore Tokyo

Photoset in Great Britain by
Bristol Typesetting Co Ltd, Bristol
and printed by Billings & Sons Ltd,
Guildford, Worcester & London

British Library Cataloguing in Publication Data

Service, Robert
  The Bolshevik party in revolution
  1. Rossiĭskaía sotsial-demokraticheskaía rabochaía
  (Bol'sheviki)—History
  I. Title
  329.9´47   HN6598.S6

ISBN 0-333-23740-4

TO MY PARENTS

Contents

Acknowledgements   viii

Introduction   1

1 The Tides of Revolution   11
  (1861–1917)

2 The Bolsheviks Advance   37
  (February 1917–October 1917)

3 Victory in Defeat   63
  (November 1917–May 1918)

4 The Alarm is Sounded   85
  (June 1918–March 1919)

5 The Battle is Won   112
  (April 1919–March 1920)

6 Defeat in Victory   134
  (April 1920–March 1921)

7 The Bolsheviks Retreat   159
  (March 1921–December 1922)

8 The Winds of Bureaucracy   185
  (January 1923–January 1924)

Conclusions   200

Maps   214

Notes and References   217

Index   239

Acknowledgements

The relief felt in dispatching this manuscript to the publishers is equalled only by the sense of gratitude owed to the friends who have helped me to reach such a position. The Russian Studies Department at Keele is an academic microcosm of peaceful coexistence. Genia Lampert, the late Katia Lampert, Joe Andrew, Roger Bartlett, Chris Pike and Valentina Polukhina have offered encouragement and advice on a broad spectrum of matters Russian and Soviet. Joe and Roger took comradely solidarity to the point of reading the draft chapters. I should also like to thank Charles Duval, Roger Pethybridge and Rick Twyman for their assistance in tackling particular problems which would otherwise have eluded me. And, collectively, the delegates to the Fourth Conference of the Russian Revolution Study Group in January of this year provoked a number of last-minute reformulations. Peter Frank of Essex University has over the years lent his wealth of expertise, energy and enthusiasm to this project. And Adele Biagi, my wife, has edited the book since its first draft, purging its pages of the more horrific (and more ludicrous) excesses of historiographical and typographical deviation.

All remaining distortions and falsifications are my own.

R.J.S.

Keele
Easter Saturday 1978

Introduction

This is a history of the Bolsheviks and their organisational development in the early era of the Soviet state. It is not an act of homage to certain leaders or factions. Nor is it an exercise in demonology. Its collective subject is the Bolshevik party as a political and social whole, as a total organisation in pursuit of revolutionary change in the former Russian empire. Its unifying theme is an internal metamorphosis. The Bolsheviks passed through a momentous transformation, organisationally as well as politically, within half a dozen years of seizing power through the October Revolution. Attitudes and behaviour which had seemed so deeply embedded in the party of 1917 were to disappear forever by 1923. The shockwaves of the process spread out far beyond the limits of the period and the boundaries of the Soviet Union. The following chapters seek to describe and explain what happened.

To this day the Bolshevik past attracts the political scientist and the historian like a great magnet. It offers the world's first example of a political party taking hold of the reins of government in the name of a socialist programme. Until 1917 the Bolsheviks had been all but unknown outside the Russian empire. They started out in 1903 as the more radical of the two main wings of the Russian Marxist movement. It was they who in 1905, a year of travail for the Romanov autocracy, helped to lead an armed uprising in Moscow; and it was they who in 1914, shortly before the outbreak of the First World War, had headed the upsurge of strikes and demonstrations which again shook the monarchy. The body politic never fully recovered from its battering and was finally felled in the February Revolution of 1917. Not that the Bolsheviks were alone in working amid the urban crowds which compelled the emperor's resignation. But what set them apart from most other socialist groups in the country was their subsequent refusal to give support to the newly established Provisional Government, dominated as it was by liberal politicians. In April the Bolshevik party proclaimed its commitment to bringing about a further revolution, a socialist revolution which might spark off a conflagration which would consume the capitalist system all over the globe. The tide of economic ruin, social dislocation and political discontent surged onward. The factory labour force wanted better conditions of life and work, the peasantry desired the possession of all agricultural land, and the soldier conscripts yearned for the day of demobilisation. Throughout the country these groups created a network of elective institutions, known as 'soviets' or councils, to represent and defend their sectional interests. In October 1917 the Bolsheviks, having at last gained a majority in them, ousted the Provisional Government by force and set up their own administration.

The steep trajectory of this rise to power contrasts sharply with the deep undulations of the party's political fortunes in its early years in government. The revolutions in Europe, in which so much hope had been reposed, failed to occur. At home the same economic and social problems that enabled the Bolsheviks to advance their cause before the October Revolution shortly turned out to be less tractable than they had supposed. Even industrial workers showed signs of political disillusionment. Despite its many achievements, the Soviet government confronted a profound crisis in midsummer 1918. Ironically, it was the invasion of central Russia at that moment by counter-revolutionary armies which facilitated its survival. Workers volunteered to join the nascent Red Army; labour discipline was reimposed in the factories; political order was introduced in town and countryside. The Civil War, which lasted until 1920, was a hard-fought affair and left society exhausted and bled white. And yet the Bolshevik leaders, still desirous of an expansion of the revolution westwards, felt confident enough to hurl the victorious regiments of the Red Army into Poland. The domestic troubles of 1918, which had been postponed by the Civil War, re-emerged. Industrial strikes, rural revolts and a naval mutiny convulsed the government. Nothing short of concessions to private enterprise could stave off prolonged turmoil. In 1921 it was decided to introduce a New Economic Policy. Numerous small factories were denationalised and the peasantry was again permitted to trade its grain on the open market. The government, in its quest for capital investment, tried to persuade foreign firms to take out leases in enterprises in the Soviet republic. By 1923 most hopes of a rapid advance to a fully socialist society had reluctantly been laid aside. Such was the transformation of Bolshevik policies since the October Revolution.

No less remarkable were the changes which had occurred in party life. In 1917 the Bolsheviks had still been coping with the initial problems of creating a mass political party. To their ranks they were admitting, with scarcely any 'vetting' arrangements, thousands upon thousands of new members—mostly persons who were working-class by occupation, skilled or unskilled. Territorially the Bolsheviks continued to be based predominantly in towns and industrial settlements (though their strength also increased in the garrisons and on the war fronts in the same year). The process of organisational separation from other Marxist groupings was somewhat sluggish: as late as midsummer it was reported that 'joint committees' were a widespread phenomenon. Nor was there a well-established system of subordination and discipline along the hierarchical chain of executive bodies stretching from the Central Committee at the apex to the primary 'cells' at the base. Tension and conflict were the rule, not the exception. If anything, committees tended to be called to account from below rather than from above. Rank-and-file members and lower activists could not only make their views known at the general open meetings but also re-elect their representatives at frequent intervals. The committees themselves managed, by and large, to supervise and control their own officials. Most decisions of importance were preceded by a discussion of some kind; few leaders succeeded in acting in opposition to the viewpoint of their committee colleagues over a lengthy period.

An internal metamorphosis had happened by 1923. Certainly the Bolsheviks remained a mass political party; but nearly all the other salient features of party life in earlier days had become greatly altered or removed altogether. 'Vetting' arrangements now accompanied the efforts to recruit new members and, to an increasing extent, were being applied to persons who already belonged to the party. Only a minority of Bolsheviks were currently employed in jobs involving manual labour. The network of Bolshevik groups had come to include most small townships and a growing number of rural areas. Subordination to higher authority was the paramount characteristic of the party's organisational condition. Disciplinary sanctions were vigorously invoked as a matter of daily habit, almost as a reflex action in cases of disobedience. It was still claimed that committees were elected from below; but in reality they were appointed from above and had been for a year or more. There was a strong movement away from collective processes of deliberation. A single official, selected and imposed by a higher body, typically directed the affairs of his local committee. The Central Committee too was affected by the trend to the extent that crucial issues of grand policy and administration were now usually handled by its inner subcommittees, the Politburo and the Orgburo. Thus the democratic anarchism of the months after the February Revolution had given way to the strict centralism of the New Economic Policy.

Many contemporary observers were so bewildered by this turnabout that they denied that there was any link between the party of 1917 and the party of 1923. They were wrong. No magical change had taken place; the principles of cause and effect had not suddenly been suspended. Other onlookers, less ready to accept that a fundamental transformation had occurred, failed to see what all the fuss was about. They too were incorrect, blinded as they were by their prejudices about the nature of early Bolshevism. It was left to the few commentators managing to retain a degree of discernment to attempt the first substantial analyses of what had happened inside the Bolshevik party. Undoubtedly the most perceptive of them were writers who themselves participated in one or other section of the Russian Marxist movement. Some were Bolsheviks, others were not. All of them were close enough to the situations and events they described to be able to attain a level of observation and commentary so dismally absent from the many rival accounts.

Traditionally there have been two main kinds of approach to the theme of the internal metamorphosis. The first lays the blame squarely upon the Bolsheviks themselves; the second seeks an explanation, and sometimes an excuse too, in the pressure of 'external' circumstances largely beyond the party's control. The most penetrating analyses stressing the role of free will were composed by non-Bolsheviks such as Yuli Martov, Stanislav Ivanovich, Fyodor Dan and Rafail Abramowitch. These four have exercised a profound influence over later generations of writers outside the Soviet Union. All highlighted the factor of personality, giving emphasis to Lenin as the founder of the Bolshevik faction in 1903 and to Stalin as the leading party administrator from the early 1920s onwards. They also drew attention to certain factional divisions among the Bolsheviks which could be traced back to 1917 and beyond. The American historian Robert Daniels has recently taken up this theme in detail. The organisational metamorphosis, he has tried to show, was largely the work of a small but tightly knit faction of leaders with an extreme leaning towards authoritarian methods, who out-manoeuvred their rival groups and ousted them from power. A further factor, investigated by Martov in particular, was said to predispose the party to this end: its pre-revolutionary ideology. Ever since 1903, it was argued, the Bolsheviks had displayed a superabundant impatience with the slow rate of change in Russian society, an impatience which was bound sooner or later to transmute itself into a ruthless intolerance of political dissent inside as well as outside the party. Much has also been made of the organisational theory which was elaborated by them before 1917 and which is said to have had a deep and direct impact upon subsequent events. Indeed Ivanovich and Dan were both convinced that well before the February Revolution the Bolsheviks had already travelled a long way along the road to an excessively centralised and disciplined form of party life.

The second kind of approach directs our attention elsewhere. Instead of concentrating upon aspects of free will and human responsibility, it picks out 'objective' circumstances as the great moulder of the party's internal transformation. Lev Trotski, who joined the Bolsheviks in 1917 and quickly rose to prominence in their midst, was the main inspirer of this outlook. Though himself an advocate of radical reform inside the party in 1923, he maintained that the changes which had occurred since the October Revolution were in large measure a reflection of the military, political and economic turmoil which enveloped the Soviet state and society in the same period. Equally important, in his judgement, was the collapse of revolutionary stirrings in the rest of Europe, keeping the Bolsheviks deprived of the political and material support upon which they had counted. To this he added the factor of habituation. Party officials who had grown used to enjoying material privileges in the Civil War and to giving and receiving military-style commands as a matter of routine would be reluctant to alter their habits immediately afterwards. The reinforcement of authoritarian methods was made more probable still, it was claimed, by the lasting effects of the social traditions and political culture which had been encouraged and strengthened under the Romanov autocracy. Thus the pressure of circumstances allegedly cleared the path for the advance of a hierarchy of pen-pushing, back-room party functionaries, by temperament conservative, and revolutionary only by self-acclaim, who were able to thrust aside that more optimistic elite of Bolshevik leaders who had led the party to its victories in the October Revolution and the Civil War. Trotski himself suggested that such an outcome would not neccessarily occur in all other socialist parties which seized power in their own countries; but many other historians have remained unpersuaded by this. E. H. Carr, drawing upon the sociological speculations of Robert Michels and Max Weber, contends that the changes in Bolshevik party life by the mid-1920s were little different from what happens in all large organisational units in modern industrial societies. Nevertheless Trotski and Carr concur that the factors determining the internal metamorphosis lay, for the most part, outside the party's control.

Predictably, not all historians may be categorised so neatly. Boris Souvarine, the French socialist leader and writer, took over as much from Martov's approach as he did from Trotski's. Isaac Deutscher too, while agreeing with most of what Trotski said, felt that factional manoeuvring had still played a part in shaping the party's condition. Yet most scholars outside the Soviet Union have taken a signally less favourable attitude to Bolshevik affairs than Souvarine and Deutscher. Robert Daniels, Leonard Schapiro and Merle Fainsod have produced the major hostile accounts. Each portrays Bolshevik ideology as the original sin and regards Lenin as the greatest sinner of all. Their intellectual debt to socialists such as Martov and Dan is beyond doubt even though they themselves barely disguise their antipathy to socialism as an idea. They wrote their books in the 1950s and early 1960s, and their interpretations reflected the expressly anti-Soviet views widely prevalent in the atmosphere of the Cold War. Since then, unfortunately, Western interest in the general topic of organisational change appears to have waned.

The same is true nowadays for official Soviet historians. Down all the years, from Nikolai Popov's early sketches to the Central Committee's latest multi-volume textbook, they have contrived to affirm that most of the talk about internal transformation was the figment of Trotski's malevolent imagination. Alterations in approved accounts since 1953, when Stalin died, have revolved around the linked problems of the behaviour of Bolshevik oppositionist groups in the 1920s and the role of Stalin. It is now recognised that Trotski and his associates were not agents and spies in the pay of foreign governments; it is now accepted that Stalin was not the model supporter of Lenin that he claimed to be (though there has been some back-pedalling here in the last decade). And so Roy Medvedev, a Soviet historian whose work is nowadays published only outside the USSR, is the only writer to tackle a new interpretation of the topic; but its principal attraction lies in his discussion of the 1930s: his treatment of the organisational changes up to 1923 follows a line not dissimilar from Deutscher's.

There was at least one belief which originally brought together all these historians, regardless of their political affiliations or predilections. This was that the Bolsheviks of 1917 had possessed a centralised, disciplined political party. The beginnings of the myth are traceable to the early 1920s. By then it had started to become official Bolshevik policy to laud hierarchical subordination as a supreme virtue in political life. Consequently party veterans, when writing about times past, were careful to avoid laying themselves open to a charge of having acted in an 'un-Bolshevik' fashion in the months surrounding the October Revolution. The party's outright opponents also had their reasons for swallowing the idea, since it was much easier to explain away the failures of the Provisional Government if it was thought that the Bolsheviks had had at their disposal a political machine of clockwork precision in its capacity to instil blind and fanatical devotion to the cause.

The first signs that the myth was losing its potency appeared in the 1960s. Leonard Schapiro's own work led the way by drawing notice to documentary collections, published not long before in the USSR, which indicated the Central Committee's problems in trying to impose firm leadership in 1917. Other scholars went still further. John Keep sketched the anarchical relations between party bodies at each level of the hierarchical structure. T. H. Rigby, in a work about rank-and-file members over the entire Soviet epoch, collected a great deal of information about the early period. Alfred Dressler revealed the protracted process whereby the Bolsheviks disengaged themselves from the remainder of the Russian Marxist movement and formed themselves into a fully separate party. Roger Pethybridge examined the huge difficulties of transport and communications facing party leaders who wished to supervise their local supporters' activity at that time. Ronald Suny, David Longley and Tsuyoshi Hasegawa cast fresh light on the springs of Bolshevik action by means of carefully researched studies of particular localities. Such investigations have greatly altered the way we have come to think about the October Revolution.

They also provoke an intriguing question: if the Bolsheviks were not after all a centralised, disciplined party in 1917, how are we now to explain the ensuing course of their internal development? It has been conventional to see the Bolsheviks through the prism of a simple contrast between the Central Committee, or a handful of its leading figures, and the rest of the party. A few studies have been undertaken of various conflicts between Moscow and certain committees in the provinces; but there still exists a need for a general account of the kinds of confrontation, and co-operation for that matter, which occurred at each and every interstice in the hierarchical structure. Only an analysis of the Bolshevik party in all its organisational complexity will suffice. Such an approach confirms, not surprisingly, that central leaders vigorously supported the policy of internal reformation; but it also shows, equally importantly, that local leaders and activists too exercised a vital influence. There were times between 1918 and 1921, indeed, when Lenin and some of his associates lagged somewhat behind a vociferous body of local opinion which urged an extension and reinforcement of the centralising and disciplinary trends already in existence. The immediate motives behind this seemingly idiosyncratic attitude were far from mysterious. Difficulties which had not been so burdensome in 1917 appeared intolerably heavy a year later at the outbreak of the Civil War. Local officials looked for central assistance to solve the enormous problems of keeping in contact with events elsewhere in the country, of acquiring material resources which were locally scarce, and of obtaining experienced, reliable personnel. A centralised, disciplined party was thought to offer the best chance of achieving this. And the central leaders, who in any case desired a greater scale of centralism and discipline, responded positively and seized their opportunity. The organisational transformation sprang from a mixture of central and local demands and requirements.

This is not to belittle the underlying factors also at work, factors which played upon and magnified the demands and requirements just mentioned. It is hard to disagree with sociologists and political scientists who state that nineteenth-century thinkers such as Karl Marx wildly exaggerated the possibilities of sustaining democratic patterns of control and accountability in large organisations in modern industrial societies. The need for a system of swift decision-making, especially in times of rapid change, is bound to lead to results which stifle criticism and diminish influence from below to some extent. On the other hand, Michels and Weber were surely misguided in their belief that the similarities between large organisations must always be overwhelmingly more important than the differences. Internal change is a matter of degree as much as of kind. The Bolshevik party's development within half a dozen years of the October Revolution took a very extreme form such as cannot be explained simply by reference to some universal law of organisational growth.

The kind of approach adopted by Trotski offers fruitful ways of exploring the question of extremity. Domestic upheaval and international isolation could hardly fail to foster a 'siege mentality', encouraging the use of authoritarian methods inside and outside the party. New habits of command, new tastes of privilege became predictably deep-rooted almost as soon as planted. Nor is it surprising that these conditions allowed pre-revolutionary modes of institutional behaviour to float back to the surface of public life. Yet such factors, while being of fundamental significance, do not explain everything. Even if the Civil War had never occurred it is difficult to imagine that circumstances at home would have allowed the party to set about the tasks of social revolution in a peaceable, tranquil fashion. It is even more doubtful that a socialist upheaval in Germany would have given the Soviet state the material succour and political relief expected by the Bolsheviks. And it still remains to be shown why on earth the central and local party leaders did so little to try to counteract both the habits which sprang up in the Civil War and the cultural traditions which re-emerged from the pre-revolutionary past.

Here the approach advocated by Martov and his colleagues is useful. It is true that it invested Lenin, Stalin and the factions headed by them with substantially more of an influence over the party's organisational transformation than they in fact wielded. But Martov was right to say that the Bolsheviks' pre-revolutionary ideology had a profound impact upon post-revolutionary events. He certainly over-stated his case. Bolshevik ideas were neither so uniform nor so unchanging as he claimed. As a consequence he did not even address himself to the question of how it was that the 'optimistic' side of Bolshevik ideology was quickly pushed out of the picture by the 'pessimistic' side after 1917. Nevertheless he hit the mark with his main point, that ever since 1903 the Bolsheviks had displayed a notable reluctance to believe in the creative potential of the Russian working class. Martov also drew attention, in the narrower area of organisational theory, to the connections between the calls for a tightly disciplined party in 1903 and the authoritarian realities of the mid-1920s. Again he over-simplified the issue. Not only did Bolshevik leaders argue that organisational methods should be changed, radically if necessary, to suit circumstances. They also gave it out that the Bolshevik party itself, like its counterparts abroad, would establish party life upon a democratic basis just as soon as the Romanov autocracy had fallen and political persecution had ceased. All this notwithstanding, however, Bolshevik leaders before 1917 were persistently and deeply naive about the dangers of extreme centralisation; they were completely oblivious of the need to build institutional bulwarks against excesses of authoritarianism.

These are the main concerns of the following chapters. A wide variety of historical sources is used: a local party archive (from the provincial town of Smolensk), contemporary party newspapers, official resolutions and proceedings, personal memoirs, and, on occasion, contemporary works of art. They have to be handled with extreme care. They are by the very nature of the subject predominantly of Bolshevik provenance and can seldom be checked against external material. Nearly all Bolshevik sources, moreover, come to us filtered through a mesh of political considerations. And even when the truth of particular episodes and situations is ascertainable it is frequently difficult to say whether they were typical of the party as a whole. Quantitative methods are sometimes applicable but just as often it is the illustrative techniques of the traditional historian which have to be used. So much more spadework needs to be done. Future research on Nizhni or Orekhovo, Tula or Ryazan, is bound to demolish a good few of our assumptions about Bolshevik history. The details are important; but it is hoped that this book will be judged not only on them but also on its general approach and argument. Its conclusions will not be to everyone's liking. This can hardly be avoided (nor is there any good reason to try to avoid it) with a theme which has always been a hornets' nest of political dispute. But in order to escape misleading the reader, I have attempted to make my own bias and predilections as plain as possible and to provide enough information to enable him or her to form an independent opinion.

1 The Tides of Revolution (1861–1917)

The Bolshevik party was born of mixed descent. On one side it traced its origins back to the human miseries of the Russian industrial environment at the turn of the present century; the factories, workshops and mines of St Petersburg, Moscow, Baku, the Donbass and the Urals were its birthplace. It was bred in a tradition, common to so many Russian revolutionaries in previous generations, which nourished the hope that economic 'backwardness' would not constitute an insuperable barrier to fast progress to a socialist society. On the other side it was directly related to forms of opposition and revolt which had sprung up in central and western Europe in the nineteenth century. It looked to Marx and Engels for ideological guidance and, until the First World War, preserved fraternal connections with the German Social-Democratic Party. In thought and action it was the product of a dynamic combination which posed a potentially fundamental threat to the political structure and social system of the Russian empire.

Socialism as an idea took shape in the last century. Its vision was of a future society free from every vestige of political inequality and economic oppression. Conservatives and reactionaries throughout the world were its earliest enemies, but liberals and anarchists too drew its fire. Liberals were criticised for their defence of the principles of private property and individualism. No worker in the factory, no peasant in the fields could ever be truly 'free', it was pointed out, until laws were enacted to redistribute society's wealth and goods and until the state intervened directly to protect and foster the collective welfare of all social groups. Anarchists were criticised on the severely practical grounds of their rejection of every kind of government. Their viewpoint, while attractive in its promises of immediate bliss and co-operation, would in fact lead to a chaos which could benefit nobody and might even facilitate the resurgence of counterrevolutionary forces.

Further than that, however, socialists discovered agreement among themselves difficult. They were at odds about which group in society was likely to offer the brightest prospects of achieving socialism. Some turned to the peasantry and upheld its supposedly egalitarian attitudes and customs as the future basis of social harmony; others, with an eye to the economic changes currently under way in many countries, felt that the industrial working class would fill the role more effectively. Strategies of coming to power also gave rise to dispute. There were two main approaches: one was directed towards a quick, violent seizure of the reins of government; a second called for a lengthy, peaceful campaign of preparatory propaganda. Even the question of internal organisation was contentious. Advocates of the need for discipline and control tended to favour a small and exclusive kind of political party; advocates of the need for open debate and discussion by and large preferred a mass party which would attract as many thousands of new members as possible. The socialists of the last century thus confronted the world with a kaleidoscopic variety of plans and proposals.

But this outwardly self-defeating variety was deceptive. Its causes lay in the social, economic and political surroundings in which each group of socialists found itself and to which it had to adapt itself if it wanted to acquire a following. Images of an ideal society based on peasant virtues were taken up most strongly in areas such as southern Italy where the largest segment of the population was still engaged in agriculture; but in countries like Britain, which had already witnessed the consolidation of capitalism as the principal sector of the national economy, the choice between a violent seizure of power and a campaign of peaceful propaganda, as well as between tightly knit and open mass parties, devolved in the main on the level of political and economic concessions granted by the ruling classes of the society in question. Spain's agricultural labourers, who toiled on the vast latifundia of Andalucia, were constantly denied the hope of an improvement of their conditions and so provided fertile soil for small groups of socialists (if they managed to evade arrest) to disseminate their calls for insurrection. But in Germany and France, where electoral reforms had been undertaken and where the middle class was persuaded to increase workmen's wages as the profits from foreign trade continued to rise, the chances of non-violent change seemed strong and it was the mass socialist movements proclaiming such a message which received most support.

The Russian empire of the mid-nineteenth century was largely an agricultural society and was ruled by an absolutist monarch. Not unexpectedly, the intellectuals who first took up the cause of socialism looked mainly to the rural areas for their following. They called themselves populists (or 'narodniki'). For them the peasant commune represented an ideal society in miniature and furnished a model for the future government of the country. The populists' reaction to the imperial legislation of 1861 liberating the peasantry from its semi-feudal ties of a personal nature to the landholding gentry was uniformly negative. It was pointed out that, so far from being better off, peasant households possessed even less cultivable land than hitherto and that they now had to endure the additional burden of 'redemption payments' in return for the privilege of cultivating it. The other great source of populist discontent was the fear that Russia was about to be engulfed by the tidal wave of capitalism. The social misery which had attended early industrial growth in Britain and Germany was to be forestalled at all costs.

The populists altered many of their initial ideas about strategy as circumstances and experiences appeared to compel. The creation of a political party was both illegal and hazardous. A number of discussion circles was set up in the 1850s, mainly in the towns and cities and especially in the universities. Most were swiftly suppressed, few managed to establish links with one another. In 1862 V. S. Serno-Solovevich, believing that a political party was essential to effective activity, gathered together various groups of sympathisers into an organisation calling itself 'Land And Freedom'. Their hopes of undertaking a long-term campaign of revolutionary propaganda were shattered by police intervention. The authorities broke up the local groups and exiled or imprisoned the leading activists. The lesson drawn by the survivors was that a campaign of propaganda necessitated the formation of a populist party along much more tightly knit, disciplined lines than Serno-Solovevich had envisaged. Terroristic attacks upon the emperor and his ministers also became widely accepted as a political strategy by the revolutionaries. The 1860s witnessed the growth and suppression of a succession of organisations displaying an ever-increasing concern with matters of internal discipline and cohesion. The extremity was reached in 1867 when the terrorist S. I. Nechaev ordered the murder of a fellow member of his group, apparently with the idea that the other members would be bound together even more closely by the pressure of collective guilt.

Disgust at Nechaev's behaviour helped to swing the pendulum of the populist movement away from conspiratorial terrorism towards peaceful propaganda. In 1869 N. A. Chaikovski organised a political circle which laid its weight behind the idea of educative work rather than sporadic violence and acted as the inspiration of a large-scale movement of students and intellectuals who 'went to the people' in 1874 in order to achieve direct contact with the peasantry. There was little local co-ordination, still less any central direction. The police again acted determinedly to sweep up the major activists. By 1876 numerous populists consequently decided that a fresh attempt should be made to create a political party. A second 'Land and Freedom' organisation was brought into existence. Unlike its predecessors, it succeeded in constructing a countrywide network of active groups; regular communications were maintained between the principal towns and cities; executive committees were set up for the conduct of local affairs and grass-roots propaganda; and, at the centre, special commissions were established to support particular aspects of work outside Moscow. The first Russian political party had at last emerged.

From the start, however, 'Land and Freedom' was bedevilled by disputes about the uses of terrorism. Efforts were made in the meantime to spread populist ideas in the towns as well as the rural areas. Industrial workers, though still a minority of the urban population, were well known for their profound discontent with their conditions and were thought predisposed to populism on the grounds that they were basically peasants merely 'on leave' from their native villages. Strikes were called in the industrial quarters of St Petersburg and Odessa. But revolutionaries who espoused the benefits of assassinating public figures felt frustrated by the slow pace of developments. A split was scarcely avoidable, and in 1879 the two factions proceeded to found their own separate parties: the terroristic People's Freedom and the propagandistic Black Repartition. Two years later the terrorists at last killed the emperor Alexander II. The ensuing repression eliminated nearly all the populist groups, whether they belonged to the People's Freedom or to the Black Repartition, across the country. A dark night descended upon the entire movement; for while the bankruptcy of terrorism was now evident to all but a handful of incorrigibles it was equally clear that the propagandistic alternative had also failed to produce the results promised by its advocates.

Yet the populists' troubles did not stem only from the efficiency of the secret police. There were deeper reasons too. They had always exaggerated the strength of egalitarian practices in the villages. Survey after survey concluded that the rich households of each commune were tending to become even richer and more influential at the expense of their less fortunate neighbours. Nor did the populists explain how to set about raising the country's low level of agricultural productivity. They apparently assumed that popular prosperity could be amply guaranteed simply by expropriating gentry-held land and turning it over to the peasantry. Scarcely ever did they question whether the traditional methods of farming, with their strip allotments and their outdated ideas about crop rotation, were adequate to the needs of the population.

An immense spurt of industrial growth was initiated in the 1880s. The factories and mines established under Peter I and his successors had remained a small enclave in the total economy. After the defeats in the Crimean War, however, ruling circles steadily became persuaded that further industrialisation was urgently required if the Russian empire was to regain its security and prestige. A vigorous programme of railway construction was undertaken to facilitate trade and communications. Large investments were made by the government in existing regions of industry. Newly found resources of minerals and petroleum were exploited for the first time in the Donbass and eastern Azerbaidzhan. Foreign companies and foreign banks were given official encouragement to play an active role in the process. By the 1890s an annual growth rate of 8 per cent was achieved in industrial output. The kind of society which the populists had striven so hard to avoid was now coming inexorably into existence.

Social changes were shifting in the same direction. In 1900 the number of workers in factories had risen to around two million. The populist notion that all of them were essentially peasants 'on leave' from the countryside no longer appeared as realistic as it once had seemed. A declining proportion of the industrial labour force, it was reported, returned annually to the villages to help with the harvest at the end of the summer. By the turn of the century, indeed, only one in every ten workers did so in factories employing more than fifty persons. It was also recognised that a swelling section of the labour force was composed of second-generation workers with little or no experience of rural life. The populists were quick to reply that, despite all this, most factory workers still kept up some kind of link with their villages. Over half of them retained small parcels of land at home by sending regular sums of money to relatives who had not left for the towns. It was also conventional for husbands to leave their wives behind in the village when they went off to seek industrial employment, since the living conditions around the new factories and mines were known to be so inhospitable. And workers who had been given the sack frequently hurried back to their families in the countryside until they could find another job. Such practices were certainly widespread and continued to occur for decades. Nevertheless it was the direction of change that mattered most: the orientation towards a town-based industrial existence was unmistakable.[1]

It was reinforced by the workers' own growing awareness of the distinctive problems and difficulties confronting them. Labour discipline was severe not only by the standards of Britain and Germany but also in comparison with the customary kinds of working relationship to be found in the peasant commune. The harsh conditions of hiring and firing, which were wholly in the employer's favour, were a further cause of continual grievance. Wage rates were often cut without prior consultation or even notification. Safety regulations, rudimentary as they were, could be flouted with impunity in many enterprises. Resentment deepened among Russian workers upon their discovery that the foreign workers who came to work in the Donbass or St Petersburg were earning much higher wages than themselves. The government made matters worse by visibly taking the side of the employer in all disputes. Until the 1870s it had displayed a certain reluctance to become embroiled in such affairs but the subsequent increase in industrial strife forced its hand. Strikes were forbidden and Cossack troops were sent in to quell disorder if the ban was ignored. Yet still the manifestations of discontent became more frequent. Only six strikes were recorded between 1862 and 1869, but the annual average alone had spiralled to thirty-three between 1886 and 1894.[2]

The political possibilities of the industrial environment were not lost upon populist groups which survived the police onslaught unleashed by the assassination of Alexander II in 1883. The remaining years of the last century were notable for a furious debate about the new course of action to be taken by the socialist movement. Some activists, after a brief time of demoralisation, reiterated the old appeal to look upon the peasantry as the most hopeful source of revolutionary change. The job of radicalising the rural poor, so the argument ran, was being done by the imperial government itself through the process of levying additional taxes in order to finance its programme of industrialisation. The famine of 1897 spread the seeds of rebellion more quickly than any pamphlets had done. Such populists regarded the outbreaks of anti-capitalist unrest as a useful aid in the struggle against the autocracy but not as the foremost area where the final battles would have to be fought and won. Modern industry, however much it now had to be accepted as a permanent feature of the economic scene, could still be contained within bounds. Local groups of this persuasion swelled in strength and numbers over the 1890s and in 1901 linked themselves together in a country-wide organisation calling itself the Party of Socialist-Revolution-aries.[3]

Other populists, however, experienced a need to submit their ideas to a basic reappraisal. By an irony of history it was they who engaged upon the first practical attempt to propagate the notion that socialism, if ever it was to sink strong roots in Russia, would have to turn its face towards things urban and industrial. Various groups and circles in St Petersburg and elsewhere started to point themselves in the new direction, cautiously sloughing off the skin of their agrarian heritage. There was no shortage of foreign writings, both literary and political, on the subject of industrialisation and its social consequences; but they were concerned mainly with historical developments in central and western Europe and said little specifically about the Russian empire. Plans and strategies had to be worked out independently. What saved the young movement from debilitating self-doubts was its conviction, bolstered by its experience of work in industrial quarters, that the current of economic change was already running fast towards the industrial society of the future.[4]

The person who did most to articulate a view of the world which could appeal to these groups was Georgi Plekhanov. He was one of the many populist leaders who was compelled to flee abroad in the 1870s to Switzerland. While in Russia he had concentrated his political energies upon practical activity among St Petersburg factory workers, leading strikes against employers and heading a demonstration against the authorities. He read the *Communist Manifesto* in 1880 and was the first eminent émigré to abandon populism for Marxism. He believed that the Russian empire was at the stage of political and economic development which had been attained by Germany in the middle of the nineteenth century. The vista he conceived was accordingly a highly optimistic one. Germany too, he argued, had in the not so distant past been a society in the initial throes of industrialisation and under the heel of an autocratic monarchy, but now she already had a constitutional form of government, however rudimentary at times, and was recognised as belonging to the first rank of the world's industrial powers. In the 1890s she also acquired a mass socialist party with hundreds of thousands of members, with a network of local bodies all across the country and with a popularity among factory workers which appeared a most favourable augury for its chances of eventually coming to power and initiating a socialist programme of transformation. Plekhanov suggested that there was no good reason why the Russian empire should not take the same path.[5]

Of Plekhanov's high estimate of the German Social-Democratic party's achievements there is no doubt. Yet he had a mind of his own and scrupulously avoided unthinking imitation of foreign models. His analysis of Russian society is a case in point. Critics tried to prove that he was merely regurgitating the ideas of his German masters, Marx and Engels. But this was an unfair exaggeration. He would probably have never won the Russian following he did if he had not addressed himself to the peculiar problems of his own country's development. His philosophical speculations, interesting as they appear, were of less practical import at the time than his summary of the implications of 'late' industrialisation. Socialists in the Russian empire, he wrote, possessed an advantage which had not been given to their counterparts in Britain, Germany or France. This consisted in their opportunity to disseminate socialist beliefs among industrial workers at an early stage in the growth of capitalism. He drew a contrast with countries abroad where industrialism had made great inroads into the social and economic structure before there was time for socialism to grow up in reaction to it. Russian workers could be equipped in advance to understand the nature of the nascent society in which they lived and to take action accordingly. Nothing, however, was going to happen of its own accord. Plekhanov stressed that Russia's retarded growth could be seen as a benefit only if the available opportunities were resolutely seized. The creation of a social-democratic party was a primary pre-requisite. Political conditions at the moment ruled out all chance of forming a mass organisation like the German Social-Democratic Party (though he cherished the hope of helping to do so as soon as the autocracy was dismantled). The Russian party would have to be an underground affair, tightly knit and disciplined. There was also a need, at least initially, to rely heavily upon recruitment among intellectuals since most workers as yet were little acquainted with socialism. It was a bold, enterprising perspective.[6]

In 1883 he felt confident enough to test his ideas with the litmus-paper of practice and to set up the first Marxist group in Russian history, albeit on Swiss soil. It called itself the Liberation of Labour Group and was composed of émigré intellectuals like Plekhanov himself. Pamphlets and articles were penned to be dispatched to potential supporters at home. The earliest success came in 1884 when an underground group in Russia associated itself with Plekhanov's. But police spies were on the alert and within a couple of years were able to inform the authorities of the names of most of its members. A succession of arrests in St Petersburg snapped the chain of contact with Switzerland. Plekhanov was pushed out into a political limbo for almost a decade, seldom knowing about the impact of his writings or the whereabouts of his sympathisers. This made work a lot more difficult for local groups in Russia but proved not to be a catastrophe. Parcels of political literature continued to arrive sporadically from abroad and ensured that Plekhanov's writings made a deep impact upon the ideological development of socialism in his native country.[7]

In any case it is usually misguided to assume that firm, regular central leadership is vital to the foundation of political movements. It was probably, in fact, of benefit to the groups of Russian social-democrats that they were able to spring up with some awareness of local conditions and to conduct their activity without being obliged to keep to a preordained pattern. The 1890s were the period of the 'circles'. Their immediate task, it was agreed, was to further the political education of their own members. Efforts were made to recruit industrial workers and to enable them to attain a level of general schooling and social awareness which would otherwise have been denied them. Time after time the same cycle of events was observed. Circles would spring up, would flourish for a while, would be detected by the police, and would be forcibly disbanded. Early social-democratic activity was perforce a secretive and introspective affair. But it is testimony to the depth of anti-autocratic feeling in the country that no amount of persecution was sufficient to snuff out the new socialist movement entirely.[8]

Yet it did not take long before local activists felt frustrated and restless. The Russian working class of the 1890s was not the passive, docile creature it had appeared in earlier times. There were many explosions of strikes and disturbance throughout the empire. They were mostly short-lived occurrences but often provoked so much bitterness as to lead to violent clashes between the workers and the authorities. The average annual number of strikes leapt from thirty-three between 1886 and 1894 to 126 between 1895 and 1903. The émigrés in Switzerland took little account of the changes under way until Arkadi Kremer, a Jewish social-democrat based in Minsk, brought it vividly to their notice in 1894 in a pamphlet entitled 'On Agitation'. He complained that excessive concentration upon internal education and discussion had distracted socialists from taking full advantage of the current wave of labour unrest. The very policy of selecting a few industrial workers to be members of each circle was not always as helpful as it seemed. Frequently their special courses of learning served mainly to isolate them from the mass of their work-mates in the factories. Kremer insisted that the solution was to step over the threshold of the circles and to take an active part in the rising tide of struggles over wages and conditions. Socialists, he urged, should be in the front ranks of those who were organising the strikes: they should not simply be joining them once they had started. Practical campaigns of economic and political agitation were now to be on every circle's agenda.[9]

Kremer's pamphlet met a need. His ideas spread rapidly to a number of social-democratic circles (although Plekhanov, to his shame, took the matter as a personal affront to his own competence as a writer and organiser). They were instrumental in the formation of the St Petersburg League of Struggle for the Liberation of the Working Class in 1895 under the leadership of two young social-democrats, Vladimir Lenin and Yuli Martov. This early attempt to unite all local circles and stir up industrial conflict was abortive. Most of its prominent supporters, including both Lenin and Martov, were swiftly arrested. It so happened that a large section of St Petersburg textile-workers did come out on strike in 1896, but they were not headed by social-democrats: police attempts to break up the circles had been too successful to allow that. A similar tale of misfortune attended the socialist movement in other parts of the country where moves were made to organise discontented workers. Yet the government was well enough informed to recognise that it had small grounds for permanent complacency. As soon as one local alliance of social-democrats was eliminated, another would be reported to be in growth elsewhere. In 1898 groups in various towns and cities of the empire, on their own initiative and without the backing of the émigré leaders, convoked a countrywide congress to found the Russian Social-Democratic Labour Party. Its proceedings had little effect in practice; most of the delegates were rounded up by the police within months. But it required no great gift of political insight to understand that the new party would remain a thorn in the autocracy's flesh as long as the working class harboured deep grievances against the environment in which it was obliged to live.[10]

Meanwhile in Switzerland Plekhanov, together with the newly arrived Lenin and Martov, was becoming worried by the ideas currently publicised by S. N. Prokopovich and E. D. Kuskova. Russian labour disputes in the 1890s were seldom accompanied by overt demands of a political nature. Prokopovich and Kuskova treated this as a sign of the working class's ideological immaturity; they urged that social-democrats should abandon political propaganda altogether and devote themselves exclusively to organising strikes and getting higher wages and better conditions for factory employees. They made no secret of their desire to get rid of all thoughts of revolution. Plekhanov, who was quick to brand such a viewpoint as 'economism', pointed out that it paralleled the campaigns by Eduard Bernstein in Germany and the Fabians in Britain to revise the strategies of social change espoused by Marxists and others in the mid-nineteenth century. He was willing to admit that most Russian workers lacked much cognisance of political questions; but that, in his opinion, made it all the more necessary to propagate socialist proposals among the small number who in fact possessed some. Plekhanov, Lenin and Martov were therefore fully determined to nip the economistic movement in the bud. They concerted a brief but vigorous campaign in Russia, bombarding the local activists with their ideas. Prokopovich and Kuskova, just beginning to multiply their following outside Switzerland, sustained a crushing defeat.[11]

Lenin, however, felt that the 'party' was still hamstrung by the absence of a clearly formulated strategy of action. The industrial boom of the 1890s was over; in 1900 a recession in trade and manufacturing led to the closure of many enterprises, both large

and small. Lay-offs of workers followed. Wage cuts were made in
many of the factories and mines which remained open. Strikes were
widespread—550 were recorded in 1903, an unprecedented total
in the Russian empire. Workers were not alone in manifesting their
discontent. Peasant riots and disturbances increased at the same
time, triggered off by the rural impoverishment brought about by
the government's insatiable appetite for revenue. There was also a
newly serious effort by liberals to organise a political movement of
their own by canvassing the support of various industrialist and
professional groupings. The autocracy was at last beginning to
appear hemmed in on all sides. Something had to give. And yet, as
Lenin saw it, the Russian Social-Democratic Labour Party had no
proper plans to deal with the situation. His fears were intensified by
reports that the Party of Socialist-Revolutionaries, not content
with spreading propaganda in the countryside, was making not
unsuccessful attempts to attract membership from among industrial
workers.[12]

Lenin spelled out his own ideas in a series of articles culminating
in 'What Is To Be Done?' in 1902. He started from a political
analysis of the Russian empire. Its middle class, relying as heavily
as it did upon governmental subsidies and support, was most
unlikely, when the final crisis came, to throw in its lot with the
forces of revolution and lead the upsurge to overthrow the
Romanov dynasty. Nor were foreign companies, which played so
large a part in Russia's industrial growth, likely to risk the loss of
their profits by backing so risky a venture. The working class, on the
other hand, was much more open to the appeals of political
radicalism by virtue of the extreme poverty and squalor to which it
was subjected. It was therefore to be regarded as the leading agent
of a 'bourgeois revolution' which would establish a parliamentary
republic and create the economic base for the full flowering of
capitalism. And its main ally would not be the middle class but the
peasantry. Lenin maintained that all types of peasant household,
save the richest, would support the ousting of the monarch when
the time came. Not all his propositions were much more than
vague leanings at this stage. Yet the overall direction of thought
was clear enough and was recognised very quickly as pointing
towards the most militant programme yet put forward by a
Russian social-democrat.[13]

The novelty of Lenin's thinking was discerned most easily in his
organisational recommendations. If workers were to head the

revolutionary movement, he argued, the Russian Social-Democratic Labour Party itself would have to adopt stricter forms of internal discipline than had been customary until then. Otherwise it would fail to discharge its responsibility as the 'political vanguard' of the working class. He acknowledged that democratic procedures were greatly desirable in socialist parties abroad, such as the German Social-Democratic Party, which were allowed to operate without police persecution. But this, he stated, was impossible in the prevailing circumstances of the Russian empire. The Russian Social-Democratic Labour Party had therefore to accept the need for highly centralised and at times undemocratic methods in its internal affairs, for an overriding commitment to hierarchical subordination and discipline. Nobody was to be allowed to belong to the party unless he or she agreed to participate energetically in party life. Only such an approach, Lenin reiterated, could ensure that the Russian Social-Democratic Labour Party set its face against compromises, held fast to its original dreams and refused to follow the shifting moods of working-class feeling; only such an approach could ensure that it supplied the leadership required of it.[14]

Much of this was uncontentious. Most social-democrats with any experience of Russian political life concurred that democratic procedures were often impracticable and that strict, unquestioning obedience was occasionally needed instead of open debate. There was also widespread agreement that moves should be made to centralise party activity across the Russian empire. Yet many, including his erstwhile associate Martov, felt that Lenin had gone altogether too far. They were distressed not least of all by his admiring remarks about the populist terrorists of the 1870s (and about the Jacobins in the French Revolution). They recoiled from his great emphasis upon the party paying the living expenses of as many 'professional revolutionaries' as possible. They thought Lenin's scheme for membership qualifications to be intolerably restrictive and likely to discourage industrial workers from joining. Their overall fear was that Lenin was trying to 'substitute' the party for the working class in the struggle for revolutionary change. Even the young social-democrat Lev Trotski opposed Lenin. And Trotski was already starting to call for a general programme still more radical than Lenin's by urging that a socialist government be installed immediately after the Romanov autocracy's removal.[15]

The Second Congress of the Russian Social-Democratic Labour Party in 1903 gave an opportunity for the issues to be discussed in detail. A passionate dispute surrounded the question of the Party Rules and it was only by a slim majority that Martov, calling for membership qualifications which would not discourage would-be worker recruits, managed to defeat Lenin's proposals. Unfortunately for Martov, however, a number of his supporters left the Congress before the end of its proceedings. Lenin, with the temporary backing of Plekhanov, counter-attacked and was victorious in the ensuing elections to the party's central executive bodies. Thus his group proudly proceeded to dub themselves the Majoritarians (or 'Bolsheviks') while Martov's allowed themselves the dubious distinction of being called the Minoritarians (or 'Mensheviks'). A Congress which had been convoked with the hope of uniting all Russian social-democrats had terminated in more disputatiousness than ever.[16]

Plekhanov shortly regretted his own behaviour. The immediate cause of his concern was that Lenin, having eventually defeated Martov at the Congress, continued to use his dominant position to bully his party opponents in a manner which to Plekhanov appeared much too ruthless. But Plekhanov also had deeper worries about the implications of Lenin's entire programme of action. By 1904 he felt it was urgently necessary to challenge the Bolshevik idea that the working class would be the leading agent of the forthcoming revolution. Most Menshevik figures agreed. In vain did Lenin protest to them that he did not want to build a party exclusively of professional revolutionaries or to rid the party entirely of debate and discussion. He was right to claim that his views had been distorted by his opponents (though he himself encouraged this by adopting so exaggerated a mode of self-expression). Yet he could never satisfactorily demolish their criticism that his extremely centralist proposals were linked to his low opinion of the creative capacities of ordinary workers. By this time, moreover, the Mensheviks had been induced to elaborate their own revolutionary strategy. Broadly speaking, it held that the middle class would indeed achieve its own seizure of power and that the working class should therefore act only as a secondary group, not as the leading force. There was no complete agreement among the Mensheviks. Martov retained his earlier doubts that the Russian middle class could be counted on to revolt against the autocracy. But most Mensheviks, following influential writers like Pavel Akselrod, took a less pessimistic view. Steadily the issues became clearer and the debate between the Bolsheviks and the Mensheviks, which in any case had never been solely about organisational questions, became a dispute which covered all aspects of party policy.[17]

The split among the émigrés, however, did not have the impact in the Russian empire that both Lenin and Martov had expected. By deserting Lenin in 1904 Plekhanov left him outnumbered in the central executive bodies of the party. Lenin reacted by calling a number of his own supporters together, most notably A. A. Bogdanov, and by setting up a central body composed solely of Bolsheviks. The plan was to arrange a congress of all Bolshevik sympathisers and create a fully separate party. But it was over-optimistic. Several local leaders and activists were now prepared to identify themselves as Bolsheviks or Mensheviks and a few local committees underwent a full organisational split. Nevertheless it seemed desirable to the leaders in most places to avoid such an extreme move. Instead they typically agreed to work together in the same committee despite their basic disagreements about the future of the revolution.[18] Since factional sympathies remained somewhat fluid it is difficult to say whether Bolshevik and Menshevik committee members differed from each other very much in their social backgrounds; but impressionistic evidence suggests that the Bolsheviks had a higher proportion of working-class and ethnically Russian followers whereas the Mensheviks were better represented than their rivals among the middle-class, non-Russian sections of the population.[19] No such comparison, however, is practicable for the ten or eleven thousand rank-and-file social-democrats belonging to the party. Later events were to show that nearly all of them were deeply hostile to the whole idea of a split. It is this that makes a mockery of every subsequent endeavour to assess the respective strengths of the Bolsheviks and the Mensheviks at the grass roots of the party.[20]

1905 was the critical year which generations of Russian revolutionaries had long been waiting for. The government had been trying fresh approaches to domestic discontent since the turn of the century. Alarmed by the reports of rural disorders, it had repealed much of the legislation discriminating against the peasantry. It also attempted to take the steam out of labour unrest by allowing trade unions to be established under the covert control of the Ministry of the Interior. Neither scheme worked; the autocracy's troubles mounted. In 1904 the emperor foolishly entered upon a war with Japan, partly in the hope of regaining popularity through a short victorious campaign. Defeat followed defeat, culminating in the utter destruction of the Russian fleet at the battle of Tsushima. And at home the strikes in the factories and the disturbances in the villages showed no sign of diminishing in number and in vigour.[21]

In January 1905 a peaceful demonstration, which was called with the purpose of making a petition about grievances to the emperor himself, was fired upon as it approached the Winter Palace in St Petersburg. This lit the touch-paper of discontent and provoked a further blaze of strikes and demonstrations across the empire. Swift military intervention succeeded in quelling the crowds for a time. But by May the industrial workers of the textile town of Ivanovo-Voznesensk, embittered by local conditions and enraged by events in the capital, set up barricades in the factory suburbs and elected their own organ of self-government. Thus was born the earliest workers' council or soviet. The Ivanovo example was picked up in other cities so that by the end of the summer it looked as if the government might completely lose control. The peasants added to the turmoil by making plain that they wanted the government to redistribute agricultural land in their favour. Worse still from the autocracy's viewpoint was the news that the crew of the Black Sea battleship *Potemkin* had mutinied.[22]

The emperor's shaken throne was secured, if only temporarily, by two main circumstances. The first was that disaffection was not yet widespread in the armed forces and that urban and rural revolts could still be suppressed by superior force; the second was that the emperor published a Manifesto in October by which he agreed to introduce constitutional reforms and establish a Parliament (or Duma). The political danger was thereby quickly defused. Liberals, who themselves were frightened by the scale of revolutionary activism among the lower classes, were naturally keen to grab hold of any concessions on offer from the monarch. Social-Democrats and Socialist-Revolutionaries, though less easily persuaded that the Manifesto was anything other than a cynical manoeuvre, could see that the tide of events was fast ebbing away from them. The Bolsheviks in fact organised an armed uprising in Moscow, but to no avail: loyal troops were moved in against them and order was restored.[23]

The Russian Social-Democratic Labour Party hugely expanded the scope of its activities and influence in 1905. Its local leaders not only led strikes and demonstrations but also supplied the cadres who helped to run the soviets, the trade unions and the factory workshop committees which sprang up throughout the country. The breakdown of governmental authority was providing revolutionaries with a long-awaited chance to create a mass party. Bolsheviks and Mensheviks vied with one another to attract as many recruits as possible (as was wholly to be expected since 'What Is To Be Done?' had never been intended as a blueprint suitable for all times and all circumstances). The number of social-democrats swelled to 150 000. The newcomers added strength to rank-and-file demands that the émigrés patch up their quarrels and start working together again. In April 1906 delegates from both wings of the party, Bolshevik and Menshevik, were sent to the Fourth Party Congress in Stockholm and formal moves were accepted to reunify all Russian Social-Democrats.[24]

Yet to say merely that the party was no nearer to being centralised and disciplined than hitherto is seriously to understate its organisational difficulties. Social-democratic activity remained primarily a local affair in 1905. There is no mystery why this was so. Communications between towns were at best unreliable and at times completely broken. The émigrés in Switzerland were known to be at loggerheads with each other and to be unable to formulate a practicable course of common action. Above all the astonishing rapidity of the transformation of the situation made it vital to stay sensitive to local issues and react immediately to their emergence. Nor did the party's formal reunification make much difference to the existing state of affairs. The émigrés did not really bury their differences. And it still happened that several local committees in the Russian empire, though by no means all of them, came under the influence of one wing of social-democratic thinking or the other. It would appear that Bolshevik activists tended to attract greater support among the less skilled, less urbanised sections of the industrial labour force and achieved a greater influence in areas of the country where employers were especially reluctant to smooth relations with their workers. Menshevik activists are thought to have made greater headway among the better-off and skilled workers and to have shown more progress in areas where rudimentary forms of industrial conciliation were practised.[25]

The October Manifesto was swiftly revealed as a sham. Nicholas II had promulgated it solely under duress and thereafter did his utmost to retract as much of it as he could. He looked upon the first Duma, which met in April 1906, as a hotbed of dangerous radicalism since its majority was headed by those liberals, most notably the newly formed Constitutional-Democratic Party, who were most intent upon limiting the monarch's power. His response was to prorogue the proceedings and call fresh elections. Yet the second Duma turned out to be no less unco-operative. The emperor again issued an act of prorogation in June 1907; but this time he also took the precaution of altering the franchise laws so as to produce a more malleable set of Duma representatives in the future. Thus the third and fourth Dumas of 1907 and 1912 could do little to act as a brake upon the will of the government. The emperor's contempt for constitutional arrangements was accompanied by a ferocious commitment to expunge all traces of the revolutionary bacillus of 1905. Courts-martial were instituted in the rural areas to round up and try the rebel ringleaders. In the towns a deliberate effort was made to close down the trade unions. Revolutionary political parties were hunted by the secret police as they had always been.[26]

This onslaught produced the immediate results wanted by Nicholas II. Social and political order was restored. It was realised, however, that a programme involving something more than simple repression was necessary. Nicholas II's chief minister, P. A. Stolypin, believed that the solution was to regain the support of the peasantry. His policies were aimed at the cutting of the social and economic ties which bound households to the commune and at creating a class of independent small-holders. Private property was to replace collective tenure, strip-field agriculture was to give way to consolidated farms. Yet progress was slower than Stolypin's expectations. Most peasants seem to have preferred a guaranteed minimum of communal welfare to the uncertainties of private enterprise. The government's reaction was to resort to laws which pressurised the peasantry to submit, but again the achievements were less than Stolypin had hoped for.[27]

The burning issue among Russian social-democrats immediately after 1905 was the Duma question. Most Menshevik leaders came down in favour of putting up candidates in the elections. Some went so far, in the days when the full extent of Nicholas II's insincerity was not yet known for certain, as to advocate abandoning illegal activities altogether and concentrating party efforts upon the legal opportunities provided by the October Manifesto.

Other Mensheviks, who were less easily deceived about the government's intentions, hoped to retain the traditional safeguards of the underground party while nevertheless exploiting the Duma, its electoral campaigns and its daily proceedings, as a useful additional vehicle of propaganda. Lenin felt the same. The intensification of police persecution of revolutionary parties, he asserted, made it extremely foolish for Social-Democrats to forego any political chance, however slim or ephemeral, now being offered to them.[28] Most Bolshevik leaders, however, saw things differently and rallied round Bogdanov when he demanded a total boycott of the forthcoming Duma elections. For a while Lenin bowed to this pressure but in April 1906, at the Fourth Party Congress (where Bolsheviks and Mensheviks formally agreed to work together again) he strongly revoiced his earlier opinion. A bitterly contested discussion found him ranged on the side of the Mensheviks against his own faction. The final vote turned out, as he wanted, in favour of Duma participation.[29]

The Fourth Congress also accepted from the Mensheviks a motion which laid down that the party should be organised upon the principle of democratic centralism. This term, which was borrowed from the usage of certain German social-democrats in the mid-nineteenth century, did not signify anything essentially novel.[30] Ever since their own Second Congress in 1903 most Russian social-democrats had been in agreement that party affairs should be underpinned by a combination of central authority and democratic accountability whenever circumstances permitted. The Romanov autocracy made this impracticable for the moment; but it was anticipated that the establishment of political freedom in Russia, when that day eventually came, would make it possible at last to create a democratically centralised mass socialist party. Russian social-democrats saw no reason why they should not in the future be able to follow the organisational path pioneered by the German Social-Democratic Party.[31]

Such concerns, however, can scarcely be said to have been the principal subject of interest to the Congress delegates as they returned home. Bolshevik leaders remained unconvinced that Lenin's support for participation in the Duma was justified. Not that this deterred him from an energetic endeavour to change their minds. Three years later he managed to get the issue reopened at a factional conference of Bolsheviks in June 1909. This time Bogdanov was soundly defeated since it had become plain by then that boycotting the Duma simply left the political field open to rival parties. Lenin was unmerciful in victory: he had Bogdanov drummed out of the Bolshevik faction.[32] There is much unnecessary confusion about what this implied. It did not mean that Bogdanov was being expelled from the Russian Social-Democratic Labour Party, since the Bolsheviks remained only one of its main wings. Nor should it be supposed that the other Russian social-democratic factions were always paragons of comradely tolerance. In fact, Russian socialists of all kinds were already notorious throughout the European movement for their wonted recourse to every organisational chicanery in the book.[33]

To many local committees in the Russian empire itself, it seemed that the émigré disputes about the desirable forms of party organisation and activity were somewhat wide of the mark. Underground activists in the factories and workshops likened the Swiss-based leaders to prisoners about to be executed who argue among themselves on what food to request for their last dinner: the problem of the Russian Social-Democratic Labour Party was sheer survival. Police repression reduced the number of party members from 150 000 in 1906 to 10 000 in 1910. Committees in the provinces were thrown back upon their own human and material resources. Such circumstances were used as a powerful argument against the few local leaders who called for an organisational split between the Bolsheviks and the Mensheviks. It was also noted that a vast proportion of the middle-class activists who had been Bolsheviks in earlier times were now streaming out of the ranks. Their exodus meant not only that Lenin's faction was deprived of a much-needed source of intellectual skills but also that it had lost a solid core of its 'professional revolutionaries' (since most of these were persons with a private income). The younger, working-class activists who took their place complained bitterly about the enormous difficulties involved in trying to keep the party alive. And a few émigré leaders, notably Lenin, could see that the change in the social composition of local committees might well be an advantage in forthcoming attempts to plant deep roots in working-class communities. At the time, however, the prevalent mood in local committees was gloomy and despondent.[34]

Yet it was not long before social-democrats began to take heart again. Around 1909 the empire's industrial economy, benefiting from the general upsurge in world trade, began to recover from the doldrums which had surrounded it since the turn of the century.

The annual growth rate between 1910 and 1913 was only a little short of what it had been in the great years of expansion between 1983 and 1900. More and more peasants had to be attracted to the towns in order to provide the factories and workshops with sufficient labour. It is reckoned that the number of workers in the metallurgical industries increased by about 50 per cent in the last half-decade before the First World War. The government, however, was alert enough to see the upturn of the economy as a mixed blessing. As factory production expanded, so the manifestations of industrial conflict became stronger and more frequent. Neither the authorities nor the employers had taken energetic measures to expand and improve the housing facilities and social amenities, which were steadily being worsened by the pressure of a quickly growing urban population. Older workers deeply resented the deterioration in their conditions; newcomers from the villages were no less embittered by the first experiences of town life. Official inspectors reported a rise in the number of strikes from 222 in 1910 to 466 in 1911. In spring 1912 the shooting of Lena goldfield workers by the police triggered off an outbreak of further unrest. By the end of the year there had been 2032 strikes and, still more ominously for the autocracy, nearly two thirds of them had been associated with political demands.[35]

All social-democrats worked hard to make the greatest possible use of these events. Ever since his defeat of Bogdanov in 1909 Lenin had been endeavouring to effect a final, clear-cut split between the Bolsheviks and the Mensheviks. The spread of industrial strife induced him to redouble his efforts and convoke a separate conference of Bolsheviks in Prague in 1912. Beforehand he and his close associate Grigori Zinoviev had complained that an excessive concern with illegal party operations had led underground Bolsheviks in Russia to fail to take full advantage of working-class discontent. The solution, they argued, was for local committees to narrow the scope of illegal activity and to employ the illegal apparatus exclusively as a means of influencing and directing affairs in legal working-class organisations such as the trade unions and sick-insurance funds. Lenin and Zinoviev claimed that this was a tactic developed successfully by the German Social-Democratic Party in reaction to being driven underground by Bismarck's anti-socialist legislation between 1879 and 1890. Prague Conference delegates from Russia itself were in fact equally keen to place themselves at the head of the strike movement; but they withheld support from Lenin's specific proposal, knowing full well that the illegal network of social-democratic committees was far from being as solidly established as he implied. All this notwithstanding, however, there was complete agreement at the Conference on the main issue at stake: that Bolsheviks should shift the balance of party work. And in order to maximise Bolshevik influence among industrial workers it was agreed to establish a separate Bolshevik Central Committee. Never again would Bolsheviks and Mensheviks sit together in the same central executive party bodies.[36]

There was no abatement of industrial conflict. The number of strikes soared to 3534 in 1914. Reports that Bolshevik slogans were the most popular among the demonstrators were everywhere. Trade union after trade union, especially in St Petersburg (where the challenge to the authorities was fiercest), fell under the Bolshevik sway. Mensheviks noted with alarm that they were losing their traditional bastions of working-class support in southern Russia and the Ukraine. Factional hostilities grew ever more bitter. The widespread and continued existence of many 'joint' social-democratic committees gave the Mensheviks little cause for joy. Nor did they derive much comfort from the Bolshevik Central Committee's frustration at being unable to direct events from abroad. The paramount fact of political life in Russia was that the moderating slogans of the Mensheviks no longer attracted much support from the working class. By July 1914 the only worry of St Petersburg Bolsheviks, who had set up their own separate committee, was that the demonstrators might be forcing the pace of change too hard. But of the existence of a revolutionary situation they had not the slightest doubt.[37]

The outbreak of the First World War in the same month and Russian involvement in it greatly helped to save the autocracy—as the emperor was doubtless hoping when he signed the declaration. Need for continued industrial investment from France and Britain, greed for territorial expansion towards the Dardanelles, and fear of Austro-Hungarian and German designs in eastern Europe had occupied a widening space in the government's calculations for some time and continued to do so in the war itself. War fever now infected all sections of society indiscriminately. Peasants, workers, domestic servants, office clerks, bureaucrats, landed gentry and industrialists all vouchsafed their devotion to the patriotic cause.

The Duma gave an overwhelming vote in favour of war credits. On the surface everything looked well again for the monarchy.[38]

But the underlying reality was very different. The liberals, who wanted to clip or altogether remove the powers of the emperor, hinted unambiguously that they were fully ready to form a government should the autocracy prove incapable of effective conduct of the war. They formed a variety of voluntary public organisations aimed at plugging gaps in official health and welfare services; they established a network of war-industrial committees which were to serve the purpose of bringing the respective representatives of employers and workers together in order to obviate current problems in the production of munitions and other vital materials. The socialist parties were not slow to denounce the imperial government's annexationist pretensions; but that did not stop many of their members from recognising the war-industrial committees as a channel through which not only to defend the country from German aggression but also to further their own political interests. This idea was highly attractive to the Party of Socialist-Revolutionaries and to large numbers of Mensheviks. It also appealed to a few Bolsheviks. With helpmates such as these the emperor might well have wondered whether he needed further enemies.[39]

Most Bolsheviks (and many Mensheviks for that matter), however, felt that the war-industrial committees ought to be completely shunned. The war itself, they claimed, was essentially a clash between rapacious, imperialist powers; it would bring nothing to the workers of Europe but death or impoverishment. They were aghast at the reaction to calls for mobilisation displayed by socialist parties in the other combatant countries. Worst of all was the decision taken by the German Social-Democrat Party, long regarded as the corner-stone of the socialist movement throughout the world, to vote in favour of war credits in the Reichstag. The Bolsheviks, like many observers of international politics since the turn of the century, had for some years been predicting the outbreak of a world war; but what they had totally failed to consider was the possibility that the very party in whom they had reposed so much faith and admiration would itself succumb to the pernicious attraction of German nationalism.[40]

Bolshevik leaders, struggling to recover from the traumatic effects of this outcome, set about explaining to themselves why it had occurred. Now at last they began to acknowledge the truth in much of what had been said by the numerous German critics, both Marxist and non-Marxist, of the German Social-Democratic Party. Rosa Luxemburg and Rudolf Hilferding had for a long time been sounding the alarm that their party was no longer aiming at the creation of a socialist society. All talk of a revolutionary transformation had degenerated into a mere cloak with which to disguise how far the party had already travelled along the road of political compromise with the country's ruling classes. Its journey had been facilitated by the worldwide expansion of the German industrial economy as a flood of cheap raw materials became obtainable from Asia, Africa and South America and as new lucrative markets for manufactured products were sought out and developed in the other countries of Europe. Rising profits induced employers to take the political sting out of domestic discontent by increasing workers' wages and starting a programme of social welfare. The German Social-Democratic Party's own paid officials, whose weekly income typically exceeded that of most workers, steadily began to identify their personal interests with policies which avoided open confrontation with the middle class. Circumstantial accounts of the resultant changes in party life were chronicled by the sociologists Robert Michels, Max Weber and Gustav Schmoller. They showed how the highly disciplined hierarchy of executive party bodies was being used to stamp out opposition to the political line of the central leaders; they claimed that professional functionaries had become so powerful as to constitute a 'bureaucracy' set in dominion over the rest of the party.[41]

Bolshevik leaders hastily recast their practical plans in the light of these ideas. The supreme task of the moment was to organise a 'war upon the war': in Russia agitation should be redoubled among workers; in Switzerland an international body should be created to co-ordinate those few socialist parties in Europe which had taken an anti-war position. Thoughts were also turned towards the longer-term problem of how to evade the path of political and organisational 'degeneration' down which the German Social-Democratic Party was lurching. The Bolsheviks by and large felt that its low wages and poor conditions made the Russian working class unresponsive to the notion that its grievances could be settled through co-operation and conciliation with either the government or the employers. But they also believed that precautionary measures ought to be taken so as to ensure that the

party might not become deflected from its revolutionary programme. As early as 1902, when the German social-democratic
leaders were still the object of his admiration, Lenin had defended
them against their own critics on the grounds not so much that they
observed the niceties of democratic procedures in party life as that
they acted with determination to defeat current moves to water
down their party's original aims.[42] The disturbing news of the
German Social-Democratic Party's reaction to the outbreak of the
First World War consequently served only to reinforce Bolshevik
beliefs in the fundamental need for a strong and dedicated
revolutionary party leadership. Specific organisational proposals
were few on the ground. Lenin and Zinoviev favoured a scheme to
keep an illegal apparatus in reserve even after the future establishment of parliamentary democracy in the country; but other
Bolshevik leaders made little mention of this topic. In any case all of
them turned a deaf ear to Michels's dire warning that every mass
organisation, regardless of the policies it professes, stands in danger
of succumbing to 'bureaucratic' features such as time-serving,
buck-passing, rule-fetishism and the absence of initiative. Such
complacency was not without its significance after 1917.[43]

Understandably, theoretical speculations were not the most
crucial aspect of Bolshevik activity in the First World War. From
the start the police waged an intensive struggle to suppress all
political groups hostile to Russian military involvement; there had
never been a more concerted effort by the authorities to infiltrate
their agents and provocateurs into Social-Democratic committees.
Underground activists who had managed to escape being con-
scripted were hauled off to prison or exile by the hundreds. Contact
between groups in Russia itself was disrupted time after time by the
raids by the authorities. Bolshevik-dominated committees were
pursued with special fervour by the police—a sign of governmental
discrimination which helped to aggravate factional hostilities
among social-democrats. Thus the war was instrumental in giving
the party a further push down the slope towards a final organisational split. This was welcomed by Bolshevik leaders in
Switzerland; but in other respects they had little cause for
celebration. Communications with the Russian empire, which had
never been close at the best of times, were now impeded by the line
of the Eastern front which ran across the breadth of Europe.
Perhaps the most effective focus of émigré action consisted in the
convocation of international gatherings of anti-war socialists in the

Swiss towns of Zimmerwald and Kienthal; but even so it proved impossible to secure enough agreement to set up an executive body capable of co-ordinating activities in all the member countries. Bolshevik fortunes, it seemed, had never reached a lower ebb.[44]

Subjectively the Bolsheviks had been severely battered and dispirited by their early experiences in the First World War. They had still not formed a fully separate party of their own; their internal affairs were no nearer to being centralised and disciplined than they had ever been. The image of a tightly knit bunch of inveterate conspirators, so sedulously cultivated by their enemies, was therefore a cruel mockery of their real condition. Indeed so much of their public reputation was wide of the mark. They did not look upon Lenin, even when he succeeded in keeping in contact with underground committees, as the only acceptable source of plans and policies. They did not regard 'What Is To Be Done?' as an organisational blueprint to be applied in all times and in all places; they in fact wanted to found a mass socialist party as soon as it was practicable. They increasingly thought of the Russian working class as potentially the most responsive to calls to revolutionary action in the whole of Europe. And yet their critics were not totally misguided. The Bolsheviks undoubtedly did adhere to highly centralist notions of party life even though they did not put them into effect. They also constantly emphasised that industrial workers could not be relied upon to follow the road of revolution unless guided and directed by the firm hand of a social-democratic party; they exhibited an extreme impatience at the slow rate of political change. Ideas alone cannot make revolution: they require social support of some kind. What scared the Bolsheviks' opponents was not the nature of their ideology by itself so much as the evidence of the impact it was having in working-class communities. By the end of 1915 the recrudescence of the strike movement in Russian cities, though weak and faltering at first, gave sign that the fate of the autocracy was again in the balance.

2 The Bolsheviks Advance (February 1917– October 1917)

The February Revolution, much predicted and long awaited, came as a surprise to the outside world. Strikes and demonstrations by workers suddenly could no longer be contained by the police in the capital; mutinies broke out in many of the city's garrisons. The emperor's first reaction was to disperse the Duma in the hope that this would somehow assist the task of suppressing the unrest in the streets; but shortly he was compelled to recognise the irretrievability of his position and to abdicate, leaving a vacuum of power which an unofficial committee of the prorogued Duma moved to occupy. Further negotiations led to the formation of a Provisional Government, headed by Prince G. E. Lvov and composed mostly of liberal politicians who had made their name either in the Duma itself or in the voluntary public organisations born in the First World War.

The new cabinet's most pressing need was to cope with the industrial unrest which had mounted to an explosive climax since late 1915. Military requirements had brought about a rapid rise in the numerical strength of the factory labour force; by February 1917, it was reckoned, there were as many as three and a half million industrial workers in the empire. The conscription of working men by the thousands into the armed forces meant that up to two million persons entered factory employment for the first time after the outbreak of hostilities. Real wages declined somewhat between 1914 and the beginning of 1917. It is true that workers in industries linked to armaments production were given marginal increases; but they too had to face the deterioration of living and working conditions experienced by the labour force in other factories. Old machinery was not being replaced with the usual regularity; safety precautions were neglected even more flagrantly than in peacetime; housing facilities were drastically over-crowded; food supplies became steadily scarcer. It was only a short while before this buffeted and deprived mass of humanity voiced its discontent. Strikes and demonstrations occurred in most Russian cities in 1916. The police succeeded in quelling them and in rounding up known Bolshevik activists and sympathisers. Yet this was no answer to the basic problem. The entire working class, both the older established skilled sections and the more numerous peasant newcomers, was united in its demand for a radical redressal of the wrongs it had suffered.[1]

The Provisional Government also had to deal with the demands and expectations expressed by soldiers. The garrisons of Petrograd (the recently de-Germanicised name for St Peterburg) had played a crucial role in the monarchy's overthrow. And now the same soldiers, still crammed into the city's barracks and held down by harsh discipline, called ever more loudly for their conditions to be improved. Already there was more than a suspicion that they would not take kindly to being mobilised for active service on the Eastern front. Nor were the peasants, by far the largest segment of the total population, likely to remain quiescent for very long. They too had contributed to the downfall of Nicholas II, admittedly in an indirect manner, since their dissatisfaction with the prices obtained for grain and vegetables in 1916 had been a cause of the food shortages in the towns. In their eyes, moreover, the destruction of the autocracy in February 1917 left them but one short step away from the achievement of their traditional dream: the seizure of all non-peasant agricultural land and its redistribution among themselves.[2]

The Provisional Government professed a commitment to social reform and national defence. It tried hard to reassure Russian industrialists and bankers that their interests would be protected; it took every opportunity to allay the fears of foreign politicians, investors and generals. But its immediate survival depended most vitally upon the measure of consent afforded to it by the socialist activists emerging from the underground who had agreed to its creation in the first place. Workers, soldiers and peasants had begun to set up their own soviets shortly after Nicholas II's abdication. The Petrograd Soviet, dominated by Mensheviks and socialist-revolutionaries, was ready to give conditional support to Lvov's cabinet and to allow it a breathing-space in which to formulate its policies and establish administrative machinery. Even the Bolshevik Central Committee, once leaders such as Lev Kamenev and Iosif Stalin had made their way back from exile in Siberia, refrained from opposition to the Provisional Government.

For its part Lvov's cabinet proceeded to submit to various requests by the lower classes. Workers were given a shorter daily shift and were permitted to bargain with their employers for higher wages; soldiers were relieved of the most irritating aspects of military discipline; peasants were given to believe that the land question was shortly to be permanently resolved as soon as the elections to the forthcoming Constituent Assembly could be arranged.[3]

Not all socialists, however, were prepared to tolerate the Provisional Government. Before 1917 only a tiny minority of Social-Democrats had maintained that power should be withheld from the Russian middle class once the autocracy. had been overturned. Lev Trotski had been the most prominent advocate of this viewpoint in emigration; a Petrograd Social-Democratic group known as the Interdistricters had attempted to spread similar ideas in the Russian empire in the First World War. Yet until the February Revolution they were regarded as wrong-headed and misguided. It was in fact the speed and ease with which Nicholas II was toppled which convinced numerous other Social-Democrats and Socialist-Revolutionaries that such an attitude had been vindicated after all. Bolshevik activists in their hundreds, in the provinces as well as in Petrograd, began to call for the installation of a socialist government. As yet they did not dominate many party committees in which they worked, but their prospects of winning widespread support were already very bright even before Lenin returned home in April and declared that he too was dedicating himself to the overthrow of the Provisional Government. A vigorous campaign of propaganda was launched against the Lvov cabinet, culminating in the Seventh Conference of the Bolsheviks at the end of the month. There it was decided to work for a further revolution which would transfer all the powers of government to the soviet administrative network and would promulgate a wide-ranging programme of socialist policies. A worldwide end to the war to be effected without annexations or indemnities; the commanding heights of the industrial economy were to be taken into public ownership; workers were to be allowed to participate in factory decision-making; peasants were given the promise that agricultural land would immediately be redistributed. The gauntlet had been thrown down to the Provisional Government.[4]

The first strain in the uneasy marriage between the Provisional Government and the Petrograd Soviet occurred in the third week

of April when it became known that P. N. Milyukov, the Minister
of Foreign Affairs, had sent a message to the Allied governments
reaffirming Russia's intention to extend her border at Turkey's
expense. The Soviet's Menshevik and Socialist-Revolutionary
leaders would not brook an expansionist policy and insisted upon
Milyukov's dismissal. Lvov complied, having also by now become
persuaded that it was expedient to include a substantial minority of
these 'moderate' socialists in his cabinet. The Bolsheviks quickly
pronounced the Mensheviks and Socialist-Revolutionaries guilty
by association. A suitable opportunity for a demonstration against
the new coalition was provided by the occasion of the First
Congress of Soviets in early June; but the Provisional Government
banned all marches through the streets for three days and when the
prohibition was lifted the Mensheviks and Social-Revolutionaries
grabbed the chance to organise their own demonstration. Yet the
Bolsheviks would not be thwarted. They called for yet another
march through the centre of Petrograd at the beginning of July.
Not only did the government forbid it to take place; it also used
force to quell the demonstrators and outlawed several Bolshevik
leaders. Nevertheless the crisis in the capital, coming swiftly upon
the heels of news of the failure of the Russian military offensive on
the Eastern front, persuaded Lvov that the time had come for the
creation of a government composed predominantly of 'moderate'
socialists. After a period of negotiation it was resolved to place the
Socialist-Revolutionary Alexander Kerenski at the head of the
second coalition.[5]

The government's policies, however, fell a long way short of
solving the problems of social discontent and instability. Though
workers were permitted to bargain for higher wages, it was rarely
possible for them to obtain agreements which kept pace with the
soaring rate of inflation. Industry was in a state of dislocation.
Transport and communications were unreliable, raw materials
were scarce, marketing facilities were poor. Both fears about the
political future and straightforward bankruptcies produced a spate
of factory closures. All this added powerful fuel to the radicalisation
of popular opinion, leading quickly to many seizures of enterprises
by the factory committees elected by the workers themselves. In the
meantime the mass of the soldiery too became more restless.
Troops in the trenches were proving no less immune to anti-war
propaganda than the men in the garrisons. And doubtless their
embitterment was aggravated by reports from the rural areas.

Most soldiers expected to return to their native villages as soon as the war was over; their aspirations were whetted by the thought that there was soon to be a redistribution of agricultural land. The prospect of an upheaval in the countryside was reinforced by the growth of peasant discontent. Grain prices were thought no more satisfactory than before 1917; official agrarian policies served only to build up the feelings of impatience in the villages. Illegal land seizures had become not infrequent by midsummer.[6]

The Bolsheviks rightly assumed that their principal hope of taking power lay in depriving the Mensheviks and Socialist-Revolutionaries of their early influence over the various representative organisations elected and sustained by the lower classes. As many as nine hundred soviets were set up by late autumn. In theory they should have shown obedience to the elective hierarchy of soviet executive bodies which was headed by the central machinery created at the First Congress of Soviets and was steadily equipped with an array of committees at the regional and provincial levels. But real authority lay elsewhere, in the grasp of the town and suburb soviets themselves. Instructions from above were adamantly rejected whenever they were deemed inappropriate to local conditions or generally unacceptable. Town soviets quickly acquired an administrative infrastructure of their own. Plenary sessions of delegates became less frequent as executive committees and subcommittees took over the task of day-to-day decision-making. Paid officials were employed at wages roughly equal to what was currently earned by skilled industrial workers. Administrative and secretarial abilities were at a premium. Thus the incidence of middle-class personnel tended to be greater at the higher echelons of authority at both the central and the town levels. Altogether a solid apparatus of alternative government was being brought to life.[7]

Soviets were not the only lower-class organisations to wield political and social power. Trade unions were not much slower in constructing machinery with which to represent the demands of their members, who came to number between two and three million. Even factory-workshop committees managed to establish a countrywide central executive body by early October. The exercise of authority in both the trade unions and the factory-workshop committees, as in the soviets, was at its strongest at the lowest tiers of the formal hierarchy; the centralist aspect of democratic centralism was piously sanctioned at congresses and conferences but largely ignored when the delegates returned to their constituencies. Soviets, trade unions and factory-workshop committees were alike in allowing their own executive bodies to be re-elected at frequent intervals. Thus the key to political advancement was to maintain direct contact with the current feelings of industrial workers and garrison soldiers. By late spring the Bolsheviks had already carried off several victories in trade unions and factory-workshop committees; by midsummer they were making substantial headway in the soviets too.[8]

Not that the Mensheviks and Socialist-Revolutionaries had resigned themselves to defeat; but there were many indications that they took the Bolshevik threat ever more seriously after the troubles of early July. Social discontent was a cause of continual disquiet in governmental circles, so much so that in August the Kerenski cabinet ordered General Kornilov to move loyal troops up to the capital. But at the last hour Kerenski was given to believe that a military *coup d'état* was in the offing. The Provisional Government, urgently needing to drum up all the support it could get, allowed the Petrograd Bolsheviks to function freely again. Bolshevik participation in the unsuccessful counter-moves against Kornilov helped their political campaign go from strength to strength across the country. Soviet after soviet came under their influence in September. The Bolshevik Central Committee at last, on 10 October, agreed with Lenin that power should quickly be seized from the Provisional Government and transferred to the Second Congress of Soviets which was shortly to meet in Petrograd. On 25 October 1917, after some hours of almost bloodless street-fighting, this plan was successfully put into effect.[9]

One of the few propositions about the Bolsheviks in 1917 which nobody has dared to challenge is that the number of their members rose enormously. Every Bolshevik, like every Menshevik and every Socialist-Revolutionary, was committed to the goal of building up a large mass organisation as swiftly as possible. Now that the autocracy was no more and freedom of political self-expression had been decreed, there was no longer any need to stick to the old underground habit of behaving warily towards all would-be recruits. Nor was there a shortage of willing entrants. Recruitment figures followed the steep rise of an exponential curve, astounding the old undergrounders and emboldening their thoughts about future ventures. Timofei Sapronov's memoirs vividly describe how the enthusiasm to join the Bolsheviks was so great at a certain Moscow factory in March that long queues had to be formed so as to register the names of all the newcomers. Never since 1905 had there been such a surge of active support throughout the country.[10]

Yet beyond this point the waters of Bolshevik history run somewhat muddier. Scholarly attempts have been made to gauge the numerical strength of the Bolsheviks at the time of the February Revolution and have thrown up estimates ranging from 23 000 to 45 000.[11] This is all sheer guesswork. How is it possible to tot up the rival followings of the Bolsheviks and the Mensheviks when it is quite unchallengeable that 'joint' Social-Democratic organisations continued to exist in many parts of the country until midsummer 1917 and even later?[12] The same problem arises with the Seventh Party Conference official report in April which laid claim to 80 000 members: even Soviet historians, who are apt to dream up Bolsheviks in every industrial nook and cranny, have expressed embarrassment at this particular estimate.[13] The movement towards an organisational schism gathered pace in the course of the year. Perhaps some greater confidence may therefore be placed in the Sixth Party Congress official report boasting that membership had touched a quarter of a million; but, even so, it was ruefully acknowledged that many of the local claims upon which it was based were probably exaggerated.[14] Nor was this the end of the matter. Central Committee secretary Yakov Sverdlov was to say in October that the number had rocketed up to 400 000. A case of non-Euclidian arithmetic is to be suspected here since in March 1918 Sverdlov put party strength at 300 000 while none the less stating that the mass influx into the ranks had continued unabated from summer 1917 onwards.[15] Consequently all that can be said with certainty about the months between the February and October Revolutions is that they witnessed an astonishing rise in membership. The Provisional Government's repression of the Bolsheviks outside Petrograd was so ineffective that there was, apparently, no immense plunge even during July.[16] It was an achievement which only the most unrestrained optimists among party officials would have predicted in the days immediately after the downfall of the autocracy.

The largest proportion or rank-and-file members was drawn from the working class. Soviet archivists have proposed that as many as three fifths of Bolsheviks were manual workers of some kind or other.[17] How precisely this reflects the truth is impossible to say; but there is little cause to question its rough accuracy. Circumstantial evidence inclines in the same direction. Not only were party members situated overwhelmingly in the country's manufacturing and mining areas, but also local committees are thought to have made a special effort to attract working-class recruits.[18] Menshevik critics were fond of carping that most Bolshevik newcomers were young lads fresh from the villages and wanting in long experience of industrial life and political activity. It was not completely unknown for Bolshevik spokesmen to come close to admitting this.[19] Yet it would be ludicrous to conclude that there were no skilled workers amidst the rank-and-filers. If it had not been for them, in fact, the party would have been reduced to a sorry plight after October 1917 in its search for personnel competent enough to take on positions of administrative responsibility.[20] In any case it is beyond serious dispute that the vast legions of working-class members, skilled or unskilled, gave the Bolsheviks firm roots in industrial communities and kept them closely in touch with shifts in popular opinion.

The remaining rank-and-filers are said to have been either peasants or persons 'on service'.[21] These are baffling categories. Official statisticians later calculated that the peasantry came to constitute a seventh of the entire party by the end of 1917; but possibly most of them were former soldiers and sailors who had joined the Bolsheviks before leaving for the villages in late autumn or early winter. Otherwise it is difficult to explain how so many peasants became members in the absence of propaganda campaigns in the rural areas by many local committees. Or perhaps the answer is that party officials tended to make brief visits to the countryside, persuade inhabitants to jot their names down for membership, and scarcely ever see them again. Still more enigmatic is the identity of persons 'on service'. Few can have been middle-class members if the barrage of Bolshevik complaints about having been deserted by them after 1905 is to be given credence.[22] Anyway entrants displaying an ounce of competence at drafting resolutions or composing articles were usually encouraged to become committee members. In consequence the largest segment of the 'service' category was probably composed of men in the armed forces who remained on the war front or in the garrisons. Perhaps it also included numbers of office staff and shop assistants; but the silence of Menshevik jibes about this is eloquent proof that such persons can have constituted no more than a tiny minority. In other words, most newcomers who were not themselves industrial workers nevertheless sprang from the lower social strata and added their strident voices to the Bolshevik demand that an end be put to every vestige of privilege and exploitation in society.

Curiosity also prompts an enquiry about the party's sexual and ethnic composition. What slender evidence there is suggests that women, though being recruited in the thousands, were still vastly outnumbered by men. Hardly any local committees are known to have conducted special recruitment campaigns among female workers. Central Committee member Alexandra Kollontai was one of the extremely few Bolshevik officials to take up such an interest in 1917; it was only in the Civil War that her ideas were accorded serious attention.[23] Sexual and ethnic divisions are in fact equally unyielding to the quest for arithmetical exactitude. The contemporary reluctance to disclose data about the representation of various nationalities in the party ranks may simply be a reflection of the scantiness of official records, or perhaps it resulted from an embarrassment that an overwhelming preponderance of members were Russians by birth. Signs of how things really stood are to be glimpsed in the party's geographical distribution. About half the total number of Bolsheviks lived in the heartland of central Russia itself; most of the remainder lived in the industrial regions lying outside it where the Russian element in the labour force was strong in numbers.[24] Not that the Bolsheviks were a mono-national party. The bodies set up by them specifically to attract support from Estonians, Lithuanians and Azerbaidzhanis were not without their successes. Latvia was well known as a pillar of Bolshevism in autumn; Jews too joined the party in thousands.[25] Yet Russians predominated, mirroring their importance within the working class and also, it may be surmised, their lack of fear that they might lose their national identity in any 'internationalist' state of the future.

The political complexion of the rank-and-filers called forth unstinted praise and wonderment from Bolshevik officialdom. It was not that they had overnight become sophisticated Marxists, erudite in their exegesis of the classic texts and bursting forth with subtleties of socialist theory. Indeed Timofei Sapronov was astonished by the crudity of their basic outlook on the world. His anxious question whether the new recruits fully understood the party's strategy and policies evoked from them the unflinching riposte: 'Our programme is the struggle with the bourgeoisie.'[26]

This kind of reply confirmed officials in their rather condescending attitude to the rank-and-file members, as terms like 'the party masses' and 'the party public' (which, incidentally, were shared by the Mensheviks, the Socialist-Revolutionaries and the Cadets) perfectly reflect. The traditional solution in the underground days had been to train and educate; but the current swirl of events scotched the opportunity of holding more than the occasional discussion circle or lecture evening. The problem had perforce to be shelved.[27]

Besides, such disadvantages were deemed to wither in the sun of the rank-and-filers' agreed virtues. Their greatest recommendation was their political radicalism. It took time before this came to full flower in several party groups across the country, but already by March 1917 it was noticed that newcomers in the industrial suburbs of Petrograd, Moscow, Saratov and elsewhere would brook no compromise with the Provisional Government.[28] Kronstadt sailors joining the Bolsheviks were well known for their revolutionary 'impatience'.[29] Over the next few months, as social and economic life approached utter dislocation, the call for Kerenski's overthrow and for a further revolution came to be voiced almost universally in the party throughout the country. Thus rank-and-file Bolsheviks, living at the levels of society where unrest was at its greatest, were a powerfully activating force among their work-mates and mess-mates (and, if they had not broken all ties with the rural areas, their fellow villagers too) who chose not to enter the party ranks. They provided a vital source of working-class energy and self-confidence without which it would have been indescribably harder for the party to have entered upon its campaign of strikes, demonstrations and, finally, the seizure of governmental authority.[30]

The men and women who galvanised all these rank-and-filers into organised channels of action were the local activists. They prided themselves as 'the leading cadre' of the Bolshevik party, and a crucial role was indeed performed by them. No worthwhile guess may be made of their number. Not the least of the difficulties in collecting statistical information is the problem that it is wrong to draw a very rigid contrast between the activists and the rank-and-file members. A less industrious activist was indistinguishable from a more enterprising rank-and-filer. The chorus of local grumbles about the paucity of experienced personnel put it beyond all reasonable doubt that the party was sorely stretched in its struggle to cope with the burdens of organisation and propaganda. The occasional town committee announced itself well-endowed with activists,[31] and presumably it was not unknown for other committees to exaggerate their own plight in the interests of being given greater assistance. By no means everything, however, is attributable to provincial swinging of the lead. The Central Committee, itself never so indulgent as to accept local reports at their face value, was kept well enough informed by its own observers to concede that a general shortage did in fact exist.[32] Some respite was secured through the acquisition of activists belonging to the various Social-Democratic groups, such as the Interdistricters, which affiliated themselves to the Bolsheviks in summer. Further help came from the numerous Mensheviks who decided to transfer their personal allegiance. Yet such windfalls, though highly prized, were no answer to a problem which was to grow still more acute after October.[33]

Most activists, like most rank-and-filers, were of working-class origins and continued to live in industrial communities.[34] The party's opponents assiduously cultivated and adorned the story that Bolshevik personnel consisted largely of 'professional revolutionaries' drawn chiefly from the middle class and financed out of party funds. The intelligentsia certainly supplied a multitude of activists. Nearly all the large party organisations managed to get hold of at least a handful of them (except in non-urbanised regions of industry and mining, such as the Donbass, where it was difficult for such persons to discover gainful employment); but smaller organisations tended to rely much more heavily upon working-class leaders, especially if a huge city like Moscow or Petrograd lay nearby to siphon off intellectuals.[35] It is also true that the incidence of middle-class activists increases at the higher echelons of the hierarchy of executive committees.[36] Yet the party would have suffered greatly if it had been unable to call upon the services of those thousands of working-class organisers who were the backbone of the party at the point of contact between the committees and the mass of the ordinary members.

Party finances are a veritable quagmire of half-truths and untested assertions. Many activists are known to have got their living expenses from the party, but the precise number is entirely in the realm of speculation. Over the years it has often been alleged, but never proved, that the Bolshevik Central Committee received a vast subsidy from the German government, a subsidy which was vitally needed to pay party officials. Throughout the raging controversy it has gone almost unmentioned that party funds were by no means the only source of livelihood for Bolshevik officials (or indeed for Mensheviks and Socialist-Revolutionaries). Many a party activist—most of them in all likelihood—took employment in the various mass institutions which sprang to life in 1917. Soviets, trade unions and factory committees were vital to the Bolshevik advance not only in offering an organisational channel for seizing power but also in supplying a wide variety of administrative jobs at the wage level of the skilled industrial workers.[37]

The shortage of experienced personnel meant that activists had to become political 'jacks-of-all-trades' on behalf of their party committees; they had to turn their hand to whatever seemed the priority of the moment. The Central Committee, anxious as ever to keep account of what was happening in the party outside Petrograd, asked the Sixth Party Congress delegates in July 1917 to complete a questionnaire about their personal backgrounds. The results, though obviously not strictly representative of the mass of all activists, are of use at least in pointing to broad tendencies. Three quarters of the delegates held two or more party jobs, a sign of the frenetic pace of party life. Much importance was attached to maintaining face-to-face contact with rank-and-file members and ordinary workers. The skills of public oratory and persuasion were highly valued since two thirds of the delegates saw political 'agitation' as one of their primary tasks. It was evidently far from being an introspective party, obsessed with matters of internal administration and bogged down in a routine of daily business. The overwhelming majority of delegates held positions of responsibility in soviet executive bodies and other mass organisations.[38] The party's watchword was to go out and compete for the social support which held the key to political victory.

Bolshevik officials were later to portray 1917 as the halcyon epoch of 'comradely togetherness' among the activists. Not all of this was rose-tinted nostalgia. There was an amicability and informality about party life before the October Revolution which swiftly departed thereafter. It would appear from the Congress survey that a very high proportion of activists were still in their twenties, were male, and were ethnically Russian; and possibly this widely shared background helped to bind them ever more closely together.[39] Be that as it may, an open and frank atmosphere certainly prevailed. The delegates to the Sixth Party Congress were not to know that this was the last such countrywide gathering to be held in an atmosphere of unembittered, non-vituperative debate until the tragi-comically stage-managed affairs of the late 1930s. Nor was the air unduly stifled by noxious considerations of status or rank. It is not too much of an exaggeration to say that activists were classified not so much according to the formal level in the party's organisational hierarchy at which they worked as according to the estimate of their personal qualities made of them by their colleagues. Much kudos was associated with membership of the Central Committee but it was not unknown for officials to be reluctant to stand as candidates in the elections to it.[40]

Such behaviour speaks of a party still in flux, still groping its way towards setting up a solid political organisation. Even so, it comes as something of a surprise to discover that until 1917 a mere 6 per cent of Sixth Party Congress delegates had previously attended a Party Conference or Conference. Still more remarkable is the fact that 31 per cent acknowledged having been Mensheviks and 8 per cent having belonged to non-Marxist parties (seemingly this referred mainly to Socialist-Revolutionaries and anarchists) before the First World War.[41] Even today there exist numerous irredeemable believers of the legend that the February Revolution beheld the emergence from the underground of a highly drilled corps of long-seasoned Leninists who alone and unaided took up the struggle with the Provisional Government. This belief, however consoling it has been to the party's foremost champions and foremost adversaries alike, appears all the more to be an act of self-delusion in the light of the knowledge that 94 per cent of Congress delegates had become Bolsheviks only in the short period since 1914.[42] Indeed a good number, most notably the Interdistricters, had made their final choice of party allegiance as recently as summer 1917. The Bolsheviks were not the jealously exclusive political sect of popular mythology; they were really much closer to being a catch-all party for those radical Social-Democrats who agreed about the urgent need to overthrow the liberal-dominated cabinet, establish a socialist government and end the war.

The forum of contact between activists and rank-and-filers were the local party organisations. The distended growth of membership and the expanding onus of political activity conspired to make it acutely necessary to establish an articulated structure of executive bodies appropriate to the particularities of the places where they were situated. The basic unit was the cell, still known sometimes as the group or circle and based predominantly in factories, workshops, pit-heads and garrisons. Cells in urban centres moved quickly to form town committees wherever they had not already been created. Suburb committees too sprang up as an intermediate unit. And with the very heaviest concentrations of party membership, as in Petrograd and Moscow, it was not infrequent to come across further executive subdivisions. This was not all. Committees were also founded to recruit entrants from specific social categories: 'sections' were set up to work among national minorities; 'military organisations' were called to life for the enrolment of soldier members. By late autumn, it is conservatively reckoned, the Petersburg City Committee bestrode a structure of fifteen suburb committees (which in turn gave birth to twenty-three lower intermediate bodies), five national sections, and a citywide military organisation (which co-ordinated as many as sixty-five subsidiary military bodies).[43] This scheme of construction was paralleled in numerous town committees across the country, though understandably on a smaller scale. Not all organisations, of course, were to be found in urban centres. Many Bolsheviks lived in the industrial settlements which sprawled around the isolated factories of the Moscow region and the scattered mining enterprises of the Donbass. In such environments it was customary for party cells to group themselves together under the aegis of district committees. As regards organisations on or near the Eastern front, the usual practice was to make use of the units of the command structure employed in the armed forces themselves. It all sounds highly complicated and replete with anomalies and exceptions. And so it had to be unless the party refused to adapt itself to local peculiarities. Difficulties of definition and enumeration are as yet far too profuse to allow experts to agree how many party organisations existed in 1917; but everyone endorses at least that virtually all the towns of the former Russian empire had acquired a Bolshevik committee by the October Revolution.[44]

Committees were usually chosen by some form of election. The simplest method was to arrange an open general meeting, attended by rank-and-filers as well as activists, and hold a vote. But this quickly proved unworkable in the numerically strongest organisations and gave way to more indirect procedures which still permitted the open general meetings to elect suburb committees and entrusted the suburb committees with the election of the town committees. There crop up a few hints that some officials in March 1917 were slow about putting such transactions under way if they thought their own political line likely to prove unpopular.[45] But it seldom took long for these laggards to be overcome. The committees themselves gave equal rights to all their members. Care was taken that the office of chairman should not acquire overriding authority. Thus the name of Sergei Minin, the Tsaritsyn Town Committee chairman, looms large in that locality's revolutionary history not because of his formal party job but as a result of a widespread recognition of his personal qualities of leadership. Attempts by individual officials to subvert committee decisions were wont to provoke an uproar.[46]

All the same it was frequently discovered that the other demands upon committee members' time and energy made it impossible for them to attend all the many sessions which were called to deal with sudden emergencies. Inner subcommittees were set up to deal with the problem; but even this measure did not do the trick. The hectic pace of political developments in the end meant that all committees and subcommittees were impelled to hand over the day-to-day running of party affairs to a small handful of officials. So pressing was the manpower shortage that the Petersburg City Committee itself had to make do with only two main administrators in August.[47] Yet somehow these improvisations worked and committee members felt confident of being able to intervene whenever they objected to the policies and decisions enacted in their name. Trouble was kept to a minimum so long as the informal group in charge of affairs stuck to the overall strategy approved by the majority of their colleagues.[48]

The committees were a law unto themselves when it came to accepting orders from above. Democratic centralism, as vague a principle of internal administration as there ever has been, was commonly held at least to enjoin upon lower executive bodies that they should obey the behests of all higher bodies in the organisational hierarchy. But town committees in practice often had the devil's own job in imposing firm leadership. The Vyborg Suburb Committee, to take the most obvious example, was not content in March 1917 simply to express verbal opposition to a Petersburg City Committee which it branded as altogether too tolerant of the Provisional Government; it went to the length of selecting its own

band of agitators to travel around the Baltic area to stimulate
wider support for its views. Another such instance was the Railway
Suburb Committee's refusal to have anything to do with the
Mensheviks despite the Saratov Town Committee's open advocacy
of the desirability of forming a united Social-Democratic party
throughout the country. Insubordination was the rule of the day
whenever lower party bodies thought questions of importance
were at stake.[49]

Suburb committees too faced difficulties in imposing discipline.
Many a party cell saw fit to thumb its nose at higher authority and
to pursue policies which it felt to be more suited to local
circumstances or more desirable in general. No great secret was
made of this. In fact, it was openly admitted that hardly a party
committee existed which did not encounter problems in enforcing
its will even upon individual activists. Recalcitrant opposition, it is
true, could be dealt with by removing the 'offender' from his or her
party job; but there was no guarantee that he or she would meekly
make peace with the committee thereafter. On the contrary, the
chances were strong that the much-needed activist would simply
move off to work in another place where his views were less likely to
provoke hostility. The Krasnoyarsk Town Committee took a
bravely feudalistic hand to such behaviour by banning all officials
from quitting the locality; but this prohibition had little real effect,
it was more a moral plea for co-operation than anything else.[50]

The notion of democratic centralism also entailed arrangements
for executive party bodies, such as town committees, to be
regularly held to account by the party's lower echelons. The main
tool devised for this purpose were the elections which took place at
the open general meetings or at conferences of delegates. Committee members whose work was thought unsatisfactory or who had
fallen out of step with grass-roots opinion stood in danger of being
hauled over the coals or, if necessary, replaced by other activists.
The electoral debates were often lively affairs with both uplifting
and unsavoury episodes from the candidates' past careers being
recounted by their supporters and detractors for the benefit of the
audience. If feelings were strong enough, the resultant vote might
produce a basic alteration of a town committee's political complexion (even though custom had it, as in Saratov for example, that
leading members of the losing faction should be allowed to retain
their places as committee members).[51] This of course did not mean
that town committees, if they so desired, could not easily snub their

nose at lower-echelon viewpoints in the time before the next election. Try as hard as they might, suburb committees and ordinary cells could meanwhile do little to rectify matters beyond telling their own representative on their town committee to speak on their behalf. Or, if this too failed, they could resort to disruptive tactics by criticising it in public and refusing it all collaboration.[52]

Such difficulties not only confirm the importance of the original election but also point at the potential influence which could collectively be exerted by the rank-and-file members. The old view, popular in the USSR in the 1930s and 1940s as much as in the West, was that ordinary party members were political putty in the hands of Bolshevik officials. And certainly nobody even today is so credulous as to believe that all party policies without exception were thoroughly debated at open general meetings. Massed crowds, for a start, do not afford the most useful forum for careful exchanges of ideas. Yet it is ludicrous to deduce solely from this that grass-roots sentiments could be brushed aside with barely a second thought. Not a few Bolshevik activists in fact testified to their own political discomfiture at the hands of the collective feelings of their rank-and-file members regarding vital issues of the day. The survival of united Social-Democratic organisations in many places until midsummer and even later was largely due to the strength of feeling among ordinary Bolsheviks that the Mensheviks should not be treated as pariahs, a feeling which ebbed only as the consequences of the Provisional Government's policies became evident.[53] The question of a socialist seizure of power too gave rise to animated discussion among the rank-and-filers. Studies of Petrograd industrial suburbs and of the Kronstadt naval garrison show that those officials and activists who called for a further revolution in March and April 1917 were lent stalwart support by the surge of grass-roots demands that the Lvov cabinet should be forcibly removed from power.[54]

Such conclusions cast a long shadow. They raise grave doubts about the customary assumption that the abrupt switchround in party policies which occurred at the Seventh Conference stemmed almost exclusively from Lenin's dynamic leadership. The elements of the traditional story are as follows: in late March an informal gathering of Bolshevik leaders, who had come to Petrograd from all parts of the country for a nationwide soviet assembly, resolved to give conditional support to the Provisional Government; Lenin arrived from abroad too late to do more than harangue the leaders for the decisions they had taken; but so powerful was his hold over their minds that by late April, at the Seventh Conference, he had won them over to his viewpoint. This would be all very well, though highly Carlylean, if it were not for the fact that merely 15 per cent of the provincial delegates to the March gathering secured their election to the Conference in the following month. Some, no doubt, failed to do so because they had been pushed aside by the more prestigious leaders recently returned from exile; others, no doubt, because they stayed on in Petrograd after the March gathering. But that can hardly be true of most of them. There would at least appear to be strong circumstantial evidence that the Conference's radicalism was a reflection of the widespread radicalism of rank-and-file members who by then had used their voting power to change the political complexion of many local committees and local delegations. Indeed the Bolsheviks of Moscow province (excluding the city itself), who constituted 6 per cent of all Conference attenders and formed part of its most vociferously anti-governmental bloc, had not even been represented at the March gathering. It would be silly to claim that Lenin's campaigning in the earlier part of April played no part in this or that the Conference resolutions do not bear the intellectual stamp of his previous writings; but equally it should not be rejected out of hand that his chances of emerging victorious would have been very flimsy in the absence of pre-existing support among the party's grass roots.[55]

Town committees, suburb committees and ordinary cells were the backbone of Bolshevik organisational life in 1917. Yet plans were also made in the course of the year to establish a tier at the level of the province, a tsarist administrative unit, so that party activity in various towns could be co-ordinated. There was no unanimity about this since numerous officials felt that provincial committees were a luxury the party could ill afford with so few activists available in any case. The Constituent Assembly electoral regulations came to the rescue of the plan's advocates when the government announced that the constituencies were to be drawn up along the boundaries of existing provinces. As the years go by, Soviet archivists dig up details about the creation of hitherto unheard-of provincial committees (though in a handful of cases there is more than a suspicion that enthusiasm to publish 'discoveries' has outstripped factual exactitude). The highest estimate to date is thirty-two.[56] But at all events the precise number does not mean very much since the provincial tier was the least authoritative in a hierarchy of command which itself left much to be desired. The fanfare of professed zeal accompanying their election at delegates' conferences was all too often a prelude to an atmosphere of indifference or even mistrust when they began work. A few strove stubbornly to overcome the shortages of finances and manpower that made their activities so difficult. Yet even the Moscow Provincial Committee, probably the most vigorous of them all, could do next to nothing about local party bodies such as the Kolomna Town Committee which refused to bow to official policies.[57]

A further reason for the unsolicitous attitude towards provincial committees was the belief, still often expressed in Bolshevik circles, that the party's business was to concentrate its effort in areas of industrial development and not to dilute them by trying to encompass each and every little township in each and every province.[58] Deeper interest was naturally shown in the formation of so-called regional committees which were meant to co-ordinate the work of local party bodies in their own respective group of provinces. The impulse came mostly from within the region itself, though the Central Committee sometimes accelerated the process, as in the Donbass, by sending down its own personnel to give assistance.[59] Two were elected by late April, six by late July, and ten by the October revolution. Almost all heavy concentrations of urban population had acquired a regional committee by the end of the year. The exceptions were Petrograd itself and the Volga area; the first did not need one since the Central Committee was close at hand, the second since the absurdities of immemorial inter-town rivalries made agreement about where it should be based impossible.[60]

Regional officials sensibly took a modest view of their practical powers; service and leadership were the words which cropped up in their correspondence, not administration and discipline.[61] Up to a score of members might well be voted on to each committee but in reality this hardly ever made any difference. A small handful of leaders would be expected to cope with the daily routine. This was no small imposition in view of the huge expanse of territory covered by them; but they tried to get round the problem by encouraging lower committees to send in a regular stream of detailed reports and by promising in return to publish a regional newspaper (which was thirsted after in those many areas where *Pravda* was not always available).[62] The Moscow Regional Bureau had every reason to take pride in its organisational achievement. Elsewhere the record left fewer grounds for complacency: the Urals Regional Committee omitted to make preparations for the seizure of governmental power in October; the South-West and the Donbass Regional Committees found it troublesome even to keep track of the names of all the party groups and committees within their formal orbit.[63]

Meagre resources and manpower shortages had much to do with this but that is only half the story. Of equal moment was the degree of goodwill and co-operation extended to the regional committees from below; for in the Russia of 1917 it was the easiest thing in the world for lower party bodies to rebut the demands and pleas by higher authority. No regional committee was without its trouble spot. For the Moscow Regional Bureau it was Ryazan, for the South-West Regional Committee it was Odessa, and for the Donbass Regional Committee it was Ekaterinoslav.[64] Disciplinary sanctions were out of the question; patience and persuasion were the only course open to regional officials if they did not seek to alienate local sentiments entirely. Not the least of the organisational problems facing them was the refusal of so many town committees, not only in traditional strongholds like the Ukraine but in central Russia too, to sever their ties with the Mensheviks. It was usually decided to settle upon the compromise of admitting united Social-Democratic bodies to the regional grouping so long as it could be shown that the Bolsheviks held the upper hand in them.[65] Yet certain issues were not conducive to give-and-take. The city committees of both Kiev and Moscow thought the Central Committee's plans for an October insurrection to be a blueprint for political disaster, and nothing would bring them to change their mind. They did everything within their practical power to put a spoke in the wheel of their respective regional committees' military preparations short of denouncing them to the government. Obstructionist tactics greatly impeded the South-West Regional Committee in Kiev in November. But in Moscow the Regional Bureau was fortunate enough to be able to rely upon active help from numerous cells and suburb committees; but this very reliance was yet another token of where power really lay in the party.[66]

A Central Committee which took no cognisance of these facts of life would have condemned itself to perpetual impotence. On the other hand a failure to make an offer of resolute, clear-headed leadership would have been equally abortive. At the time of the February Revolution the much-depleted Central Committee in Petrograd, known as the Russian Bureau, had been left with only three members. Alexander Shlyapnikov was the leading figure and Vsayacheslav Molotov and Peter Zalutski were his adjutants. Their policies were not as aggressive as the Vyborg Suburb Committee's but they would brook no toleration of the Provisional Government. Meanwhile other Central Committee members were struggling their way back from Siberia and gradually produced a majority in favour of less radical policies. This was not accomplished without a battle. Shlyapnikov managed for a while to secure the election of an inner subcommittee which shared his views, but Iosif Stalin and Lev Kamenev fought on remorselessly and by mid-March had arranged fresh elections and carried off a victory which gave them the majority and allowed them to announce their conditional support for the Lvov cabinet. It was a political reorientation which called forth fulsome praise from the provincial leaders who came together for the first informal countrywide Bolshevik gathering in March.[67]

Yet the party was still obviously a house divided against itself and further debate and elections were an evident necessity. The Seventh Party Conference, coming down strongly on the side of Lenin's radicalism, threw up a nine-person Central Committee reflecting the turnabout in aims. The radicals, as the drawn-out vetting of the candidates showed, did not get everything their own way. Not all the nominees defended by Lenin and Zinoviev succeeded; not all those attacked by them failed. Yet the eventual victory was substantial enough. Its sweetness remained even though three leading moderates in the persons of Kamenev, Milyutin and Nogin had secured places; and Lenin cannot have been unduly worried because he had spoken in favour of Kamenev's candidature. The election results were also a symbol of the confidence reposed in Petrograd-based leaders: only Nogin was due to leave the capital after the Conference.[68] Thus the conditions were laid for the operation of a closely knit and vigorous Central Committee. This was practicable in May and June but was forced to be abruptly abandoned at the beginning of July when the Provisional Government drove Lenin and Zinoviev into hiding and arrested Kamenev. Feelings thereupon ran high, at the Sixth Party Congress, that the Central Committee had botched its responsibilities by paying excessive attention to Petrograd and not enough to the provinces. To prevent it happening again it was agreed to increase the number of full members to twenty-one together with several 'alternate' members who could step into their shoes if necessary: local interests were to be protected by the inclusion of representatives from the provinces; an inner sub-committee of eleven Petrograd-based leaders was chosen to oversee day-to-day affairs. Politically too there were further changes since most of the newcomers were of the radical persuasion. The most notable was Lev Trotski who at last decided to bury his old differences with Lenin and to join the Bolsheviks.[69]

The inner subcommittee hardly lasted a month, since the Kornilov affair witnessed the return of prominent Central Committee members like Kamenev, Kollontai, Trotski and Zinoviev from prison or hiding.[70] None of them would reconcile himself to taking a secondary role; everyone wanted to put his stamp upon events. Controversy was the lifeblood of Central Committee activity in 1917. First there had been the question of support for the Provisional Government in March; then conflicts arose about the preparation of the demonstration of early July; and finally in September and October there were the bitterest wrangles of all to do with the proposal for an armed insurrection. Collective loyalty did not always bear up under the strain of disagreements. Stalin broke discipline in early March by publishing Kamenev's name at the bottom of articles in *Pravda* despite the Russian Bureau's explicit orders to the contrary. In August the Central Committee's injunction to all its members to keep silent about Lenin's call for an uprising against the government was defied by Sverdlov. Worse still, Kamenev and Zinoviev did their utmost to ruin the preparations for the seizure of power by divulging them to the non-Bolshevik press.[71]

The Central Committee's administrative business was handled by its Secretariat. Elena Stasova was its first head but she was joined by Sverdlov after her failure to gain election to the Central Committee at the April Conference. Their close rapport came in especially useful after the July Days when the Secretariat had to be split into two sections in different parts of the city for reasons of security. Half a dozen assistants were all the staff that they were spared throughout the year. By and large the Secretariat remained the loyal executor of the Central Committee's wishes (though Sverdlov was apparently not above exaggerating the official membership figures in his possession in October in order to gain acceptance for Lenin's policy). This was not true of that other vital central agency, *Pravda*.[72] Stalin was again the main culprit. He not only displayed a forbidden indulgence to Kamenev in early March but also published Zinoviev's letter of self-defence in October despite knowing that the Central Committee was certain to express its disapproval.[73] But such episodes were exceptional and short-lived because the editorial board was quick to step in and insist upon official policies being observed. The same was not true of the Central Bureau of Military Organisations. Founded in March by the Petersburg Committee to co-ordinate activity among the city's garrison Bolsheviks, it was taken over by the Central Committee and entrusted to do a similar job throughout the country's garrisons and upon the Eastern front. A conference of military organisations was held in June to formalise the position by electing a Central Bureau. But the results were not as the Central Committee had intended; for as well as refusing to accept a Central Committee nominee to its line-up the Bureau proved a sharp thorn in its flesh in July by continuing to call upon rank-and-filers to demonstrate against the government at the very time when the Central Committee was attempting to cool the crowds down.[74]

Thus it is not true that the Central Committee was somehow less efficient than town-level party committees after the February Revolution. In fact it seems to have done just about as much as came within its capacity and its resources. Its meetings were held frequently enough to elaborate clear-cut policies and to adjust them to swiftly changing circumstances. It kept *Pravda* in regular circulation, sometimes having to put it out under a different name but raising its circulation to around 90 000 in August. Its Secretariat sent out over 2000 letters before the October Revolution, not to mention the innumerable messages which reached the provinces by word of mouth.[75] Of course there were lapses. Local committees constantly complained that neither letters nor *Pravda* could be relied upon to arrive from Petrograd; but such comments were unfair since the fault lay with the country's postal services, not with the Secretariat. Politically, however, the Central Committee had less to feel proud about. In particular there was some truth in the oft-repeated charge that the Central Committee's early encouragement of the July demonstration, however much it later came to regret it, was based upon calculations which in the main were relevant only to Petrograd and took little account of events elsewhere. Yet the lessons of this fiasco were not lost upon the Central Committee. Care was taken in October to ascertain that a seizure of power in the capital would not flounder through the absence of political support in other places.[76]

The central leadership was constantly on the look-out for acts of indiscipline. It often summoned disobedient local officials and administered a spirited dressing-down; it sometimes discussed sterner measures such as removal from party posts.[77] But heavy words were untranslatable into disciplinary action. Compliance, if it was to be obtained, would come only through argumentation and cajolement. In the first place there were the thousands of rank-and-filers who for so long set their face against an organisational schism and who, when they changed their mind, did so in their own good time and not out of fear or respect of the Central Committee.[78] Activists were equally likely to jib at directives from above. Disagreements over politics made things difficult enough but, as Sverdlov ruefully recounted, the Secretariat also faced the problem that a mere third of those asked to change their jobs or to work in a different part of the country would consent to do so.[79]

Suburb and town committees could be just as hostile to Petrograd. It was not simply that they often refused to go along with official policies such as the demand for a complete break with the Mensheviks but also, and more disturbingly, that they sometimes took it into their heads to engage in a campaign of active obstruction and disruption. The Kronstadt Committee became notorious for its efforts to push on with the July demonstration despite Central Committee remonstrations; the Moscow and Kiev City Committees, though the news of their activity was not widely broadcast at the time, took every possible step to baulk local preparations for the seizure of power in October.[80] The provincial and regional tiers followed a similar pattern. Not a few provincial committees adamantly rejected central suggestions for the lists of Bolshevik candidates in the Constituent Assembly elections.[81] Regional committees too were known to take independent lines of their own. Some, like the Far-East Regional Bureau, could scarcely help doing so since the Central Committee was unaware of their existence; but others, like the Moscow Regional Bureau in its acrimonious allegations of the Central Committee's indecision about overthrowing the government in the autumn, kept close contact and pulled no political punches.[82]

Centrifugal forces dominated party life in 1917. Yet already beneath the calm and gleaming surface of local self-confidence there were seismic shifts which threatened to generate such strains and tremors as would cause serious difficulty to the party when it at last seized power. At the time these intimations were made light of. Even Lenin, whose revolutionary optimism before the February Revolution had always been tempered by a large measure of political caution, was temporarily carried away by the surge of feeling that the Bolsheviks would have little difficulty in coping with the tasks of government.[83] Thus it came about that the indications of the many basic weaknesses in the party's organisational capacity were played down with a zest that might otherwise seem amazing. Not that the Secretariat was unaware of the problems. Nearly every day its mail was full of letters begging for manpower to be despatched from Petrograd without delay. Equally urgent entreaties were made for newspapers, pamphlets, articles and information sheets. What is more, it was not unknown for local party bodies, most notably the smaller and newer ones, to plead for detailed guidance about how to proceed as regards matters both great and small.[84]

The Central Committee did whatever it could to assist but a complete solution was out of its control. Galling as it must have been to him, Sverdlov could often do little more than advise his pleaders to turn to the pages of *Pravda* for general guidance and to formulate their own specific local schemes accordingly. By the time of the October Revolution his messages reached the extremes of pithiness: 'You understand, comrade, that it is difficult to give you instructions any more concrete than "All power to the soviets". This is apparently all that can be said, except to add that it is of supreme importance to take charge of the post and telegraph offices and also the railways.'[85] This did not mean that the Central Committee was shrugging off its proper responsibilities or underestimating local difficulties: it was essentially a recognition that if the party was ever to take power it was up to the lower committees to make the best of things by relying upon their own manpower and resources and by trusting in their own political instincts about the particular problems facing them in their area. As Sverdlov wrote to the Orsha Committee: 'There is no point in writing to you in detail about work methods. What is needed is lively participation in activity on the spot.'[86]

In any case we should be running ahead of events if we were to assume that local demands for central intervention were the salient feature of Bolshevik life before the October Revolution. Anarchic attitudes to higher authority were the rule of the day. It would have been imbecilic of the Central Committee to have seriously taken issue about this; no Bolshevik leader in his right mind could have contemplated a regular insistence upon rigid standards of hierarchical control and discipline unless he had already abandoned all hope of establishing a mass socialist party. It was not simply that centralisation was rendered impracticable by the problems with transport and communications; it was not even merely that town committees, suburb committees and ordinary cells were too engrossed by the technical business of setting up their own administrative infrastructures to be able to spare either the time or the energy to take much heed of orders from above. More than anything else it was the general climate of opinion, not only among the Bolsheviks but in all the other lower-class mass organisations of 1917, which shaped the internal workings of the party. Patterns of collective decision-making and democratic accountability were not the subject of elaborate ratiocination; they were just part of the unquestioned mental equipment with which politics was conducted in those months. Thus the edge held by the Bolsheviks over the Mensheviks and the Socialist-Revolutionaries did not result from their fictitious obsession with matters organisational. Nobody can deny that the Mensheviks and the Socialist-Revolutionaries were plagued to a greater extent by factional quarrelling, but this was not of decisive importance. What really counted was that the Bolshevik political programme proved steadily more appealing to the mass of workers, soldiers and peasants as the social turmoil and economic ruin reached a climax in late autumn. But for that there could have been no October Revolution. As the Bolsheviks grasped at the reins of government, so the eyes of the world were watching to see whether they would last any longer than their predecessors. They were stepping out into uncharted territory. The question on everyone's lips was whether this party, riven as it was by anarchic and centrifugal forces, would ever be able to bring order to the chaos of Russian society and its economy, let alone unleash a revolution across the length and breadth of Europe.

3 Victory in Defeat (November 1917– May 1918)

Power was wrenched from the helpless hands of the Provisional Government and presented to the Second Congress of Soviets on 25 October 1917. Kerenski's faltering attempt to pre-empt the Bolshevik uprising by closing down their newpapers and harassing their open activities had come to naught. The victory achieved in the capital by the Petrograd Soviet's Military-Revolutionary Committee was complete. Most Menshevik and Socialist-Revolutionary delegates to the Congress had no doubts about the response required of them: they walked out immediately in protest. Undaunted, the Bolshevik Central Committee undertook to form a new government which was to be called the Soviet of Peoples' Commissars (or Sovnarkom). The desertion of the Congress by most other socialist groups was treated as reason for refusing to offer them the olive branch of a coalition. Only the Left Socialist-Revolutionaries, who had just now broken away to found their own separate party and who had remained in their seats at the Congress, were deemed worthy partners. But for the moment the Bolshevik Central Committee discovered them less than willing to align themselves quite so unconditionally with the October Revolution.

Kamenev and Zinoviev felt that only a still broader coalition would protect the Bolshevik party from the danger of political isolation. Their fear appeared justified when the central executive body of the Railwaymen's Union called for a strike until such time as a government representing all shades of socialist opinion was instituted. After a heated debate the Bolshevik Central Committee again decided to stand its ground even though a number of members of Sovnarkom were worried enough by the warnings given by Kamenev and Zinoviev as to lay down their offices. Steadily the reports were flowing into Petrograd that the soviets of the major towns and cities of central Russia were

announcing their support for the Provisional Government's removal. In Moscow and elsewhere there were brief bouts of heavy
fighting but by and large the transfer of power was accomplished
with surprisingly little bloodshed. True, the Ukraine and the Trans-
caucasus still withheld their consent. Yet the overall movement
of events was unmistakably in Sovnarkom's favour, so much so that
the Left Socialist-Revolutionaries overcame their reservations and
resolved to throw in their lot with the Bolsheviks in mid-November
1917.[1]

Sovnarkom, under Lenin's leadership, made no secret of its
dedication to fostering socialist revolution throughout Europe.
How this was to be effected was not entirely clear; official
declarations oscillated between hopes that Bolshevik propaganda
would foment mutinies inside the German armed forces and vague
intimations that a 'revolutionary war' might be unleashed on the
Eastern front to hasten the process along. To outward appearances
the government's intentions as regards the Constituent Assembly
were no less divided between allowing the long-awaited elections
to proceed and suggesting that, whatever the result, Sovnarkom
should continue to be recognised as the sole legitimate authority.
Industrial policies were clearer. The banks were nationalised,
foreign trade was brought under tighter supervision, large-
scale factories and mining enterprises were taken into public
hands. The government also elucidated its views about 'workers'
control'. Elected factory committees were to be permitted to
oversee the general conduct of production but were debarred from
interfering directly in the day-to-day business of management. In
addition the Bolshevik Central Committee saw that it would be
politically suicidal to go ahead with its old scheme for the
nationalisation of all agricultural land; instead it resolved to hand
over the job of redistribution to the peasants themselves—a change
which played no small part in persuading the Left Socialist-
Revolutionaries that the coalition could be worthwhile. Sovnarkom
pinned its hopes of expediting the delivery of food supplies to the
towns upon the peasantry's gratitude for being granted its age-old
desire. Teams of propagandists and grain-collectors were to be sent
into the rural areas to make bargains which would ensure that the
urban population would be adequately well fed in the coming
winter.[2]

The legislative and administrative machinery for this programme took time to be consolidated. There were early troubles

with the civil servants inherited from the Provisional Government who recoiled from taking orders from Peoples' Commissars. In the meantime Sovnarkom relied heavily upon the executive apparatus created by the Petrograd Soviet's Military-Revolutionary Committee. The initial chaos was a prelude to a rapid proliferation of central governmental bodies designed to plug the administrative gaps. Little endeavour was made to demarcate the functions of the new institutions to any great extent. It was not unusual for contradictory instructions to be issued by the many branches of Sovnarkom and by the Provincial Committee of the All-Russian Central Executive Committee of the Congress of Soviets. But in the main the Bolshevik Central Committee managed to lend some coherence to the broad lines of policy whenever inter-departmental conflicts broke into the open and threatened to distract officials from the urgent tasks at hand.[3]

It was less easy, however, to eradicate friction and hostility between central and local authorities. The Bolsheviks had ridden to power on the back of local discontent with the Provisional Government and now they too confronted protests and demands from the provinces. Acts of non-co-operation and downright opposition were undertaken by soviets at the regional, provincial, town and suburb levels alike. Every Peoples' Commissariat, from November onwards, encountered obstacles in trying to get its own local adjuncts to toe the line; and, needless to remark, trade union bodies and factory committees felt no compunction about standing up for their members' special interests, often to the detriment of Sovnarkom's wishes. Conflicts broke out in every interstice between the many levels in the formal hierarchy of power. Local institutions, when they were not quarrelling with Sovnarkom, were likely to be engaged in disputes among themselves. Nobody tried to cover this up. Official spokesmen were among the first to admit that the entire structure of authority was being sapped and mined by a persistent reluctance of soviets in the provinces to forswear their habit of tossing all orders of which they disapproved back in the face of the government. The positive side of this was that local energy and initiative was being used to the full to tackle the country's problems; the negative side was that nationally co-ordinated campaigns were often out of the question.[4]

The plight of industrial workers grew worse over the winter. The long summer of economic disorder produced a bitter harvest of factory closures which led to the lay-off of hundreds of thousands of men and women. The textile enterprises were the worst affected, being brought almost to a countrywide standstill by late autumn. Bargaining for higher wages caused dilemmas in such a situation even though the heady pace of inflation made it all the more vital. Workers in some factories needed so desperately to keep up a minimum of output that they were ready to accept a number of redundancies so long as the elements in the labour force with close rural ties were the first to lose their jobs. Real wages fell disastrously; they were already below the level of subsistence requirements in not a few towns. Small wonder that hordes of workers fled to the countryside to escape the prospect of urban starvation. Between summer 1917 and summer 1918 the number of persons in factory employment plummeted from three and a half to two and a half million. The Bolshevik Central Committee put on a brave face. It said that the ex-peasants who had returned to the villages were in any case a politically unreliable section of the labour force, that their departure had helped to strengthen the resolve and solidarity of those who remained. It also took solace that not all those who abandoned manual employment in the factories did so in order to go off to the countryside; many thousands in fact had been transferred to responsible administrative posts in the new Soviet state. Yet no amount of self-reassurance in this vein fooled anyone. Urban conditions were certain to get a lot worse before they got better.[5]

Soldiers and peasants too had afforded social pillars of Bolshevik strength before the October Revolution. Unlike the workers, they had immediate desires which could be quickly satisfied by governmental action. By turning a blind eye to military desertions and by organising large-scale demobilisations, Sovnarkom was able to solve the most burning grievance held by the mass of soldiers almost at a stroke. Former conscripts streamed in their millions back from the Eastern front and from the town garrisons to their native villages. Their journeys were made all the more urgent by the knowledge that if they tarried they were likely to have no say in the redistribution of agricultural land. The peasantry, with governmental consent, was moving fast to expropriate all the possessions of the landowning gentry. Officially, the large-scale capitalist estates were supposed to remain intact; but in practice the communes usually decided to break them up and parcel them out among the local households, and the Peoples' Commissariat of Agriculture did nothing to stop them. Stolypin's pre-revolutionary

plan to raise the technological standards of Russian grain production fell victim to the resurgence of communal customs and strip-
field methods.[6]

Sovnarkom's programme had mixed effects. The policy which
encountered least resistance was the decree on land redistribution,
but this was scarcely startling since in practice it amounted to
appeasement. Other issues caused greater ado. The Constituent
Assembly elections did not supply the Bolsheviks and the Left
Socialist-Revolutionaries with a majority. Sovnarkom forcibly
dispersed the Assembly in January. It also empowered its newly
created secret police (or 'Cheka') to move ruthlessly to clear the
towns of all 'counter-revolutionary' activity. Spokesmen would
accept no criticism. The lists of electoral candidates, they indicated,
had been drawn up in early autumn before the Left Socialist-
Revolutionaries had broken away from their parent party and
therefore could not be taken to reflect the political order of battle in
following months; and the November elections occurred in
advance of swings in popular opinion towards the Bolsheviks in
numerous towns and villages. No words of self-justification,
however, disguised the fact that the dispersal was an act of political
violence. And it was clearly not the end of the matter: counter-
revolutionary armies were already being trained in the south of
Russia.[7]

Meanwhile it was the First World War which placed Sovnarkom
in its most intractable predicament. Its early summons to the
workers and soldiers of the world to overthrow their governments
and to compose 'a peace without annexations or indemnities' fell
upon distracted ears. The Bolshevik Central Committee opted for
a truce with the German and Austro-Hungarian armies with a
view to giving time for its propaganda to take effect; but it shortly
became clear that the Soviet government was alone in its serious
intention to put a permanent stop to the fighting. The solution to
this dilemma, according to most members of the Bolshevik and the
Left Socialist-Revolutionary Central Committees, was to trigger
off popular uprisings in Europe by means of a revolutionary war.
Lenin opposed this as foolhardy and drew attention to the
exhausted, demoralised state of the Russian forces. By February
1918 he succeeded in winning half his own Central Committee to
his side. Trotski, who until then had hoped to keep the negotiations
going with the German representatives indefinitely, now realised
that an invasion of Russia could be staved off only by bowing

immediately to the Central Powers' ultimatum. His casting vote gave Lenin his victory in the Bolshevik Central Committee, a victory which was ratified by both the Seventh Party Congress and the Third Congress of Soviets in March. The governmental coalition snapped under the strain. The Left Socialist-Revolutionaries resigned in a bloc from Sovnarkom, promising to use all means at their disposal to overthrow the Bolsheviks. Within his own party too Lenin faced acrimonious opposition; for the advocates of a revolutionary war, led by Nikolai Bukharin and known as the Left Communists, laid down their positions in government and Central Committee. Yet the deed was done; the treaty of Brest-Litovsk was signed. Sovnarkom relinquished its claims to sovereignty over the Ukraine, the North Caucasus and the Baltic states. Vast reserves in industrial and agricultural production had been given away at a stroke, to say nothing of the millions of persons involved: it remained to be seen whether this humiliating peace would give the 'breathing space' for which Lenin hoped.[8]

The Bolshevik Central Committee, reeling already from these blows, took a further welter of heavy punishment from the social discontent which gathered fresh vigour in spring 1918. The peasantry, while content with the redistribution of the land, was still notably reluctant to release sufficient grain and other foodstuffs to the hungry towns. Urban detachments failed to make much impact upon the state of affairs by the methods of persuading and haggling. Sovnarkom, hard pressed to do something decisive, turned to sending 'plenipotentiary' expeditions into the countryside and directed a blind eye to the ensuing reports of violent conflict. The honeymoon between government and peasant was coming to an end. This rupture was bad enough for the Bolsheviks but it was made even worse by the growing hostility towards them exhibited by numbers of industrial workers. The continual dislocation of production and the galloping rate of inflation pushed factory committees into demanding a scale of nationalisation which far outstripped Sovnarkom's wishes. Workers in many enterprises, no longer willing to put up with the self-restraints demanded of them from above, empowered their committees to take matters into their own hands by getting rid of the owners and managers once and for all. Economic grievances were starting to acquire an explicitly political coloration. The Mensheviks, freed from the burdens and responsibility of public office by the October

Revolution, made gains in the elections to several local soviets; the Left Socialist-Revolutionaries were engaged in organising terrorist campaigns and even armed uprisings against the Bolsheviks in certain provincial towns. By May 1918 a tidal wave of unrest and discontent, in the towns and in the rural areas, threatened to engulf Sovnarkom in the immediate future.[9]

It is hard to say how many Bolsheviks there were in 1917–18. Sverdlov, whose arithmetical shenanigans have already been noted, put the number in March 1918 at 300 000; later archivists, though able to approach the task with greater circumspection, have lamentably failed to come remotely near to agreeing among themselves. Estimates range from 115 000 to 390 000.[10] There will probably never be a definitive solution since local party committees still had a strong incentive to exaggerate their membership figures as a means of being allowed to send more voting delegates to Party Congresses and Conferences. The culprits did not always escape detection. An official enquiry at the Seventh Party Congress embarrassed the Sevastopol delegates by suggesting that their claim to represent 3500 Bolsheviks overstated reality by as many as 3000. But a lot of the less blatant cases must have slipped through the net because the Secretariat's channels of information were too defective by far to permit it to keep tabs on all that was going on outside the capital.[11]

But all is not lost. It would take a surfeit of scholarly scepticism to deny that the number of Bolsheviks continued to rise between late summer 1917 and the beginning of 1918. Numbers in the Urals region, to take the clearest example, appear to have increased twofold in that period.[12] Whilst absolute figures are unreliable it would not be stretching our credulity too much to accept that local reports are roughly correct in what they tell us about relative trends. At all events it is perplexing to explain why so many Bolshevik officials harped so often upon the risks involved in continuing to admit vast hordes of 'October Communists' into the party unless such admissions were indeed happening on a large scale. A moment's thought confirms the point. Since seizing power the Bolsheviks had become the party of government; it would have been astounding if persons who had previously felt lukewarm towards them or who now saw the chance of personal advancement did not attempt to enter their ranks. Thus the rise in membership, which had enjoyed universal approbation before the October

Revolution, was now for the first time beginning to be seen in a disturbing light.[13]

But equally disconcerting was the decline in numbers which occurred from early 1918 onwards. This started happening, contrary to what is usually assumed, some months before the Central Committee's decree in midsummer that the party should be purged of its 'undesirable' elements. Thus the Bolsheviks of the town of Ivanovo-Voznesensk, who had gathered together nearly 5500 members by August 1917, were reduced to 4000 in the province as a whole by May 1918. Many drop-outs did not go through the rigmarole of tendering a formal resignation; they simply stopped contributing anything to or doing anything for the party. And so a large proportion of rank-and-filers in the local registers were really, as the Urals Regional Committee ruefully put, 'paper communists'.[14] A few officials contrived to welcome this voluntary exodus on the grounds that it relieved the party of 'ballast' which it could ill afford to go on carrying; but in the main it was realised that the fall-off in Bolshevik strength, if it continued, would pose grave problems.[15]

Local committees shrank from discussing why the difficulty had arisen. They are not likely to have shown such reticence if the bulk of the drop-outs had been composed of middle-class members; for this would have given officials a chance to expatiate upon the revolutionary solidarity of all working-class Bolsheviks. It is more probable by far that it was industrial workers who were leaving in droves. After all, it would have been strange if the growing unpopularity of Sovnarkom in factory milieux had been confined exclusively to non-Bolsheviks; for governmental policies affected the working lives of men and women inside as well as outside the party. But political disenchantment was not the only factor. There was also the problem that, with the best will in the world, ordinary Bolsheviks who remained in the towns must have found it onerous to sustain active membership at a time when they could barely manage to fill their own stomachs. Indeed a good number of members, especially those with close rural ties, almost certainly resorted to speeding off to their villages in search of food (as well as a possible share in the redistribution of land, no doubt), thereby allowing their party affiliation to lapse.[16]

The effects upon the party's social composition quickly sank home in the minds of Bolshevik officialdom. As the proportion of working-class members declined, so that of entrants from the middle class rose; the steady drift towards a party in which industrial workers no longer numerically predominated was under way. It was reinforced by the fact that many working-class members of 1917 found themselves promoted away from the factory bench after the October Revolution. The Central Committee Secretariat was well aware that resolute counter-measures were required if Bolsheviks in manual occupations were not to turn out as second-class citizens within their own party; it was so easy for educated, bourgeois recruits to inveigle their way into administrative jobs inside and outside the party in a way that was difficult for ordinary workers. Sverdlov therefore announced the need for a programme of political and cultural education which would equip all Bolsheviks with the wherewithal to take upon themselves every kind of governmental responsibility. The rank-and-filer, he urged, who had been so useful in participating in the demonstrations and uprisings against the Kerenski cabinet, must now be given the training necessary to cope with the more complicated and more positive tasks of government.[17]

Such hopes were doomed to be held in abeyance for some time; economic chaos, social dislocation and political turmoil put it out of the question for the moment to contemplate ambitious schemes of party schooling. Throughout 1917 the Bolsheviks had been an outward-looking party; they had constantly concentrated their energies upon making headway in all the elective grass-roots mass institutions like the soviets. Work inside party committees continued to be sacrificed, understandably, in the same fashion after the October Revolution. If Bolshevik officials devoted special attention to practical issues of the party's internal operations, it is to be glimpsed in their endeavour to establish as many party cells and committees as possible in those areas not yet covered by the existing network. Sverdlov announced that 125 new 'organisations'—again he omitted to define the term—were set up between late October 1917 and early February 1918; most were based in the armed forces but some must also have been in far-flung towns and cities such as Tashkent where the Bolsheviks had hitherto achieved little success.[18] Nonetheless the Topsy-like growth of the organisational edifice was slowing down. Indeed there was probably some contraction by spring inasmuch as military demobilisation necessarily led to the disbandment of many party groups in the armed forces. If this is true, then the party was becoming even more overwhelmingly a town-rooted affair than in the previous year; for there is no evidence that party recruitment was yet making much headway in the rural areas.[19]

Bolshevik activists were being tugged into public office on a scale unseen since the Mensheviks and Socialist-Revolutionaries had dominated local soviets in March 1917.[20] Although nobody thought of questioning this as a priority, yet there were signs that several party officials were coming round to believing that things were being taken too far. It was fair enough to allocate enough manpower to keep the soviets, the trade unions and the factory committees in Bolshevik hands; but by midwinter it was not uncommon to hear complaints that party bodies at all levels had become almost denuded of personnel.[21] Evgeniya Bosh, working in the South-West Regional Committee, was not the only party chairman who was expected to cope on her own for days on end. Administrative staff was pared to a minimum; secretaries were expected to deal with all technical business with little or no assistance. Committee members were greatly taken up with their soviet responsibilities and found it even more difficult than in 1917 to attend regular formal meetings.[22] Important decisions were hammered out increasingly on the basis of behind-the-scenes consultations; every effort was made to stress that the party should not be turned into a 'talking shop'. Nonetheless certain issues were deemed so fundamental to the future of the revolution as to merit thorough debate. The Brest-Litovsk affair in particular witnessed party committees sitting long into the hours of the night, often at the expense of urgent tasks of local government, to settle official policy. Such episodes aside, however, it was not entirely unwarranted for pessimists to warn that, if current developments persisted, the party's organisational identity stood in danger of being effaced by the burdens of its public commitments.[23]

Optimists tried to see the positive side. They argued that the parlous condition of the party's internal administration was an expenditure worth bearing so long as the Bolsheviks sustained their existing level of achievement in the soviet sphere. Indeed scarcely a day went by without an official spokesman stating that party representatives in public institutions should be encouraged to get on with the job at hand without being pestered into referring each and every snag back to their party committee. The opportunities for initiative were elastic, not to say boundless. Mark Minkov is a case in point. Ordered to march a troop of Petrograd Red Guards down to the Donbass to deal with the military threat of Cossak counter-revolutionaries, he seems to have construed his assignment as permitting him to take the lead in organising a Bolshevik seizure of power in Kharkov.[24] Actions of this sort also highlight the growing risks of political involvement as the possibility of a civil war became a probability in early 1918. It was not merely that Bolshevik officials, whether they earned their wages from the party or from the soviets, were scarcely more immune from the rigours of economic inflation than ordinary manual workers; it was also that their party affiliation would be treated as no light matter by the White armies, should they ever fall into their hands. It says something for the determined atmosphere inside the party that problems with political renegades do not appear to have been unduly numerous.[25]

Yet the charge that party work was being neglected was irrefutable. In Vologda, an eyewitness later recalled, it was the Bolshevik 'fraction' of the town soviet, rather than the party committee itself, which dealt with most decisions of importance; and such was the measure of agreement between them that this arrangement suited everyone concerned.[26] Elsewhere, however, conflicts were often deep and bitter. Many a local soviet, trade union or factory committee took advantage of an unwary party committee by issuing instructions which flagrantly contradicted its wishes.[27] Troubles with Bolshevik representatives in public institutions could of course always be met by transferring the delinquents from the posts they presently held. But this was less likely to be the end of the matter if a lower-level party committee decided that its town party committee had acted precipitately or unjustly. Events in Astrakhan, Penza and Nikolaev illustrate how things stood in reality. An Astrakhan official by name of Trusov took his political quarrels with higher authority to the lengths of forming his own organisationally separate group of party members which refused to show allegiance to the Town and Provincial Party Committees. But his stand could not have lasted long if he had not been able to count upon lower echelons within the party. The contrast with circumstances in Penza is conspicuous. There the Town Party Committee, discovering that the editor of the soviet newspaper had defied its wishes in an editorial comment, pounced immediately and ensured that it did not happen again. His campaign quickly fizzled out in Penza for want of the kind of following enjoyed by Trusov in Astrakhan. Not every official, of course, was willing to take such a defeat lying down; but if support among the lower ranks of the party was lacking, then the only remaining option for further opposition was to leave the vicinity and take up work with another party committee. This had happened so frequently in the town of Nikolaev that beleaguered committee leaders described it as a malaise of epidemic dimensions.[28]

The image of a disciplined hierarchy of party committees was therefore but a thin, artificial veneer which was used by Bolshevik leaders to cover up the cracked surface of the real picture underneath. Cells and suburb committees saw no reason why the October Revolution should oblige them to kow-tow to town committees; nor did town committees feel under compulsion to show any greater respect to their provincial and regional committees than before.[29] Exceptions there were. In May 1918 the Northern Regional Committee succeeded in constraining a group of Novgorod Provincial Committee members to be transferred to posts in other localities. Even so, this obeisance to higher authority was not quite so straightforward as it might appear. The Regional Committee would never have dared to chance its arm if it had not already been invited to arbitrate in a Novgorod dispute by most members of the Provincial Committee itself.[30] At any rate the mainstream of party life flowed on in the same anarchic fashion as in 1917. Zinoviev was not too far wide of the mark when he said that the Northern region's hierarchy of Bolshevik committees, which he had observed at close quarters, was facing total disintegration; Sverdlov recoiled from expressing himself so apocalyptically but concurred nonetheless that the basic description was equally applicable to the party as a whole.[31]

Central Committee members were often to be heard declaiming, in stentorian tones and abstract phrases, that the party urgently needed to construct its own smoothly functioning countrywide hierarchy of command; but their rhetoric would have been listened to with more attentive ears if they had shown readiness to put their own house in order in the first place. The internal administration of the central party machine remained as improvised as ever. Central Committee meetings were still about a dozen strong in attendance and were still conducted at the frenetic pace necessary if the mountain of official business was to be moved. Kamenev, Nogin and Zinoviev resigned in protest at the early refusal by Lenin and Trotski to go along with their vision of a broadly based governmental coalition of all socialist parties; but the absence of these competent committee-men and administrators in no perceptible way lowered the Central Committee's prodigious work-rate. Geography too, in those days before transcontinental air travel, kept down the number of participants. S. G. Shaumyan and P. A. Dzhaparidze, based in distant Baku on the shores of the Caspian, were not the only provincial leaders who would not have taken kindly to orders requiring them to make regular train journeys to the capital. But the heavy burden of soviet duties, from which only Stasova and Bukharin were exempted so as to enable them to devote themselves exclusively to party activities, would anyway have made it inconceivable that the Central Committee should have operated in a less hand-to-mouth fashion than before the October Revolution.[32]

Sverdlov stayed nominally in charge of the Secretariat but his newly-received governmental post as chairman of the All-Russian Central Executive Committee of the Congress of Soviets meant that Stasova was expected to transact most affairs on her own initiative. Yet he had grown in political stature since April 1917 (when Lenin expressed doubts about his calibre as a Central Committee member). Thus whenever the Secretariat became involved in serious disputes with local party committees it was he who stepped back in to handle them.[33] There was never the barest glimpse of political dissension between the Central Committee and the Secretariat since Sverdlov was among Lenin's most ardent associates. Stasova later confessed to having had misgivings about the desirability of a separate treaty with the Germans; but, as if to make up for this, she was the most vociferous of the Central Committee's advocates once it had finally decided its policy. Her conversion of mind was so enthusiastic that she was not averse to sending out garbled accounts of events in Petrograd as part of her campaign to secure provincial approval of the treaty.[34] All this makes the Secretariat sound a den of high-powered Machiavellianism. It was not. It was still the over-worked, under-staffed and poorly equipped little group of activists, mostly women (and thereto hangs a Bolshevik male-chauvinist tale), that it had always been. The only improvement in its working conditions since the October Revolution was that it had been housed in a single set of offices for the first time since the July Days and that it had untrammelled access to state communications facilities for the first time in the party's history. Such was destined to remain its fate so long as the Central Committee was happy to allow Sovnarkom and the All-Russian Central Executive Committee to retain their roles as the primary organs of governmental administration.[35]

In fact the hectic character of central party activity was reinforced in early 1918 when a German attack on Petrograd was imminent. The capital was moved hastily and permanently to Moscow. But Petrograd's importance was not forgotten and the Central Committee took care to leave five members behind when it decided to move in February.[36] The Seventh Party Congress supplied a chance to examine whether a more settled system of central decision-making could be devised. But the delegates were too bothered by the life-and-death problems of Brest-Litovsk to involve themselves in a debate about administrative reform. The only change to be agreed upon was the reduction of the Central Committee to fifteen full members and eight alternates. In the past the dispersion of so many leaders across the length and breadth of the country had obviously offended Sverdlov's eye for executive neatness; for he now argued that a smaller number of elected officials, achieved by lowering regional representation, would ease the arranging of regular quorate meetings.[37] Through no fault of his own, things did not work out precisely as he had intended. Bukharin, Kiselev and Lomov from the beginning declared their unwillingness to have anything to do with a Central Committee wedded to the policy of a separate peace with the Central powers; it was some time before these Left Communists would agree to return to the fold. Yet Sverdlov's main intention was realised since there were still eleven full members and two alternates available for work in the new capital, Moscow. It was to take the rigours of the Civil War to bring Bolshevik leaders round to thinking that a much more radical reconstruction of the central party machine was necessary.[38]

The Central Committee found no respite from the disputatious proclivities and disorderly behaviour of local committees after the October Revolution. Both its rejection of the Mensheviks and the Socialist-Revolutionaries in November 1917 and its break-up of the Constituent Assembly in January 1918 had the salutary effect of binding the party, with the exception of a handful of central and provincial leaders, round its flag; but various other issues evoked acts of insubordination as bitter as any in Bolshevik history. The Left Communists, firmly ensconced in most regional committees, adamantly declined to temper their criticisms not only as regards

Brest-Litovsk but also in respect of industrial and rural legislation; they felt that too little opportunity was being given to workers to control the factories and that too much indulgence was being shown to richer peasants in the redistribution of the land.[39] The same was true of dozens of town committees. At every rung in the hierarchical ladder of command there were plentiful instances of determined opposition to decrees and instructions handed down from the capital: suburb committees and ordinary cells were no less reluctant than hitherto to stand up for their own opinions. Bolsheviks in the provinces considered that 'their own' revolution was just as important as what had happened in Petrograd and Moscow since the seizure of power. Local freedom to discuss and to decide was guarded as jealously as ever. The words spoken by M. I. Vasilev, the deputy chairman of the Saratov Town Soviet, testify resoundingly to that ebullience of self-confidence which animated the party everywhere: 'Our commune is the beginning of a worldwide commune. We, as the leaders, assume full responsibility and fear nothing.'[40]

Yet the paradox remained (though it is a paradox only if we maintain extremely limited expectations of human behaviour) that officials often, while fending off the Central Committee with one arm, went on beckoning it with the other to come to their assistance. Quite a number of town committees which publicly anathematised Lenin and his colleagues as traitors to the revolutionary cause were simultaneously composing letters to them in the hope that they would prove angels of mercy. Relief was sought from the pressures of the manpower shortage and requests were sent to make an improvement in communications.[41] There was also a stream of pleas—again especially from committees with small followings—for specific directives about particular policies. The Secretariat received a most touching message from the party cell in Tersy, deep in the heart of Saratov province: 'Send our village some texts for learning and, if at all possible, some apostles. Educate us, open our unenlightened eyes and instruct us in the wisdom of this teaching.'[42] How hard-bitten atheists like Sverdlov and Stasova responded to the biblical undertones of this letter is unknown; but we may be sure that they were as little able to satisfy the practical needs of the Tersy comrades as they were in the case of more prestigious and sophisticated regional, provincial and town committees. Even Evgeni Preobrazhenski, who throughout his party career (unlike so many of his Left Communist associates) retained a healthy wariness of excessive centralisation, was ready to concede that circumstances warranted more strenuous intervention from above in local affairs. As the food and transport crisis deepened, so it was becoming accepted to a wider extent that the Central Committee, which alone was in a logistical position to find out where the major trouble-spots lay, needed to be accorded greater power if it was to surmount the social and economic obstacles in its path.[43]

Party leaders in the capital would gladly have answered these sentiments with an all-round programme of centralisation; they were constantly calling for a new emphasis upon discipline and self-restraint. But they were also realistic. They knew that it would be all too easy to go charging in like a bull in a china shop and create still more havoc than already existed. Asked to give a ruling in the protracted dispute between the Donbass Regional Committee and the Bolshevik military commander Antonov-Ovseenko, the Secretariat issued the following explanation why it could not immediately clear things up: 'Bear in mind that it is impossible for us to take any direct measures without also hearing the other side's case.' Sverdlov on occasion threw his hands up in despair at the swirling fog of contradictory data through which he had to pick his way. The wrangle between the Astrakhan Provincial Committee and the defiant Trusov was a Byzantine intrigue which defeated him altogether; he refused point-blank to act as arbitrator. It was a sensible decision. To have done otherwise would undoubtedly have heaped hot coals upon his head from one side or the other.[44]

By early 1918, however, the cry was going up from numerous party bodies in the provinces that the Central Committee's sedulously cultivated 'low profile' was disingenuous in the extreme. Sovnarkom quickly acquired a habit of appointing plenipotentiary officials to tackle specific problems such as the transport breakdown or the grain shortage, a habit which was given the full approval of the Bolshevik Central Committee. Party leaders throughout the Urals and Siberia were aghast at A. G. Shlikhter's fierce campaign to requisition agricultural supplies under these auspices and were quick to make strong complaints about what they took to be a flagrant infringement of their own spheres of competence. The plenipotentiaries were greeted with equal hostility in the Ukraine. The Nikolaev Provincial Committee opposed them on the practical grounds that they lacked any acquaintance with local conditions; but party bodies in neighbouring provinces were much less restrained and unequivocally denounced them as alien 'occupiers'.[45] Such abusive language had hardly been known inside the party before the October Revolution. Try as hard as it could to hide behind the back of Sovnarkom, the Bolshevik Central Committee was clearly engaged in an endeavour to put its relations with local party committees on a new footing. Its labours were restricted to a few critical bottlenecks but there was nothing tentative about its approach. A way was already being cleared towards centralisation even before the onset of the Civil War.[46]

But we must not run ahead of events too far; for in most other respects there was little change in the pattern of conflict between the Central Committee and party bodies in the provinces after the seizure of power. The Brest-Litovsk controversy had Bolshevik officials on tenterhooks about the possibility that the party might at any moment be split asunder by the disagreements convulsing it. Never since April 1917 had so many local committees given notice so stridently that they would not be pushed around by the central party machine. The advocates of a separate treaty with the German government faced a daunting struggle in January 1918. Most town committees and nearly all regional committees were sternly declaring that revolutionary war was the only possible option for the party if the truce should break down on the Eastern front. The turnabout which was to follow was as striking as what had happened in the previous year before the April Conference. Within weeks of the Central Committee's decision to reverse its policy and to accept the humiliating German terms it was being reported that town committee after committee was falling in line with Lenin's viewpoint.[47]

Why was this? Soviet authors maintain that the Left Communists' stranglehold upon the party earlier in the year had been illusory and that they had been doomed to be felled as soon as they were constrained to expose their ideas to the cut-and-thrust of open debate. This view, while having much to recommend itself, errs through its abundant overstatement. Far from being cowed by the Central Committee's change of mind, the regional committees of the Urals, Moscow and the Ukraine continued to oppose the peace treaty well after the date of its signature. The Urals Regional Committee published a stream of editorials condemning the Central Committee for its actions. A regional meeting of Ukrainian

Bolshevik officials, who had fled south to Taganrog to escape the invading German troops, took its opposition a stage further by resolving that party committees in the Ukraine should henceforward remain independent of the Moscow Central Committee and should give allegiance only to an international executive body which was to be drawn from communist parties across the globe. The Moscow Regional Bureau, with its usual forthrightness, proclaimed simply that all true Bolsheviks should completely sever their organisational links with the Central Committee. It will clearly not do to pretend that the Left Communists were a tiny oppositionist group whose objections to the treaty were easily brushed aside in March 1918.[48]

It is tempting to conclude that the crucial factor was the disparity in political stature, nerve and leadership displayed by the two sides in the controversy. Bukharin shuddered at the thought when he asked himself: 'Am I of sufficient stature to become leader of a party and to declare war upon Lenin and the Bolshevik party?' His natural diffidence, which dogged him all through his career, had its parallels among local officialdom. Tsaritsyn for a time was a hotbed of Left Communism. One of its guiding figures, a certain Erman, was seen suddenly to drop his opposition to the Central Committee in early March. His about-face astounded his erstwhile associates but their efforts to persuade him otherwise fell on stony ground. He so much doubted the Left Communists' ability to carry the party with them that he felt that a decision to go to war with the Central powers would inevitably involve Bolsheviks in 'knocking each other's heads in beforehand'. It was this kind of half-heartedness that filled Stasova with contempt. The Left Communists of Petrograd, she wrote, ought not to be taken seriously, 'since they speak many loud words but behind those words there are hidden no active measures to prepare a revolutionary war'.[49]

Yet this explanation of the Brest-Litovsk dispute, when taken very far, rests upon a fallacy. To say that Left Communist leaders at central, regional and town levels failed because of their personal inadequacies begs the question whether they could have imposed their viewpoint upon the mass of the party even if they had had the nerve and the skill to try. The answer must be no. It would have required the existence of a disciplined hierarchy of command stretching down from the regional committees to the party cells. That had never existed in Bolshevik history, as the Left Communists were well aware. The Moscow Regional Bureau, easily the most truculent, found itself flailing impotently against a wall of lower-echelon hostility as soon as debate reached the public arena. Its members took to paying brief visits to towns whose party committees had come out in favour of a treaty; Varvara Yakovleva, its secretary, was a well-gifted orator who managed to sway not a few Bolshevik audiences in places such as Yaroslavl. But these achievements, more often than not, were quickly swept aside in the wake of visits by Central Committee supporters. Apart from sending its members back round the same towns there was nothing that the Moscow Regional Bureau could do about it.[50]

The basic cause of the demise of Left Communism was in fact the hostility towards it shown by the overwhelming bulk of party members. Bukharin and his supporters had caught a strong whiff of what was afoot by the third week of January 1918; they had become so despondent about their chances of victory in public debate that they tried, unsuccessfully, to persuade the Central Committee to call off its plan to convoke a Party Congress in order to gauge Bolshevik opinion across the country.[51] The town of Tsaritsyn gives us a clear view of how town committees could be brought over to support the peace treaty. Throughout January the editorials of the local newspaper had beaten out the message that no compromise was to be tolerated in the negotiations with the Central powers at Brest-Litovsk; it was assumed that Sovnarkom would engage in a revolutionary war in the event of a rupture of the truce at the front. But then an open general meeting of all the town's party members was arranged and a debate was held about foreign policy. The result was a victory for the advocates of a separate peace (and it was a victory, incidentally, which preceded Lenin's triumph in the Central Committee). The role played by the Tsaritsyn Town Committee remains obscure; it is just possible that it had privately decided to support a treaty shortly before calling the open general meeting. Even so, there were still plenty of Left Communists around who continued to put the case for a revolutionary war. At the very least the episode shows that most of the town's active rank-and-filers in Tsaritsyn no longer favoured a resumption of military operations on the Eastern front. There is little reason to doubt that their feelings were shared by the lower orders of the party, at least in central Russia.[52]

This makes it laughable to contend that Lenin bludgeoned his party into submission. To be sure, he got up to a trick or two. He and Sverdlov seem to have arranged somehow that the Moscow and Petrograd Bolsheviks composed a much larger segment of the Seventh Party Congress than their numerical strength as a proportion of the party as a whole should have allowed.[53] But the tide of party opinion was already in any case running fast in Lenin's favour. He would eventually have won the debate even if the Left Communists had beaten him at the Congress (so long as they had permitted him to go on propounding his views). The localities were remarkably well informed about the issues at stake. Left Communists in Ivanovo tried to pretend in public that Lenin in fact advocated revolutionary war; but such connivances never worked for very long.[54] Too many emissaries of either side were busily travelling up and down the country for local activists and rank-and-filers to be kept perpetually in the dark. For their part the Left Communists were always on the lookout to publish material incriminating the Central Committee with applying administrative sanctions against its opponents; but they could dredge up nothing except a few demands that local committees should call their own troublemakers to order. In their hearts they knew that they had lost because the party, after hearing both sides of the question, had of its own volition rejected them.

Their own practical experiences left them in no doubt why it had happened. It required no great insight to recognise that pro-Bolshevik soldiers, once demobilised from the Eastern front, were too exhausted and demoralised to resume the military struggle with a foreign foe as powerful as the German armed forces still were. By April 1918 it was not unknown for Left Communists in Ekaterinburg to acknowledge the fact in public. They also realised that no amount of fiery resolutions composed by party committees carried any weight if active support could not be attracted from industrial workers inside and outside the party. It all depended, in the words of Preobrazhenski, upon whether the working class would agree to engage in 'a most active and feverish preparation for the inevitable combat at hand with the German marauders'.[55] Nothing printed in following issues of his newspaper gave any sign that any such enthusiasm existed. Even if it had, indeed, the obstacles in the way of forming regiments and keeping them in the field would have been enormous unless assistance was obtained from Sovnarkom in Moscow. The Left Communists in control in Ivanovo-Voznesensk raged about the constraints placed upon their activities by the local shortage of food supplies.[56] No wonder that the vast majority of Bolsheviks, their noses pushed down into the harsh realities of military unpreparedness and economic ruin, inclined heavily in favour of a separate peace. Lenin's achievement was not his much-vaunted but entirely mythical ability to bring his party to heel simply through a display of ranting and raving leadership. Nobody can deny that he ranted and raved a good deal; but that was not what secured him his victory. His real accomplishment lay in winning over most Central Committee members to his side and thereby ensuring that the opinion of the party as a whole was consulted. Once this was done, it was a foregone conclusion that the policy of accepting the German terms would be confirmed.[57]

Yet as late as April 1918 there were still party committees which refused to give up their denunciation of the Brest-Litovsk treaty. This might have been predicted with Bolshevik officials who had to evacuate the Ukraine in order to evade the clutches of the invading German forces; but certain town committees in Russia too (such as Ekaterinburg, Ivanovo-Kineshma, Ivanovo-Voznesensk and Perm) held on to the Left Communist cause with just as much determination. It seemed that nothing would shake their belief that a revolutionary war should be waged. In fact, what finally effected a rapprochement between them and the Central Committee was not so much a change of heart as a change of circumstances. By the beginning of May it was obvious that the political and military security enjoyed by the Bolsheviks in the heartland of Russia since the October Revolution had come to an end. Political insurrections were being planned in a number of towns and military invasions were being made ready in several peripheral areas. Arguments about Brest-Litovsk were no longer relevant to the immediate crisis. Not that recalcitrant Left Communists felt inhibited even now in criticising tactical aspects of the Central Committee's foreign policy.[58] But the general aim of winning the forthcoming Civil War overrode everything else and relegated the issue of a separate peace to the dustbin of history.[59]

The Bolshevik party, which before the October revolution had seen the worldwide overthrow of capitalism as near at hand, now looked over its shoulder and came face to face with the prospect of a domestic bloodbath. Party officials maintained a stiff upper lip in public but they would have been fools to discount the ordeals that lay ahead of them. The way had been strewn with unanticipated pitfalls ever since the seizure of power. The industrial economy was in straits as dire as ever; the shortage of food supplies in the towns had never been more acute. Bolshevik leaders were well aware that nothing undertaken by them in the social and cultural spheres could be of much use unless they also managed to rescue the material situation from disaster. And yet the party gave many signs that it was about to share the fate meted out to the Mensheviks and Socialist-Revolutionaries in the previous year. Already the working class had shown that it was far from happy about the government's handling of affairs. The social composition of the Bolshevik party itself was changing as thousands of industrial workers left its ranks. The immense burdens of public office offered little chance of salvaging matters in the near future. Indeed the Brest-Litovsk controversy, though it had produced a resounding victory for Lenin's side, had for a time nevertheless brought the party to the edge of the abyss of total disintegration. It had pulled up short; but only just. The early months of government, far from putting out the flames of insubordination and indiscipline, fanned an even greater conflagration. The Central Committee had admittedly belied its apparent weaknesses by using Sovnarkom to exercise vigorous control over the operation of transport services and grain requisitionment. But it was treading this path carefully. The knowledge that so many local party committees were crying out for its assistance, its guidance and its intervention did not delude it into thinking that a faster pace of centralisation was worth the risk of provoking a storm of provincial opposition. The question hanging over the Bolsheviks in October 1917 had been whether their anarchic party had taken on too much in promising to consummate a socialist revolution in the wake of economic ruin and social dislocation. The answer was still awaited in May 1918.

4 The Alarm is Sounded (June 1918–March 1919)

The Civil War greatly outstripped the Eastern front in sheer savagery and brutality, if not in the number of casualties and fatalities. It began almost accidentally. Czechoslovak units of former prisoners-of-war who were being sent back to their native country via the Trans-Siberian railway suddenly came to blows with the Bolsheviks of Novonikolaevsk in May 1918. The Red Guards were no match for them. Within a few days it was reported that most cities to the west of the Urals had fallen to the Czechoslovaks. By mid-June they had reached the Volga and occupied Samara and Kazan. It could not have happened at a worse time for Sovnarkom. British expeditionary troops, who had first set foot on Russian soil in April, were steadily reinforced by contingents dispatched to the northern ports of Archangel and Murmansk in the summer. French warships had docked in Odessa; American forces were already ashore in Vladivostok. Germany had still not been brought to her knees in the First World War and her armies still enforced her dominion over the Baltic States and the Ukraine. Not that the Bolshevik government lacked domestic opponents. An administration of Socialist-Revolutionaries who had been elected to the Constituent Assembly was installed in Samara in the wake of the Czechoslovak advance. Armed uprisings were being organised by groups of Left Socialist-Revolutionaries in Yaroslavl and elsewhere. Most ominous of all, General Denikin decided to march northward with the Volunteer Army which had been assembling under his command all winter and spring. By August 1918 he had stormed Krasnodar.

The Bolsheviks improvised a hasty defence against all these threats. Trotski came into his own as the official in charge of the creation of a Red Army which could beat off the pressing danger posed by the rampant Czechoslovaks. In some respects he was a traditionalist. He wanted his forces to be placed under centralised command and he would have nothing to do with the suggestion that troops should elect their own officers. But he was also an innovator. Recognising that few party officials had military experience, he made a policy of attracting men who had attained high rank in the army of Nicholas II. In order to obviate the risks involved he laid down that every officer should operate alongside a 'political commissar'. This was designed not only to help with the dissemination of socialist ideas among the soldiers but also to keep a sharp lookout for the slightest sign of treachery on the part of the command staff. Yet Trotski had reckoned without the widely held opinion inside the party that Soviet society contained no members more suspect than the tsarist officer class. Matters came to a head at the Eighth Party Congress in March 1919 when the so-called Military Opposition, encouraged behind the scenes by Stalin, proposed that the lack of formal qualifications should not be allowed to preclude Bolshevik activists from filling the posts of command. By then, however, Lenin had resolved to give Trotski the backing he required. The Congress permitted itself a day's dispute on the subject but there was never much doubt that the current system would be confirmed.[1]

In any case the real battles were on the banks of the Volga. Trotski rapidly gathered together sufficient forces to turn the Czechoslovaks back from Sviyazhk. Kazan was once again in Red hands in late summer 1918. Moreover, the armistice between the Allied and the German governments in November paved the way for an invasion of the Ukraine by Bolshevik troops in the first two months of the following year. Yet such achievements were outweighed by further advances made by the Whites in other directions. The main source of trouble was the army formed in Siberia, at the very time when the Czechoslovaks were pressing on into central Russia, under the leadership of Admiral Kolchak. At first Kolchak aligned himself politically with yet another group of delegates to the ill-starred Constituent Assembly styling themselves as the Directory and holding a base in Omsk. But in November 1918 his own officers, who shared his predilection for restoring bankers, industrialists and landlords to their former position in society, staged a *coup d'état* and designated Kolchak himself as 'Supreme Ruler of All the Russias'. By December his swift strike through the Urals had brought him the coveted prize of the town of Perm. Misfortune upon misfortune attended Sovnarkom and the Bolshevik Central Committee. Denikin held the

Kuban; German forces were no idle threat around the Baltic; the Japanese straddled the eastern end of the Trans-Siberian railway; Finnish units patrolled a border not thirty miles from Petrograd. The prospects for the survival of the October Revolution, hemmed in by an iron ring of foreign and domestic foes, were grim in the extreme.[2]

The Bolshevik response was nothing if not determined. While the early contingents of working-class volunteers made their way off to join the Red Army it was left to the remaining party and soviet officials to keep the wheels of the economy turning. Factories and workshops which had until then remained in private hands were quickly nationalised. Production targets were set for all trades and industries vital to the war effort; strict labour discipline was demanded of the work force. Sovnarkom grasped at every opportunity to see that all other institutions of public authority, whether central or local, did what it told them. Soviets, trade unions and factory committees were asked to swallow the pride of their independence and, come what may, obey the directives sent out from Moscow. Conflicts did not disappear at a stroke; but, on the whole, the priority given to uniting under a single organ of government was accepted with little trouble. The recurrent emergencies of the first months of the Civil War also lent strength to the argument that Sovnarkom itself was too large and unwieldy to take decisions with the speed required of it. It was permitted to set up its own inner subcommittee, known as the Council of Workers' and Peasants' Defence, and empowered to take charge of civilian as well as military affairs. This drift of authority into ever fewer hands was not confined to the capital. Local soviets and trade union branches too were obliged to prune their staffs in order to supply their quota of personnel to the man-hungry ranks of the Red Army. The one goal that gripped everyone's imagination was the need to sustain an effective war effort.[3]

Food shortages in the towns still represented a deadly danger for the Bolsheviks. The party had always been distrustful of all but the poorest sections of the peasantry and now decided that the time had come to take measures against richer households suspected of hoarding surplus stocks of grain or engaging in speculation on the urban market. Encouragement was given for the formation of 'committees of the village poor'. By dividing the peasants among themselves and by allowing impoverished households to police the doings of their more fortunate neighbours, Sovnarkom hoped to establish a cheap and effective method of foodstuffs procurement. In practice, as everybody knew well, it amounted to an extension of the permitted use of force. For the moment, however, a blind eye was turned to reports that the 'committees of the village poor' had few scruples about turning their attention upon the middle-range as well as the richer households. It took until the Eighth Party Congress for such activity to be officially condemned; for in 1918 what mattered most to Sovnarkom was the delivery of grain supplies. Its expectations, at least in the short term, were not fulfilled: the quantity of wheat and barley reaching the towns, once the Red Army had taken its share, continued to be miserably inadequate to prevent malnutrition.[4]

Yet life in the towns remained a harrowing experience. To the deepening crisis of hunger and disease was added the fear that any one of the rampant White armies might suddenly break through the Red Army's defences and occupy central Russia. When faced with Kolchak's threat to restore the factory owners, most workers identified their own interests with the Bolshevik cause. The growing disenchantment of early 1918 quickly evaporated when the choice between Red and White was posed so starkly. Industrial centres like Petrograd, Moscow and Ivanovo-Voznesensk readily supplied contingent after contingent of ill-trained but enthusiastic volunteers for active service. As the months wore on, the government resorted with greater confidence to conscripting recruits from town and countryside. Qualified personnel, whether skilled workers or engineers, were usually exempted from the draft in order to retain sufficient expertise in vital areas of industrial production. Nevertheless the number of factory workers was bound to fall: between the autumns of 1918 and 1919 it probably dropped from two and a half to one and a half million. Initially the exodus of the young men into the armed forces meant that the work force on average was much older than it had been in earlier days. But this was quickly counterbalanced by the infusion of wives and adolescents to fill some of the empty places in the factories. The Civil War had already wrought enormous changes in the life and composition of the working class.[5]

Before May 1918 the Bolsheviks had treated the Mensheviks and the Socialist-Revolutionaries as the greatest danger to their political hegemony. The Czechoslovaks and Kolchak changed all that. The Bolshevik Central Committee knew that those Mensheviks and Socialist-Revolutionaries who took the side of the

Whites constituted only a minority of their own parties. It was also obvious that most moderate socialists would be only too willing to play a constructive part in the Red war effort if the Bolsheviks were prepared to make concessions. Coalition was out of the question: neither Lenin nor his close colleagues felt any pressing need to subject their policies to such a compromise. But the Bolshevik Central Committee was realistic enough to understand that no great harm would be done to its plans if it allowed the Mensheviks and the Socialist-Revolutionaries the freedom to conduct their own propaganda (which was in any case vigorously anti-White) and even to put up candidates in the fresh elections to the local soviets. In the international arena too the Bolsheviks sought to come to an accommodation with certain enemies. The Americans were rightly spotted as the weak link in the chain of hostile powers surrounding the Soviet state and were courted, in a series of semi-covert negotiations, with a view towards terminating the military offensive and economic blockade maintained by the Allies since the October Revolution. Yet the Bolshevik Central Committee was wise enough not to put all its eggs into this political basket. It continued to sanction and subsidise revolutionary propaganda across Europe in the hope of sparking off anti-capitalist upheavals. By March 1919 it had succeeded in organising an international congress of sympathetic socialist parties in Moscow and in getting agreement to the creation of a supreme executive organ to co-ordinate their affairs in the future. Thus was born the Communist International.[6]

Nearly every facet of Bolshevik party life was affected body and soul by the tribulations of the Civil War. One of the few areas where no change is observable lies in the reliability of party membership 'statistics': they were as inaccurate as ever. Zinoviev leads the field by estimating that there were 700 000 rank-and-filers in early 1919; Strumilin the historian trails in last, as usual, with his figure of 251 000.[7] There is no saying who is correct. Everyone privileged enough to gain access to the archives, however, agrees that there was an overall increase in the late months of 1918. Certainly the Bolshevik cells of Petrograd had little difficulty in attracting recruits by the end of the year. It was a remarkable change since the time in spring and early summer when party officials had been seriously concerned about the number of rank-and-filers permitting their membership to lapse. It is all the more remarkable if we remember that the Central Committee decreed in May 1918 that the party was to rid itself of 'idlers, hooligans, adventurers, drunkards and thieves'. In fact, this early resort to the idea of a purge cannot have had much effect in practice. No local party body ever claimed to have pursued it with either thoroughness or enthusiasm. Nonetheless it is worthy of note that the Bolshevik party was managing to expand its ranks at the very moment when it was officially being asked to do the opposite.[8]

The influx into the party cells was not without its untoward characteristics. Most newcomers were not of working-class origin. It was said to be the easiest thing in the world for a middle-class careerist to obtain administrative employment simply by applying for party membership the day before applying for the job itself.[9] A few years later, when the dust of the Civil War was beginning to settle, party leaders set a team of archivists the ungrateful task of discovering what changes in social composition really had occured in 1918. They came up with the answer that the proportion of Bolsheviks of working-class origin fell from 57 per cent at the year's beginning to 48 per cent at the end. The team did not specify how many Bolsheviks were still employed as manual labourers; but the number must have been far smaller than in 1917 since rank-and-file workers had left in droves for administrative jobs, for the countryside and for the Red Army. Not for nothing did party officials continue to feel nervous that the active working-class base was being eroded. They did not need telling that middle-class newcomers had every incentive to conceal their true origins and that the movement away from a predominantly working-class party was even more pronounced than the party files attested. Some consolation might be drawn from the knowledge that the proportion of peasant rank-and-filers rose by 7 per cent in 1918. But this was not sufficient to sweeten the bitter pill of the constant increase of middle-class entrants. Lenin tried to soothe his troubled colleagues with the thought that the party needed all the help it could get in the Civil War and that it could not afford to turn up its nose at applicants simply because their parents had been well-off. He added that a clean-out of social undesirables could easily be undertaken once the Whites had finally been beaten into the ground.[10]

Every rank-and-filer in late 1918 knew what to expect. He or she was left in no doubt, from the start, that a Bolshevik's main duty was to do what he was told and see that his fellow members did the same. It was quite a turnabout since the anarchic days before the Civil War. The Central Committee had always advocated the virtues of obedience and co-operation; but the rank-and-filers of 1917 had cared as little about such entreaties as they did about appeals made by other higher authorities. The wartime emergency now supplied an opportunity to expatiate on this theme at will. It laid down, in terms more emphatic than ever before, that no Bolshevik should be permitted to avoid doing work for the party. More to the point, it demanded that all party members should undergo a course of military training in case it should become necessary to mobilise the entire party against the Whites.[11] Local committees needed no persuading about the urgency of the situation and the measures required to deal with it. The mood of the times is well illustrated by the Petrograd City Committee's blanket ban on rank-and-filers leaving the vicinity without its permission. The Samara Provincial Committee, which found itself uncomfortably near the front line of the fighting, announced its decision to mobilise all its party members into the armed forces (though it cannot have enforced this to the letter, or else there would have been a complete collapse of the civilian party machine in the area). Yet the rank-and-filers of Samara were not presented with a *fait accompli*. Their views had been consulted at an open general meeting and they had responded with a resounding vote of approval.[12] It may be that ordinary Bolsheviks not wishing to bow to the new disciplinary mood had already cleared out of the party; it may also be that the newspaper reports, penned by officials, exaggerated the disciplinary enthusiasm among those who remained. Even so, there is no sign of a mass exodus from the party ranks in the early months of the Civil War. And it remains difficult to explain the huge rise in the party's numerical strength across the country if there was not at the very least a widespread acceptance, however unenthusiastic, of the need for order and cohesion.[13]

The new discipline was taken to unparalleled lengths in the Red Army. Mutiny and desertion were not the only actions which incurred the death sentence. Trotski also ordered exemplary executions of military officials, especially if they happened to be party members, who displayed cowardice in the face of the enemy. His summary shooting of commissar Panteleev, being one of the first of such instances, caused many leading Bolsheviks to complain that Trotski had gone altogether too far. His high-handedness kicked up such a storm of protest that he probably was not allowed to pursue the policy. Even so, party life in the armed forces in the Civil War contrasted sharply with what it had been before the October Revolution. The days were long past when a Bolshevik soldier was encouraged to use his initiative in resolving the political problems affecting his own unit. Submissiveness was now the order of the day. The martial spirit which had once been so mocked and despised inside the party was becoming the model to which it was expected that all rank-and-filers should aspire. About 30 000 Bolsheviks were on active service in the army or navy by spring 1919; a further 30 000 served in units to the rear of the fighting and were occupied with supplies, transport and training.[14] This was no mean segment of the party as a whole. The authoritarian environment which suddenly enveloped them upon enlistment may well have reminded many rank-and-filers of the kind of treatment they had received in their factories, their villages or their offices under the regime of Nicholas II. Much pressure was probably needed to get ordinary Bolsheviks, used to speaking their minds, to agree to buckle under. Yet only most obdurate cynics would deny that those rank-and-filers accepting the new discipline did so not only through administrative fiat or through force of cultural habit but also because they consciously believed that this was the only way to win the life-and-death struggle against the Whites.[15]

Party activists, inside and outside the Red Army, were relied upon to set an example in all fields of endeavour. Once again the Central Committee took its chance to lecture them on the need to attend cell meetings with greater regularity and also to make sure that they knew one end of a rifle from the other. To many officials, laden with posts in public institutions, it seemed that too much was already being asked of them even without these fresh demands. But the Secretariat's response was stubborn and uncompromising (as it had to be unless all hope of keeping the party alive as an organised entity in its own right was to be abandoned). Lists were periodically made of activists in Moscow who disregarded the Central Committee's imprecations. Reprimands were occasionally delivered in the pages of *Pravda*.[16] This approach, though it caused little more than mild embarrassment to the officials exposed, met with a good deal of sympathy and encouragement among party committees in the provinces. Activists still caused bother by insisting on being able to choose their geographical place of work, a bother which was aggravated when party and soviet institutions in the newly liberated parts of the Ukraine made matters worse by unashamedly 'poaching' personnel from central Russia.[17] On top of all the other annoyances affecting party life, this was thought too much by town and provincial committees. A stream of pleas for disciplined behaviour poured forth from their offices. Every argument in the book was used to shame the 'delinquents' into co-operating, ranging from straightforward though ineffectual threats of punishment to more subtle and possibly more influential reminders that they were disappointing the hopes of the rank-and-file workers they left behind. Nobody pretended that habits had changed overnight, but there was more than enough evidence that things were indeed turning in the direction of that 'truly iron party discipline' which was required of the activists by committees at every level of the organisational hierarchy.[18]

The vivid memoirs of a man like Stepan Milnichuk testify admirably to the personal convulsions and tribulations demanded of all activists in the service of the party and the soviets. Wounded in Kiev early in the Civil War, he was transported out of the Ukraine to a hospital in Samara. But a few weeks later Samara itself was taken by the Czechoslovaks and he was compelled to flee up the Volga to Kazan. When this town too fell to the invaders he made for Simbirsk and then for Saratov. The need for thorough convalescence brought him for a short spell up to Moscow. From there he was ordered back to Samara as soon as the Red forces had retaken it and re-established a Bolshevik administration. The Samara Provincial Committee picked him to take charge of matters relating to the numerous prisoners-of-war in the vicinity. Yet he had barely had time to settle down to his new duties when he was redirected to the Ukraine and placed at the disposal of its Central Committee (or did he simply drift off to Kiev of his own accord?). Once arrived, he was dispatched to Kherson where he was appointed chairman of the Provincial Cheka. In spring 1919 he was mobilised into the Red Army when the local Bolsheviks were threatened by the swift-moving, marauding bands of the Cossak leader Grigorev. The emergency quickly passed and he was ordered first to Kiev and then to Odessa as a specialist in prisoner-of-war work. When he came to write his war memoirs he managed to relate his travels and assignments in a style which rivals *The Good Soldier Schweik* in its matter-of-fact terseness. But whereas Schweik spent the First World War devoting himself to the avoidance of physical violence, Milnichuk was hurled willy-nilly into the bloodbath of the Russian Civil War. It is not hard to imagine how deeply the experience of this time of vicious conflict affected the psychology of persons like Milnichuk who were witnessing war directly for the first time.[19]

Predictably it was in the armed forces where the changes were most marked. From the start of the Civil War it was obvious that the Central Committee was very unhappy about the potential havoc that could easily be wreaked by any elective party body in the Red Army that took it into its head to defy directives from Moscow. Bolshevik leaders in 1917 seldom worried what was done by their military organisations at the front as long as they were being as troublesome as possible to the Provisional Government. But Sovnarkom wanted no repetition of their disorderly conduct. The need to keep a close watch on the activity of former tsarist officers had led to the creation of 'revolutionary-military soviets' at each level of command in the Red Army itself. A typical soviet of this kind would consist of the staff officer and two or three commissars who supervised him and conducted propaganda among the troops. It was realised that the commissars were being asked to take on a heavy burden of responsibility and that it was only reasonable to furnish them with 'political departments' which were to consist of a number of reliable assistants. This was all very well but it did not meet the question of what was to be done about the multitude of elective party committees that were springing up in the nascent units of the Red Army. What was to be the relationship between the commissars appointed from above through Sovnarkom and the Bolshevik bodies elected from below by rank-and-file members on active service?

The answer arrived at by the Central Committee has until recently been so ill-documented that it has evaded the attention of scholars entirely. After a few months' hesitation it decided quite simply to abolish the elective party committees lock, stock and barrel above the level of the party cell.[20] Never in Bolshevik history had the Central Committee had the confidence to trample on the feelings of lower-party bodies so blatantly. Henceforward, it was made clear, there was to be a fusion of soviet and party posts in the armed forces. The commissar, who strictly speaking was subject only to Sovnarkom and had nothing to do with the Bolshevik Central Committee, was to be looked upon nevertheless as 'the representative of our party' and was to be obeyed accordingly. In practice this often meant that those commissars who did not themselves belong to the Bolshevik party could easily find themselves in the invidious position of having to pass on party directives to the Bolsheviks who were in their regiment. But again the Bolshevik Central Committee did not mind about these niceties so long as things got done as ordered. Party cells were strictly forbidden to inhibit the commissar in the pursuance of this policy; their job was to spread socialist ideas, explain what the war was about, raise military discipline, and do everything in their power to see that rank-and-file Bolsheviks complied with higher instructions. Constraints of this kind would have been tossed back into the face of the Central Committee in 1917; but the awesomeness of the struggle with the White armies was sufficient to achieve in a short while what no amount of pleading by party leaders had yet managed.[21]

Unluckily, we do not know what went on behind the closed doors of the Eighth Party Congress, in March 1919, when the question of party activity in the Red Army came up for discussion. By then the Military Opposition had become so steamed up that the Central Committee took precautions, once the proceedings were over, to keep secret the acrimonious words spoken on that occasion. The main bones of contention were the shooting of Panteleev and the employment of pre-revolutionary officers in soviet regiments; but it is quite possible that the abolition of elective party bodies in the armed forces also drew a chorus of criticisms. Nevertheless, if such a controversy really did take place, it is most remarkable that so few hints about it should have crept through the barriers erected to hide it from public view. By the beginning of 1919, in fact, party leaders in Moscow were already congratulating themselves that the reorganisation had been accomplished with so little fuss. Only a few elected party committees outlived 1918 in the armed forces; only a small number of party cells, usually led by especially strong-headed chairmen, dared to contravene the wishes of the commissars set above them (though reports of clashes continued to irritate the Secretariat right through to summer 1919).[22] The new discipline was everywhere. Even the Red Cavalry, by all accounts the most ebullient and anarchic of the Soviet armed forces, reflected the changed temper of Bolshevik life. Their leader, Semen Budenny, was later to recall with pride how, when on the move from one battle to another, they used to get the men in the front ranks to fix letter-boards on to their backs so that those in the rear ranks might be taught how to read.

Such preoccupations left scant opportunity to engage in the untrammelled political disputes of days gone by.[23]

Civilian party committees too immediately registered the impact of the Civil War. Needless to say, the Central Committee was far too canny to try to reorganise them along the lines already imposed upon party bodies in the armed forces. It would have provoked an unimaginable shemozzle, at a time when the Bolsheviks could least afford it, if orders had arrived from Moscow that henceforward all functionaries were to be appointed from above and that elections to party office were to be abolished. What is more, it was realised, although it was not spelled out in so many words, that civilian party committees could not be expected to cope with the bewildering complexities of political and economic affairs in their locality unless they were granted a degree of autonomy which had been snatched away from their counterparts in the Red Army and Navy. Keeping an industrial economy in productive shape was a much more difficult operation than keeping troops in battle readiness. Information percolating through to Moscow about local developments was scanty and irregular at the best of times; the Central Committee was well aware that it had to let the Bolsheviks in the provinces get on with things as they saw fit if there was to be any administrative effectiveness whatsoever outside the capital. Disaster would have struck far more often if this policy had not been followed. The initiative displayed by the party cells of Tula, when the army of Denikin was menacingly near and volunteers had to be found who would build defences on the outskirts and patrol the munitions factories, was the strongest of all arguments in its favour.[24]

Yet civilian party committees could not reasonably expect to carry on exactly as before the Civil War. Even now, with the benefit of hindsight, it appears quite remarkable how quickly the Bolsheviks, who for years had talked idly of instituting a strict hierarchy of command inside the party, at last began to put ideas into practice. The provincial tier in particular underwent an astounding rise in stature. If for no other reason, the Red Army's thirst for hundreds of thousands of peasant conscripts made this a sensible step. In 1917 the party had possessed few cells in the countryside to speak of. Official schemes to foster the installation of party committees at the level of the rural district and subdistrict had thereupon come to grief on the rocks of the other priorities engaging the attention of local Bolsheviks after the October

Revolution. It says something for the reorientation produced by the outbreak of hostilities that nearly every rural district had acquired a party body within a year of May 1918. And astride this structure stood the previously much-despised provincial committees: they saw that enlistment teams were sent round all the villages to dragoon the able-bodied peasant males into the armed forces, and they too helped to direct local requisitionments of supplies of grain and other foodstuffs.[25]

But their newly found authority was not limited to the countryside. Party bodies from the town committees themselves down to the ordinary cells in the factories were ready to submit their activity to control from above with a rapidity that could hardly have been predicted in the tumultuous days of 1917. Sverdlov was quick to encourage this. Not only did it appeal to his idea of an orderly party; it also helped to relieve the work-load of his Secretariat if he could call upon the provincial committees to deal with the pleas for assistance reaching Moscow from a multitude of town committees.[26] The main reason why the provincial tier was now welcomed from below, however, had less to do with Sverdlov's chafing remarks than with a grudging recognition by the Bolsheviks in the localities that they could no longer go on in the old way. There had to be some agency in each province to co-ordinate the various town committees if a cohesive war effort was ever to be attained. It was not an altruistic commitment to some hierarchical principle that had produced this change of heart (though a few enthusiasts had no doubt felt this way all along). More practical factors were at work. Above all it was the aggravation of all those long-standing difficulties, of manpower and of resources, which finally snapped the proud self-confidence of the town committees and brought them to an acceptance of the provincial committees. Wars not infrequently have this unifying effect. Indeed the transformation of attitude sometimes occurred so abruptly that it caught the provincial committees themselves on the hop. It must have been most galling for the Penza Provincial Committee to listen to charges by local activists that it had acted with insufficient vigour in co-ordinating party work in the area; it must have been little short of amazing for the Ivanovo-Voznesensk Provincial Committee to hear that the town committees in its area consented to its being allowed to deal with the alleged indiscipline of the Bolsheviks of Kineshma as it saw fit.[27]

'Total centralisation' of local party life was the slogan invented by the Novgorod Provincial Conference to describe what was required. The general idea took hold throughout the party.[28] Of course, the first to trumpet the news of what was happening were the provincial committees themselves. Their boasts would merit a lot less faith were it not that many lower party bodies confirmed that what they said was substantially true. A visitor to Archangel from Moscow observed that local Bolsheviks depended so strongly upon their Provincial Committee that party activities were likely to come grinding to a standstill unless it succeeded in keeping up a stream of detailed directives about all the issues of the day.[29] Yet it did not take long before town committees learned the lesson that once power is handed to a group of leaders it is often a tricky business to prevent them using it on a more extensive scale than had originally been envisaged. Activists and officials in Nizhni Novgorod were alarmed that their Provincial Committee had no scruples about imposing its policies without bothering to hold public debates beforehand. Behaviour of this kind was not what they were used to, and they resented it.[30] In much the same fashion, the Severo-Dvinsk Provincial Committee gave a ruling that its Town Committee should submit to fresh elections on the grounds that squabbles among the latter's members were disrupting constructive work.[31] Again it was hardly something which could have happened in 1917. Nobody, not even in Archangel or Nizhni or Severo-Dvinsk, was so deluded as to think that a smoothly operating line of command had been created once and for all from the provincial tier downwards; but, equally, nobody doubted that a profound change had indeed taken shape.

Regional committees advanced their own interests with similar resolve. In 1918 a number of 'new' communist parties were established in parts of the former Russian empire inhabited predominantly by non-Russian nationalities. The Bolsheviks of Turkestan were the first to announce the existence of their 'party' and were swiftly followed by those of the Ukraine, Lithuania, Latvia and Belorussia. The change was tactical. It was calculated that the chances of the Red Army gathering social support in such areas would be massively enhanced if every occasion was seized to allay suspicions that Bolshevism was essentially Great-Russian chauvinism in a new guise. The Central Committee in Moscow was alert to the risks it was now taking upon itself. It laid down strongly, though as discreetly as possible (for fear of intensifying the very doubts it sought to dispel), that the newly born parties were to retain their status simply as regional organisations of the All-Russian Communist Party. Federalism was ruled out from the start by official decree. Concessions enough, it was emphasised, had been made to nationalist sensibilities even without further hacking away at the cherished ideals of socialist internationalism.[32]

All regional committees, whether or not they were in non-Russian areas and calling themselves Central Committees, wanted to affirm their authority over lower party bodies. This no longer involved the protracted wrangles which would have been necessary before the Civil War. The question of hierarchy and discipline was discussed at length at the founding Congress of the Turkestan Communist Party. No one challenged the proposal to entrust the new regional party body with an energetic campaign to co-ordinate Bolshevik affairs throughout the area. The Turkestani Central Committee, according to one of its future members, should be given a free hand and should be granted 'dictatorial, plenipo-tentiary powers' to get on with its job. His phrase was omitted from the resultant resolution but his broad plea for hierarchical subordination was accepted in its entirety.[33] The same story was unfolded at other regional gatherings. Arguments continued to rise to the surface whenever town committees felt that their regional representatives had not taken their opinions into account. But of the desirability of strengthening the regional tier there was no hint of disapproval; the old condescension towards it had evaporated in the heat of the early months of the fighting.[34]

Regional committees were not slow to make the most of the opportunities handed to them. Taking the bull by the horns, the Moscow Regional Committee openly claimed the right for each of its members as individuals to supervise the affairs of all party bodies or activists in its area. This naked statement of intent did not have the counterproductive results which would have occurred in the earlier months of 1918. The litmus-paper test of its true influence was observed in the obedience it could count upon even from its two bitterest critics, L. M. Kaganovich and M. K. Muranov, whom it dispatched on official missions around the region (partly, no doubt, to remove the nuisance they caused).[35] The Ukrainian Central Committee demonstrated that it could rely upon an even greater measure of co-operation from subordinate committees. The question perplexing the Bolsheviks in that area after the treaty of Brest-Litovsk was what to do about the German occupation: should they foment a popular uprising or should they wait upon events in the hope that the Red Army would eventually make its way southwards to liberate them? Opinions were divided. The All-Russian Central Committee in Moscow warned in no uncertain terms that the Germans might well use any outbreak of violence as the pretext for invading central Russia. The Bolsheviks in the Ukraine, for their own part, knew full well that an uprising was not a course of action lightly to be entered upon; it could so easily invite reprisals which would devastate the party locally. Yet not a single town committee stood in the Ukrainian Central Committee's way once it had decided that the time for a revolt against German rule had arrived.[36]

If the Civil War triggered off massive changes in party life, it also consolidated many processes observable for some time beforehand. Nowhere was this more evident than in the internal operation of local committees. Shortage of experienced personnel had presented acute problems immediately after the October Revolution, but these now seemed almost trivial when judged alongside the huge responsibilities laid upon the party's shoulders through the onset of hostilities. The main drain on its exiguous resources of manpower was caused by the need to allocate thousands of activists and officials to military work. There was no let-up in this priority. As the Red Army continued to expand its numbers and as the counter-offensives of early winter took their inevitable human toll in Bolshevik fatalities, it was to be expected that local committees would be asked to give up an ever larger proportion of their own members to fill the gaps. Yet at the same time they were also being required to disperse their hard-pressed reserves of party function-aries all over those rural districts which previously had scarcely ever seen a Bolshevik. Food supplies and peasant recruits were altogether too important for the war effort to allow party committees to bury themselves in the towns and cities. The urgency of this was appreciated by all. But it meant that each committee was quickly pushed back upon depending on an ever tinier handful of active officials to cope with administrative work, which was itself growing more onerous every day. Local leaders penned letters full of strident requests to be spared further depredations or even to be granted additional manpower to deal with particular difficulties. Yet everyone knew that activists and officials would continue to be siphoned off to the armed forces and to the countryside until such time as the war was won.[37]

An indirect but momentous result of this process was a drift away

from collective modes of deliberation and decision. Party committees were not the only ones to suffer. Soviets, trade unions and
factory committees were subjected to the same denudation of
human resources. The investment of individuals with administrative powers that had recently been the prerogative of collective
bodies was not to every Bolshevik's liking. Some, like Lenin, saw no
objection to the idea in principle, but they had to use all their
rhetorical resourcefulness to get others to accept it.[38] It was the
party committees in the less urban, less industrial areas which were
placed in the least enviable position as regards manpower. The
Novosil District Committee reported dolefully that an unfortunate
activist named Milyukov (no relation, presumably, to the Milyukov
who was the Cadet leader in 1917) was obliged to do the work of
'committee chairman, newspaper editor, committee treasurer,
sometimes even its secretary, lecturer and agitator too—in fact,
anything you care to mention'. The gloominess of the report leaves
little doubt that it was also Milyukov who was obliged to write the
report in question.[39] Committees at the provincial and regional
levels never felt the pinch quite so tightly as this, but their situation
was far from being comfortable, certainly a great deal less
comfortable even than in the early half of 1918.[40] In the
circumstances it was a predictable step to supply the office of
chairman with powers to handle day-to-day party affairs without
having to go running to consult the opinion of committee
colleagues who were themselves getting fewer in number and
trying to cope with increasing workloads of their own. The
dominance exercised by L. M. Kaganovich and N. K. Ostrovskaya
over the provincial committees of Nizhni Novgorod and Archangel
became almost proverbial locally. The Petrograd City Committee
went to the extent of passing a formal measure that a single official
should be made responsible for party work in each suburb.[41] There
were even rumours in the air that a Bolshevik committee in Saratov
province had appointed its own 'dictator'. These rumours were
hastily and embarrassedly denied but their very existence indicated the transformation of party life within a few months.[42]

There was never any chance that the Central Committee would
entrust all its weighty business to one person. Not even Lenin, who
was not known to underestimate his own talents and capacities,
ever dreamt of bidding for such supremacy. Despite this sensible
restraint, however, the early months of the war witnessed an

inexorable reduction of the core of central leaders available for regular meetings in Moscow. The Central Committee claimed no privilege for its membership to be spared all involvement in military duties. The price it paid in return was that only six full members and two alternates remained uninterruptedly in the capital in the latter half of 1918. Never a day went by without the creation of some new bottleneck, some new emergency requiring swift decision and action. Alongside the continual threats from Kolchak and Denikin there were the equally menacing problems of food supplies, industrial production and foreign relations to be resolved. Formal meetings were held less often than ever. There was a flurry of them in July but no further attempt was made to convene the Central Committee until the end of the year.[43] It was left to Lenin and Sverdlov to handle the daily transaction of affairs. Their detractors complained that the two men occasionally omitted to initiate all their colleagues into the current development of issues as important as the negotiations with the American government. But it was unfair to represent this as an organisational *coup d'état*. Both leaders, at least for the most part, were aware enough of their absent associates' sensibilities and made ample use of letters, telegrams and telephone conversations to consult their views.[44] Nobody could properly accuse them of pulling a fast one by pressing forward with schemes they knew would have failed to gain a majority in the Central Committee.[45]

It would have been unrealistic, however, to expect anyone to be able to expunge all traces of rancour and disputatiousness from a group of party leaders who had so recently been locked in political combat over the Brest-Litovsk treaty. No person on earth could reconcile the irreconcilable. Stalin, who led a growing body of opposition to the employment of pre-revolutionary officers in the Soviet armed forces, was the principal obstacle to harmony. But it was a token of the high value placed upon maintaining the appearance of unity in public that he confined his criticisms to closed meetings of party officials. Lenin and Sverdlov in the meantime did their utmost to assuage his troubled feelings. Their work as mediators was shared by Nikolai Krestinski, a sympathiser of Trotski's, who had already shown his mettle as a tactful defuser of explosive disputes in March 1918 when the Left Communists looked as if they might rend the party. It did not go unnoticed, either, that Lenin and Sverdlov had effected a great change in their own styles of political discourse since those heady days of 1917 when they had closely rivalled each other in the abrasive tone used to defend their opinions. There is nothing to show that either man had undergone a transformation of personality; in fact, Lenin's later outbursts were to show that he was still capable of unleashing cannonades of vituperation whenever he felt his ideas to be under serious attack. The rigours of the Civil War called for a closing of the ranks. Lenin, Sverdlov and Krestinski were intelligent enough to perceive that need and suppress the fractious side of their natures accordingly.[46]

The Central Committee, such as it was in 1918, continued to get on well with its own Secretariat. Sverdlov had lost the collaboration of the industrious Stasova in February 1918 when the capital was transferred to Moscow and she was left behind in Petrograd. His own wife Klavdiya stepped into her shoes and was formally appointed as his deputy. It was as well to have someone whom he could trust to act in accordance with his wishes since he had to devote the bulk of his energy to his job as chairman of the All-Russian Central Executive Committee of the Congress of Soviets. She and her handful of assistants were expected to deal with the ordinary run of party business by themselves and to call upon Sverdlov's services only when important principles were at stake or when important controversies were in the offing. Her staff never totalled more than a dozen members—and this at a time when any People's Commissariat would have considered itself hard done by unless it could count its employees in their hundreds.[47] Klavdiya Sverdlova in her new post quickly decided that the Secretariat could not make a satisfactory job of its increasing workload if it was not allowed to take on many more assistants and to set up an internal system of departments of its own. Even by the end of 1918, however, she had precious little to show for her plans, only a rudimentary office for party activity among women under the leadership of Alexandra Kollontai. The conclusion is hard to resist that Sverdlov was still not fully convinced of the need to equip the Secretariat with an infrastructure which would enable it to handle administrative functions on the scale entrusted to the soviet executive framework.[48]

Let it be emphasised, however, that the Central Committee and its Secretariat had never bulked larger in the daily life of local party committees across the country. Party leaders in Moscow pushed their weight about, from the outset of the Civil War, with a keenness heightened by years of frustration with anarchy and indiscipline. The omens were more than good for such a foray into the depths of the party. Indeed the Central Committee was bombarded with a series of requests that it take a much stronger line both in directing the Bolsheviks at lower levels and in calling them briskly to order whenever they erred from the paths it had marked out for them. The stream of pleas for information, manpower and guidance continued unabated, Even so, it perhaps caused some surprise to the central leadership to receive invitations from a few party bodies, such as the Pereslavl-Zalesski Town Committee and the Kostroma Provincial Committee, to act as an arbitrator in disputes currently afflicting local affairs. It may well have given the Central Committee still greater pleasure to learn that Bolshevik officials in Ivanovo-Voznesensk, whence had come so many of its problems earlier in the year, were now so worried by their own incapacity to secure adequate food supplies that they had joined the front rank of the advocates of centralisation.[49] Not even the most starry-eyed apologist for the Central Committee could pretend that the manner in which it set about its task did not cause serious offence in many quarters; yet nowhere in the mass of contemporary testimony is it possible to discover an official, based either in Moscow or in the provinces, who rejected the basic idea of centralising the Bolshevik party as quickly as possible. Practical exigencies, not abstract principles, were cutting deep rivers of change which were to flow more and more strongly in the course of the Civil War.

The central leadership accelerated the movement with an energy which belies any suggestion that it was only the tide of local requests which had galvanised it into action. The will to construct a centralised party had been in the minds of Lenin and his colleagues for a long time before 1918. The decree of the Central Committee on the abolition of elective party committees in the Red Army and Navy was just the tip of the iceberg of its campaign to clip the powers of subordinate bodies at every level of the hierarchy. It revealed a particularly lively concern that the newly consolidated authority of the regional tier did not detract from its own. Its self-confidence went beyond all previous bounds. It did away with both the Moscow Regional Committee and the Northern Regional Committee entirely, not without encouragement from local centralisers like L. M. Kaganovich and N. K. Ostrovskaya, on the grounds that its own geographical proximity enabled it easily to do the job that they were doing.[50] The Urals

Regional Committee went the same way after an investigative commission had held it culpable for the capture of Perm by Kolchak in December. In its place the Central Committee set up the Siberian Bureau, which was to direct party work in the Urals and Siberia and was to have a membership appointed from Moscow. The Turkestani Central Committee's fate was slightly different but no less hurtful to it: it was permitted to survive on condition that it accepted its subordination to a 'Turkkomissia' selected by the All-Russian Central Committee. Nor did the Ukrainian Central Committee succeed in evading Moscow's toils. Annoyed by the apparent recklessness of the uprising against the Germans in late summer, the All-Russian Central Committee insisted that two of its nominees should be elected to the Ukrainian Central Committee chosen at the Second Ukrainian Party Congress.[51]

Provincial committees got off more lightly. There were no abolitions, there were no compulsory nominations. The sorest troublespot in their relations with Moscow in fact concerned the quotas of local Bolshevik personnel reassigned to the Red Army. Not a few party bodies proclaimed that they had specially mitigating circumstances requiring them to hang on to a higher proportion of activists than was needed by their counterparts in neighbouring provinces. The Nizhni Novgorod Provincial Committee was more than a little incensed by Sverdlov's failure to bother to inform it that he was transferring one of its leaders, a certain Kraevski, to the armed forces—a failure which Sverdlov was honest enough to admit publicly.[52] Yet local party bodies in the main kept to verbal remonstrations and forswore active opposition. A certain amount of passive resistance was also in evidence: very few provincial committees provided the Central Committee with regular reports, no doubt partly in the hope of concealing the exact number of activists on their books.[53] Sverdlov for his part tried to assume a tolerant demeanour. His visits to the localities confirmed the impression he had gained from his exchange of correspondence with them that all provincial committees without exception supported the idea of some kind of centralisation in principle. He also recognised that the party's cause would not be helped if the central party leadership did not allow some rein for local initiative. His advice to assistants in the Secretariat was to avoid entanglement in every little disagreement which reached their ears from the provinces; his slogan, it was later recalled, was: 'There is no point in attempting to do the impossible.' Sverdlov's self-restraint in his dealings with the provincial committees enabled him to capitalise enormously on the deep fund of support for centralisation which existed throughout the party.[54]

But here came the rub: centralisation is a word covering a multitude of organisational possibilities. Numerous local leaders came to conclude by the end of 1918 that the Central Committee was taking altogether too narrow a view of its task at hand. Nobody ventured to deny the desirability of strengthening hierarchical control and discipline; but there was the other side of the coin too to be considered. Party committees at regional, provincial and town levels saw centralised methods as a vital means of obtaining regular and reliable services of information, guidance and succour from Moscow. There was a growing feeling that the Central Committee had fallen a long way short of satisfying this aspiration. Local critics who had some acquaintance with the central party apparatus declared that the remedy lay in doing away with the hand-to-mouth, improvised techniques in existence and going over to a more systematic, planned approach to the running of the party. The old 'amateurism' had to give way to a new 'business-like' attitude. It was realised that such moves were bound to tighten still further the central leadership's grip on local party life, but this was felt to be a reasonable price to pay for the relief obtained. Not for the first time in the Civil War did the harsh practicalities of political and economic problems in the provinces begin to have a decisive impact upon the organisational condition of the party as a whole.

Lazar Kaganovich of Nizhni Novgorod, well acquainted with the Kraevski affair, was first to enter the field with his criticisms. In his view the failure to found a sleek hierarchy of uniformly organised party committees, each with a uniformly organised secretariat of its own, would ultimately cause the party to lose even its separate identity as the leading force of revolutionary change. He was also a local apologist. All too often, he maintained, the reason why a provincial committee seemed to contravene official policies was that it had not been kept in touch with what they in fact were. The solution was to introduce the 'strictest centralism'. Asserting that it was pointless to expect the Central Committee to meet frequently enough in wartime, he urged the creation of two subcommittees to take over from it between its sessions. One was to oversee politics, the other was to deal with organisational affairs. At the same time it would be necessary to expand the size of the Secretariat and to entrust it with building up files about local party life. He emphatically affirmed his opinion that the central party leaders had not put a foot wrong in their decisions about foreign and domestic politics. His faith in their capacities was so deep that he was ready to supply them with plenipotentiary authority in all matters. He argued that Bolshevik life was still excessively permeated by a concern for democratic niceties. According to Kaganovich, it did not matter what local sentiments had to be trampled under foot so long as a highly disciplined, tightly co-ordinated party machine could be created.[55]

Unbeknown to Kaganovich, ironically enough, plans were already by early 1919 under way among central party leaders to introduce a central infrastructure not unlike the one he advocated. As early as January, indeed, it was decided to set up two subcommittees and to call them the Political Bureau (or Politburo) and the Organisational Bureau (or Orgburo). It was not the most radical of reforms: inner subcommittees had existed both in 1917 and 1918. All the same, how the new system operated before the Eighth Congress is mainly a matter of guesswork, although the Orgburo was certainly active in arbitrating in a dispute over a theatre in Petrograd between the Northern Regional Party Committee and the Peoples' Commissariat of Enlightenment.[56] The Secretariat in the meantime was left in its pristine state. The tentative ideas for expansion and departmentalisation mooted by Klavdiya Sverdlova back in summer 1918 still had not left the drawing-board. Yet this did not prevent her from casting a hostile eye upon the complaint that a suitably organised central party apparatus had yet to be established in Moscow. She correctly predicted that no formal scheme to liberate members of the Politburo and Orgburo from all other duties would prove practicable; she could see that the shortage of manpower would continue to oblige every party leader to shoulder a number of posts simultaneously: in the foreseeable future there would never be a time when either of the new subcommittees would have the leisure to run party affairs as suggested by Kaganovich. But her sharpest comments she reserved for his disdainful attitude to local initiative.[57] Poor Sverdlova! She was not to know that it would be Kaganovich's arch-centralism rather than her own milder version which would pervade the Bolshevik party. Kaganovich on the other hand must have had a shrewd idea that developments were already turning in his favour; for he signally refrained from organising his sympathisers from Nizhni and elsewhere into an oppositionist group of 'Strict Centralists' to do battle with the Central Committee at the Eighth Party Congress.

From another source, however, an oppositionist group did in fact emerge. Its initial adherents were based in Moscow and shortly became known as the Democratic Centralists; its leaders were Timofei Sapronov, Vladimir Maksimovski and Nikolai Osinski. They too felt that they had suffered from the 'inertia' and 'lack of planned leadership' exhibited by the Central Committee. Many practical proposals voiced by them would not have been looked upon with disfavour by Kaganovich the Strict Centralist. They wanted a vast increase in the number of general directives and instructions sent out from Moscow; they called for the construction of detailed files on personnel working in the provinces. They asked that at least five members of the Central Committee be assigned to concentrate all their energies upon the central party machine. They envisaged a Secretariat with much more authority than at present, able to give rulings to local committees 'even in questions of principle' and to give orders to a team of fifteen party officials who were to rove round the country making on-the-spot inspections. But the other side of their suggestions did not appeal in the slightest to Kaganovich (or to the leading members of the Central Committee for that matter). The greatest malaise in party life, according to them, was the sharp decline in elective offices and collective decision-making since the outbreak of the Civil War. Worst of all was the mounting difficulty faced by the rest of the party in calling the Central Committee to periodic account, a difficulty which the Democratic Centralists hoped to resolve by holding Party Conferences every three months. A healthy party, they declared, necessitated a balance between hierarchical co-ordination and discipline on the one hand and patterns of democratic accountability on the other. Nothing could be further from the stern authoritarianism beloved of Kaganovich.[58]

Not all the local critics of the Central Committee, however, presented so comprehensive an indictment; but their ideas were of considerable moment nonetheless. I. M. Vareikis, chairman of the Simbirsk Provincial Committee, proclaimed indignantly that if the central party leadership wished to eradicate local opposition to its policies it could make no better start than by keeping provincial committees more closely informed about its recent decisions. His picture of Sverdlov as a functionary who spent all his time filing minutes was monstrously overdrawn but his proposal that the Secretariat should have a more influential role struck a chord with many local officials.[59] The line taken by the Simbirsk Provincial Conference was paralleled elsewhere. The Ryazan Provincial Conference, after complaining that the central party leadership was isolated from practical local problems, proposed that a couple of central 'representatives' be placed at the disposal of each provincial committee. Less ambiguously, the Orel Provincial Conference favoured the installation of a special agency to inspect the activity of local party bodies.[60] Such ideas did not stem from organisational masochism, from an inner desire to lie prostrate before the Central Committee and beg it to rule with a firm hand. Party officialdom in the provinces took up the cause of centralisation first and foremost because it seemed to offer the quickest, surest means of obtaining necessary aid and support. True, many provincial leaders of early 1919 had worked in other towns in 1917 and had been cross-posted in the centrally-directed turnover of personnel at the start of the Civil War. But that did not make them stooges or toadies. In any case their highly practical pleas for help were echoed by those many other leaders who had not changed towns since 1917. Local pleas for central help were a general phenomenon.[61]

Central party leaders at the Eighth Party Congress in March 1919 made every effort to court the feelings of the mass of local officialdom. Sverdlov, his health ruined by overwork, died of Spanish influenza a few days beforehand and Zinoviev took his place as Central Committee spokesman on organisational affairs. The Central Committee must have decided that its best bet was to admit that there had indeed been shortcomings in its past performance and that a measure of internal reform was overdue. What is more, Zinoviev stole a march on his critics by incorporating a number of their practical proposals, such as the idea of an inspectoral agency, in his own projected resolution. Both Zinoviev and Lenin, whilst declaring that wartime conditions would still on occasion make it necessary to rely upon the informal methods of yore, tried in the main to reassure their listeners that the Central Committee and the Secretariat would henceforward approach their jobs in a more planned and organised fashion. Their efforts were not in vain. Most delegates, by the end of the proceedings, were convinced that the central party leadership had at last taken cognisance of local needs and could be depended upon to change its behaviour accordingly.[62]

As could have been predicted, neither the Strict Centralists nor the Democratic Centralists were entirely satisfied by what they heard. Kaganovich repeated his view that a formal central infrastructure of deliberation and administration really was totally feasible; he was ready to reduce the number of Politburo members from five to three in order to achieve this. But he did not want to upset the applecart by insisting too strongly upon his opinions. He had already received much of what he had originally desired; furthermore, he did not wish to assail the central leadership at a time when it was under attack from its other principal critics, the Democratic Centralists.[63] Sapronov and Osinski predicted that the Politburo would entirely undermine the Central Committee's authority unless preventive measures were taken. To this end they suggested that the number of Central Committee members should be increased to twenty-five, that it should include some factory workers in its composition, and that the Politburo should have at least a dozen members. Quite how such measures would act as a brake upon excesses of centralising zeal was not explained.[64] For the time being it required only the barest minimum of oratorical adroitness on Zinoviev's part to treat the Democratic Centralists as rather eccentric and hare-brained quibblers who had nothing serious to say about the state of affairs inside the party. Zinoviev in fact did much more than that. He averred that the Civil War called above all for unity and discipline and that those Bolsheviks who failed to close ranks unequivocally around the Central Committee were guilty of utter disloyalty.[65]

The party had undergone a momentous transformation since the outbreak of hostilities. Hierarchical discipline and obedience were now accepted on a scale and with a speed which made an amazingly abrupt contrast with the organisational looseness of early 1918. It had taken merely a few months for customs of collective deliberation and democratic accountability, which until recently had seemed so solidly established, to succumb to radical erosion. The elective party committees were done away with entirely in the armed forces. Civilian party bodies were spared this ultimate step but still found their powers unprecedentedly restricted by higher authority. The preoccupation with reorientating Bolshevik life along orderly lines was accompanied by a continuing neglect of the problem that the proportion of rank-and-filers who were factory workers remained on the decline; but party officials were in any case relieved that the wartime emergency had at least taken most of the venom out of the anti-Bolshevik discontent noticeable since spring 1918. No Bolshevik, moreover, could dissent from the view that the winning of the Civil War was the paramount priority of the moment. The central party leadership in fact encountered little resistance to its appeals for more regulated forms of behaviour. Quite the reverse: local committees enthusiastically welcomed the new spirit in the air, if only in the hope that it would bring about some alleviation of the burdens that they had been carrying since 1917 and which were daily growing heavier. Thus it came about that the Bolshevik party began to fashion itself into the shape which characterised it throughout the 1920s and to acquire a separate organisational identity which enabled it to dominate the country's politics even more firmly than before.

5 The Battle is Won (April 1919–March 1920)

The outcome of the Civil War was decided in 1919. The auguries for a Red victory had seemed most unfavourable at the beginning of the year when Kolchak was still pressing on remorselessly westwards through the southern passes of the Urals, when Denikin was putting the finishing touches to his plan to launch a two-pronged invasion of central Russia through the Donbass, and when Yudenich was on the point of moving his army from Estonia in a lightning strike on Petrograd. Yet the Bolsheviks did more than hold their own. The main body of their forces was turned first upon Kolchak and it was not long before his army, which had hitherto threatened to wreak the complete destruction of the Red Army, was itself streaming back over the Urals to Siberia as fast as it had come. Denikin fared no better. Initially he succeeded in making great inroads into Soviet-held territory and pushed some regiments as far north as Orel; but the Red counter-offensive, once Kolchak had been dealt with, quickly turned back the tide of the White advance and had Denikin marching southwards through the Ukraine in retreat. The Bolsheviks, while pressing home this victory, felt confident enough to transfer numerous troops to the environs of Petrograd to meet Yudenich. The Red Army was triumphant. Yudenich, whose army already faced serious problems with desertions before the crucial battles, was defeated without difficulty in October 1919; Denikin, who had managed to pull his bedraggled forces through to the Caucasus, fell into despair and evacuated them to the Crimean peninsula in March 1920.

In the international arena too the Bolsheviks had reason to feel safer than before. In spring 1919 the party's hopes for the dissemination of socialist revolutions across Europe were greatly buoyed up by the establishment of soviet republics in Bavaria and Hungary. Such high optimism, however, evaporated very rapidly.

Freikorps units seized Munich in May and smashed the Bavarian republic; Rumanian troops lent their support to Hungarian counter-revolutionaries in August and brought down the Hungarian republic. Yet the Bolsheviks could still cheer themselves with the knowledge that the Allies had at last resolved to terminate their military intervention in the Russian Civil War. This turnabout was not a sign that the British and French governments had decided to welcome a Bolshevik-dominated Russia back into the comity of nations. It resulted in fact from fears about the possible results of continued intervention. There were mutinies in the French naval and army units landed at Odessa; there were outbreaks of political unrest at home in Britain and France; there were domestic problems with post-war economic reconstruction which could only be aggravated by the additional onus of fighting a protracted war in eastern Europe. Lloyd-George, furthermore, asserted in November 1919 that a resumption of trading links with Russia would help to strengthen anti-Bolshevik elements in Soviet society. He was given backing not only by socialists and trade unionists but also by the influential lobbyists of the many business companies which cast an eager eye towards Russia in search of large profits. In January 1920 the Allied Supreme Council, after much vacillation, declared an end to the economic blockade of Russia.[1]

Bolshevik leaders welcomed these events as further evidence of the weakening power of capitalism worldwide. But they were also aware that the domestic difficulties confronting them were no less substantial than at the time of the October Revolution. The rural populace took as terrible a battering in 1919 as it had in 1918. The Eighth Party Congress had called upon local requisitioning units to relent from plundering the grain stocks of the so-called 'middle peasantry'. Yet the depredations continued in practice to affect the broad mass of peasant households. It is difficult to say whether it was the Reds or the Whites who treated the peasantry more brutally; both sides looked upon the countryside primarily as an easily tapped wellspring of foodstuffs and conscripts. For the most part the peasants put up little resistance. Yet the idea of revolt was not completely absent: later reports by Cheka officials suggest that nearly a hundred 'insurrections' had to be put down in just twenty provinces of central Russia. Such outbreaks were local affairs and were rarely accompanied by attempts to put forward an elaborate alternative political programme. At all odds it seems that the bulk of the peasantry was as yet loathe to raise its hand against the Bolsheviks. They apparently preferred the future uncertainties of life under the Reds to the certitude that the former landlords would try to regain their land and possessions in the event of a White victory in the Civil War.[2]

Townspeople too lived through grim times in 1919. Food supplies, clothing and medical services were always grossly inadequate; it is reckoned that between 10 and 15 per cent of the urban population died of disease or malnutrition in the two years of the fighting. Workers were also still being asked to join the ranks of the Red Army. Many needed little encouragement since they not only wanted to secure the annihilation of Kolchak and Denikin but they also knew that military service would at least ensure an improvement in their food-ration. At the same time it was being reported by local soviets that the flight from the towns into the villages continued, unabated even by the common knowledge that life was rough in the countryside too. Factory production had by then fallen to its lowest ebb since the nineteenth century. Priority was given to the manufacturing of munitions and other military requisites; but such was the run-down of industrial activity that the Red Army would have been sorely short of supplies if the Soviet government had not been able to draw upon stocks of materials it had taken over from the Provisional Government. The number of factory workers dropped to one and a quarter million by the end of 1919. There would probably have been even fewer if enterprises had not been able to attract thousands of women into employment; it was boasted that female labour constituted nearly half the entire industrial workforce of Petrograd. The Civil War had indeed proved a powerful locomotive of social change.[3]

The Bolsheviks had grown to take it for granted that the working class would support the Red cause. The Cheka, which was the main policing agency and which acquired almost unbounded authority to carry out its duties, harassed the town population's middle-class elements in order to pre-empt attempts to lend assistance to the Whites. Neither the Reds nor the Whites held back from taking and, if need be, shooting innocent hostages as a means of enforcing social control. The conditions experienced by industrial workers in areas under White occupation were alone sufficient to rule out the possibility that they would ever voluntarily fight in the armies of Kolchak, Denikin or Yudenich. Yet it also became obvious in late 1919, as the end of the war hove in sight, that the working class was far from being happy about Bolshevik policies. Trade union officials were already warning that dissatisfaction with the rigours of labour discipline as well as with the horrendous collapse of the standard of living was likely to become a serious problem in the near future. Not the least cause of discontent was that soviet and party functionaries everywhere, though hardly living in luxurious circumstances, were allowed considerably better food-rations than the rest of the population. The traditions of working-class defiance, muted when the issue of the war remained undecided, were not yet stamped out entirely. Strikes broke out in major industrial centres such as Ivanovo-Voznesensk, Nizhni Novgorod and Tula. There were already signs that the same was about to happen in Petrograd, the pillar of Bolshevik strength in 1917. Governmental spokesmen asserted that the party had not been given a fair chance and that only the termination of hostilities would afford the opportunity to make the necessary improvements. Yet the party had undoubtedly suffered a shock. The memory of the incipient comeback of the Mensheviks and the Socialist-Revolutionaries in 1918 was too recent to be forgotten: the political complacency which had begun to pervade the ranks of the Bolsheviks was in urgent need of removal.[4]

An obvious way to rally and organise popular support for the party was to launch a drive to attract more rank-and-file members. But first it was decided to get rid of all undesirable elements. In April 1919 the Central Committee announced the opening of a campaign to expel every Bolshevik who had committed 'acts unworthy of a communist', deserted from the Red Army, violated party instructions, failed to attend party meetings or omitted to pay party dues. The number of editorials devoted to the subject in *Pravda* left local party bodies with the impression that this 'purge' was meant to be a much more thorough affair than the clean-out called for in 1918. The Secretariat reckoned that the number of party members had plummeted to 150 000 by August 1919.[5] No doubt a goodly segment of the decrease consisted of rank-and-filers who had left voluntarily at the height of the Denikin offensive out of dread of what might befall them should the White army emerge victorious. 'Paper communists' was the Roslavl Town Committee's contemptuous description of such backsliders. There must also have been thousands of unfortunate ordinary Bolsheviks who perished in the fierce battles leading to the final rout of Kolchak,

Denikin and Yudenich. Yet everyone agreed that the biggest fall-off in the party's numerical strength was produced by deliberate expulsions and that the party's internal condition had been greatly improved by them.[6]

In September 1919 the Central Committee declared itself content with this operation of major surgery and ordered local officials to set about grafting 'healthy proletarian and peasant' skin on to the body of the party. An all-out recruitment drive was announced. The speed of the subsequent influx surprised even those activists who were engaged in rounding up newcomers for the party ranks. By March 1920 the Secretariat was claiming that the number of Bolsheviks had shot up to 600 000. The 'party weeks' which had wrought this exponential rise were carefully recorded by local committees so that it is quite possible that a fourfold increase did in fact take place.[7] Care in docketing numbers, however, was not paralleled by care in registering changes in social composition. Pride was taken in the claim that most persons ejected from the party in summer were of 'petit-bourgeois' origin and that most persons entering from late autumn onwards were either workers or soldiers. But a later investigator of the archives repudiated this. It would appear that the proportion of rank-and-filers of working-class origin, far from increasing in 1919, in reality continued to dip. There are few grounds for believing that very many industrial workers had in fact decided to leave the party (although this had undoubtedly been a problem in the previous year). What probably happened was that those who remained in the party ranks were numerically swamped by a vast influx of peasant lads who were persuaded to join the Bolsheviks upon enlistment in the Red Army. Nor can it be ruled out that local committees were a lot less effective in getting rid of middle-class entrants than they liked to believe or pretend. At any rate the central leadership's first attempt at social experimentation inside the party did not give rise to the results anticipated.[8]

This is not to say that the campaign was a total failure. Quite apart from its huge success in boosting numbers, it was also instrumental in introducing more women than ever before into the ranks of the party. Bolshevik officials had had little time to devote to special efforts to proselytise the female section of the industrial work force since 1917. Indeed there are signs that many activists were not at all keen to engage in exclusively women-oriented activity. But the soaring importance of female labour in wartime factories made it doubly vital to get women to join in the great influx into the party in late 1919. According to the findings of the Secretariat, about three in every ten civilian entrants in fourteen large towns were women. The proportion was reportedly as high as one in two in Moscow and Petrograd. Even so, not all party bodies could be brought to take female recruitment as the serious business it should have been. The Yaroslavl Provincial Committee admitted to one of the most dismal performances, having managed to attract only two women among the 390 recruits it had obtained in its 'party week'. In most other areas, however, the party had every right to proclaim that it had greatly expanded the dimensions of its social revolution.[9]

New rank-and-filers, particularly if they happened to belong to the traditionally downtrodden sex, were unlikely to be effective opponents of official policies. The party, which had once been overgrown with disputes and dissensions, was fast becoming a domain of submissiveness. This was nowhere more evident than among the ordinary members. The Secretariat undertook a sample survey shortly before the 'party weeks' and discovered to its horror that fewer than one fifth of all Bolsheviks could trace their party affiliation back to before the October Revolution.[10] The published results described the state of affairs only in the towns; they reveal nothing about the current composition of the party in the front-line troops of the Red Army. And doubtless the methods used to choose the sample were not such as would satisfy the standards of present-day statisticians, but at the time they were certainly adjudged reliable enough to cause a degree of worry in official circles. The survivors from the pre-October period, into the bargain, were on the point of being inundated by a flood of nearly half a million entrants in late 1919. It would of course be surprising if many new recruits were not really newcomers at all but were men and women who had abandoned the party at the lowest ebb of its fortunes in the winter of 1918–1919 and now crept back into it once Kolchak and Denikin had been seen off; yet that cannot have been true of most of them since young peasants and women together constituted so large a part of the influx. In any case all accounts agree that the recruitment campaigns gave birth to a new generation of docile and not unco-operative rank-and-filers who could be depended upon to cast their vote for whatever was asked of them by higher authority. The ordinary Bolshevik of the pre-revolutionary epoch, with his custom of saying exactly what he thought and acting accordingly, found himself swimming against a tide of mass submissiveness at the party's grass roots.[11]

Most party officials were willing to accept this process as the inevitable cost of enforcing discipline at a moment of the utmost military danger. But not everyone agreed. Concern was expressed that few rank-and-filers had anything beyond the merest smattering of Marxism. This was not true just in the far-flung regions of Central Asia: it was reported with equal worry in Petrograd. K. Shelavin, like one of the elect aghast at the apparent irredeemability of the damned, lamented to his fellow officials: 'The overwhelming majority of new members live basically under the influence of old habits, are imbued by a petit-bourgeois psychology, cling to long-outmoded. patterns and are still not liberated from a multitude of prejudices.'[12] The only complete solution, as party theorists often affirmed, was to set up a long-term programme of all-round education. Little progress was possible while the war was raging. In the meantime it was usually decided that the party would have to accept a low level of 'socialist consciousness' as the unavoidable toll to be paid for getting access to the active support of members who could be counted in the hundreds of thousands. This did not salve every official's ideological sensibilities. The Smolensk Provincial Committee spent not a little while debating what to do about an otherwise unexceptionable and useful recruit who made no secret of his Christian faith. A way was found out of the embarrassment when a smart functionary pointed out that 'at no place in the party rules is it stated that every party member must definitely be a Marxist'. Religious feelings, moreover, were a much less widely diffused affront to contemporary Marxist scruples than the materialistic acquisitiveness evinced by many newcomers.[13]

A good number of ordinary Bolsheviks, however, saw this as a fine example of the pot calling the kettle black. In their eyes, the deprecatory remarks made about them by party officialdom would have been more acceptable if there had been much sign that the deprecators themselves were straining at the leash to help to improve the situation. F. Sominskaya, an official in Tula with an understanding of rank-and-file feelings, diagnosed the increasingly 'boring' quality of party life as a major source of trouble. Her choice of adjective was sarcastically mild; she knew, and let it be widely known, that the unadulterated authoritarianism creeping into office-holders' behaviour was not going down at all well with many long-standing grass-roots members.[14] Bolshevik cells still exerted direct influence over social and economic affairs in urban suburbs, particularly as regards industrial production; but it was increasingly the cell chairmen who made the most important decisions, even though care was taken to secure a rubber-stamp vote from the mass of rank-and-filers subsequently. It was also extremely irritating to ordinary members to hearken to criticism that they failed to attend meetings regularly when everyone was well aware that exactly the same accusation could be levelled against most officials and activists. But that was not the end of the matter. Rank-and-filers were also being asked to put up with the sight of party functionaries avidly stretching out for privileges such as better food-rations and the like. Such insensitivity at a time when malnutrition and disease were so rife in the towns and cities of Russia makes it difficult to resist the conclusion that Bolshevik officials had grossly exploited the consent and trust accorded to them by ordinary members since the outbreak of the Civil War.[15]

Some observers tried to describe the change by drawing a contrast between the true 'communist' official of 1917 and the nakedly 'Bolshevik' functionary of wartime.[16] Descriptions of this kind in fact err by underestimating the strong predisposition of a great number of party office-holders towards very rapid large-scale attempts at social engineering even before the October Revolution. It is nonetheless true that few party leaders, local or central, were like Sominskaya and kept alive that fully egalitarian spirit which had pervaded behaviour inside the party before it seized power. Two notable exceptions were Alexander Shlyapnikov and Yuri Lutovinov. Holding ascendant positions in the Metalworkers' Union in Moscow, both men felt that what was happening amidst the ranks of the Bolsheviks was a symptom of a dangerous malaise afflicting Soviet state and society in its entirety. Hierarchies of committees in all public institutions and organisations held sway over their members and employees with ever tighter methods of control and discipline. Even the keenest centralisers in 1917 had held some belief in the creative potentiality of the working class as an independent social group; but now, it seemed to Shlyapnikov and Lutovinov, every ember of grass-roots initiative was being snuffed out by higher authorities worried by what they saw as anti-centralist tendencies. Neither of them had yet elaborated a closely argued political programme. Both, however, suggested that the first step out of the currently worsening impasse would be to strip away the encrustations of authoritarianism and privilege choking the political scene and to reaffirm the party's faith in industrial workers in general and its own rank-and-filers in particular.[17]

Most Bolsheviks officials shrugged off these arguments as pie-in-the-sky thinking; few leaders did anything more than mouth a stream of platitudes about the need to re-establish personal contact between officialdom and the mass of the party. Constructive action could not have been further from their true intentions. For all that, however, it would have been startling if there had been no embarrassment at existing developments. The Petrograd City Committee, according to the visiting foreign anarchist A. Berkman, went to the length of assigning a specially secluded dining-room to high-ranking party and soviet functionaries so that they might consume their superior meals unobserved by the unprivileged. The excuse usually offered was that officials physically needed more coddling than the population at large in order to survive their long hours of exhausting work.[18] Transfers from one end of the country to the other were a further burden which caused I. V. Mgeladze of Simbirsk to say that officials were being transformed into nomads. Our friend Milnichuk, who had covered so many thousand miles in 1918, was granted no relief in the following year. After engaging in prisoner-of-war work in Kiev, he was sent down to Odessa; but this was precisely the time when Denikin was launching his summer offensive: Milnichuk was obliged to flee northwards again. On arrival in Moscow he was reassigned to Samara to take charge of food procurements and to suppress a peasant rebellion. Finally in March 1920 he was smitten by typhoid and transported for his convalescence to a Moscow hospital. It was this kind of enforced mobility that stimulated office-holders to claim a certain indulgence. And quite apart from everything else they argued that wage differentials had already in 1918 been widened in all other large public organisations and that the party's functionaries deserved to be treated similarly.[19]

The all-absorbing concern with hierarchical discipline meant that party officials themselves were experiencing tauter forms of control from above: there had never been a time in Bolshevik history when committees at every local level, from the region right down to the suburb, could count upon so much obedience from lower party bodies. This is not to say that conflicts no longer exploded even in 'well-ordered' provinces such as Nizhni Novgorod.[20] Yet they never got out of hand as they had in previous years. Indeed more than a

few officials noted that military styles of command were steadily
creeping into the daily jargon of civilian as well as military bodies.
Such thoughts also lay behind the various apparently bland
statements deploring the failure of higher committees to keep up
'direct, live contact' with subordinate ones.[21] The Penza Provincial
Committee, which in 1918 had been charged with having
intervened too seldom in the affairs of lower party bodies, was now
roundly accused of erring in the opposite direction and displaying a
singular heavy-handedness. Even K. I. Shelavin, otherwise an
unflinching apologist for the party officials of Petrograd, tacitly
admitted that militaristic administrative methods were being
employed on an unjustifiably extensive scale.[22]

Reinforcing this trend was the persistent drift towards putting
local committees under the leadership of single officials. According
to the Smolensk Provincial Committee's chairman, a simple
reprimand from his lips was sufficient to reduce disobedient
activists to tears and persuade them to mend their ways in future.[23]
The schoolmasterly picture he drew was a caricature. We know
from the Smolensk party archives that the chairman's colleagues
were never so reverential or subservient as to render him the
doting collaboration he liked to pretend to in reports to Moscow.
However that may be, the position of chairman at all local levels of
the party hierarchy was indeed gathering greater influence unto
itself. From Penza came the news that a convocation of district
party committee chairmen (admittedly, together with their
counterparts in the soviet structure) had in April 1919 been held in
lieu of a normal provincial conference. The Novgorod Provincial
Committee, when called upon to mobilise activists to the front
against Yudenich, went so far as to appoint its own 'dictator' to
handle its affairs whilst all his colleagues were away at the fighting.
The official in question was brought down from his omnipotent
height as soon as the crisis had passed; yet it is an instructive
sidelight on the emerging pattern of party life that he should have
been thus elevated in the first place. Collective forms of deliberation and administration were slowly but surely being eroded by
expedients introduced for the wartime emergency.[24]

'Appointmentism', by which was meant the lapse of elective
procedures in the choice of officials, was simultaneously on the
increase. It cropped up in various shapes and appearances. Firstly,
certain local committees made up for the loss of mobilised office-
holders by co-opting new committee members. Next to nothing

would be known about this, which in itself signifies a certain discomfiture about going against the grain of past practices, if just such a case had not been recorded in the Smolensk party archives.[25] A second way of breaking with elective custom was noticeable when local party bodies nominated individual officials to take charge of lower committees. Here too there was a reluctance to parade so basic a contravention of tradition; but the historical chronicle is saved for prosperity by the swagger of the Tula District Committee, which was to become somewhat notorious for its relish in applying authoritarian methods to party life in 1920, in announcing that it was appointing 'a special plenipotentiary comrade' to assume control of each subordinate party body in its area.[26] Yet appointmentism probably reached its greatest extent in a further and less direct fashion. Sovnarkom, in co-operation with the Bolshevik Central Committee, had introduced it own plenipotentiaries to expedite the delivery of food supplies since shortly after the October Revolution and had stretched the arrangement to include military conscription and the suppression of peasant disturbances after the start of the Civil War. The centrally-appointed plenipotentiaries, once they had arrived from Moscow, set about selecting their own teams of officials. Food supplies, conscription and the maintenance of social order were matters so close to the heart of the Bolshevik war effort that elected local party committees were bound to find the boundaries of their competence encroached upon so long as the central party leadership clung on to the arrangement.[27]

Such effects indicated the civilian sector of the Bolshevik party to be moving rapidly towards many forms of organisation already adopted in the armed forces. Only in the territory under White occupation, ironic though it seems, did party bodies fail to start sloughing off collective and elective procedures to any great degree. If the writer Victor Shklovski is to be believed, the Bolshevik committee members in Odessa responded to the White presence by stealing out to a pre-arranged hiding-place on the city outskirts where they lived together until the Red Army recaptured the area.[28] Mass cohabitation must have acted as a sharp brake upon whatever monocratic ambitions may have been harboured by individual officials. Nor could rank-and-file opinion be easily overridden. Formal methods of discussion and consultation were naturally ruled out by fear that the White forces might get wind of what was happening. Yet the viewpoint of ordinary Bolsheviks had somehow to be taken into account if only because they played so crucial a role in stirring up industrial strikes and in sheltering party officials on the run. The stakes of political involvement were immensely high in the Civil War; the Whites executed captured Bolsheviks in much the same way as the Reds did away with captured enemy officers.[29] Few party rank-and-filers were going to risk their necks in such circumstances simply because ordered to by higher officials. Indeed, underground activity by its very nature could never be expected to conform to the hierarchical standards which were currently being introduced throughout Soviet-held regions. Communications were as unreliable as at any time before 1917. This, as the Urals-Siberian Bureau indicated, was not for want of effort on the part of provincial and regional bodies; but the net result was inevitably that local committees were pushed back once again on their own initiative.[30] Such conditions, far from strengthening the self-confidence of underground Bolsheviks, evidently persuaded them to accept the highly co-ordinated, disciplined framework of party life in the rest of the country as soon as the Red Army had driven out the Whites.

The leadership in Moscow meanwhile worked indefatigably to impose stricter control over every level of the hierarchy. Care was taken that the new system of Central Committee executive organs should present a common face to the world and should try as far as possible to act as a single unit. The Central Committee announced their composition soon after the Eighth Party Congress. The Politburo was assigned five Central Committee members (and a further three to be alternates); the Orgburo too was given five such members; and the Secretariat was put in the charge of Central Committee member Stasova. An interlocking arrangement was adopted to ensure close working links. Krestinski and Stalin were given seats on both the Politburo and the Orgburo; Stasova had a place on the Orgburo while carrying out her duties in the Secretariat. Even at this late date, however, little was done to establish the new network of Departments within the Secretariat despite the Eighth Congress's urgent plea for action. Most central leaders nevertheless lost few opportunities to emphasise that the organisational changes just made in Moscow were designed specifically to bring the Central Committee into closer contact with the party at large and to enable it to direct its affairs all the more effectively.[31]

But it might have been predicted that the system would not turn out quite as preordained. The Central Committee had nineteen full members and eight alternates; yet wartime responsibilities once again made their impact, leaving only ten members, of whom two were alternates, resident most of the time in the capital. To avoid this would have required a decision to exclude several men of outstanding political stature such as Stalin, Trotski and Zinoviev since it was known that they would be away from Moscow for lengthy periods. Such a step was unthinkable: they were already too well established as bright stars in the political galaxy to be dispensed with so carelessly. As a consequence, it was declared, there could be little hope of holding plenary sessions of the Central Committee on the fortnightly basis laid down by the Eighth Party Congress. Circumstances at home and abroad changed with bewildering rapidity in 1919. The ten convocations of the plenum before spring 1920 were transparently insufficient to re-establish the Central Committee as the regular body of paramount status inside the party.[32] Not that its decisions and announcements on a variety of major issues were not of the highest importance. Yet it did not require observatory powers of more than ordinary acuity to see that the Politburo, by virtue of domination of grand policy in the month-long gaps between plenary sessions, was eating away at the practical boundaries of the Central Committee's deliberative competence. It was a case of gobbling, not nibbling. By early 1920 the Politburo had settled itself comfortably into a range of duties including the conduct of foreign diplomacy, the management of the economy, the formulation of military strategy, the mediation of disputes between highly placed soviet and party bodies, and the selection of personnel for high-ranking offices.[33]

The Politburo's institutional identity was built up with remark-able speed. Other Central Committee members were initially allowed to attend its meetings if they so desired, but were not granted voting rights.[34] At an early stage it was also realised that ample resort would have to be had to telegrams and telephone messages if Stalin and Trotski were not to be disenfranchised by the accident of their prolonged absences from Moscow.[35] The Politburo in fact recorded much greater success in achieving a stable kernel of leaders than the Orgburo. Apparently neither Krestinski nor Stasova, who were the Orgburo's regular stalwarts, used the telephone to consult their colleagues and draw them into their deliberations. Perhaps this is a token that they lacked the personal standing and prestige in the Orgburo enjoyed by Lenin in the

Politburo; be that as it may, there was concern that the Orgburo should begin to set its house in order, a concern that found its expression in December 1919 in a Central Committee decision to reshuffle the members. In the event, however, a curious choice was made. Beloborodov, Serebryakov and Stalin were to be replaced by Dzerzhinski, Kamenev, Rakovski and Trotski as the Orgburo colleagues of Krestinski and Stasova. Why it was thought that the new line-up would be any more likely than the old one to be present in Moscow is mysterious. As might have been predicted, the Orgburo continued to hobble along in its erstwhile manner well into 1920.[36]

And perhaps the Politburo, not relishing the potential rivalry of a strong Orgburo, saw no reason to give it proper reinforcement. Lenin certainly enjoyed dabbling in the Orgburo's daily affairs: he could well have therefore preferred to keep things as they already were. There was no rigid distinction between the respective functions of the Politburo and the Orgburo. Day-to-day work was usually divided according to a rule of thumb whereby the Orgburo handled all matters of an organisational, administrative nature except in such instances as appeared to call for a prior decision about high policy, domestic or foreign. Even so, this did not debar the Politburo from taking it upon itself to deal with quite trivial issues like the choice of a new commandant for the Kremlin guard. And just in case the arrangement of interlocking membership failed to hold the Orgburo in check it was decided to supply the Politburo with the right to veto its decrees and resolutions at will. Comforting as all this must have been to a person with Lenin's desire to have a finger in every pie, it did not signify wholehearted compliance with the Eighth Party Congress's explicit call for a fully articulated framework of central executive party machinery.

Much the same semi-neglect befell the Secretariat. The 'responsible secretary' was Elena Stasova and her deputy was Klavdiya Sverdlova. An ambitious scheme of internal reorganisation was announced involving the installation of nine new sub-units. The precise division of functions among them was baffling even to many party leaders in Moscow itself, so that several pages of explanatory material had to be issued to the party at large. Initially only five sub-units in fact left the drafting stage: the Organisation-Instruction Department with duties to guide local committees in interpreting and implementing policies; the Files-Assignment Department with duties to collect detailed data about all officials with a view to facilitating job transfers across the face of the country; the Information-Statistics Department with duties to gather, sift and disseminate all manner of intelligence about party life in the provinces; the Province-Inspection Department with duties to establish a team of peripatetic officials to supervise the activity of local committees; and the General Department with duties to service the workaday business of the Secretariat as a whole. A so-called Special Department was also projected in the hope of conducting party propaganda amid certain social groups; but progress was slow: all that had been achieved by late 1919 was a section for the national minorities and a section for women.[38]

Stasova tried to present her record as a substantial success. Under her leadership, she pointed out, the Secretariat had at last carried out its long-awaited expansion of staff and now had over two hundred assistants. She also produced pages of diagrams and statistics to show that a rapid rise in the quantity of letters written and decisions taken had been achieved. But her depiction of a well-ordered, well-articulated administrative apparatus was not a fair picture of reality. She must have known about the many teething problems, especially the absence of a clear demarcation of functions among the Departments. Worse still was the failure to take a sensibly broad view of the Secretariat's responsibilities. In the light of the reports indicating the increasing disenchantment of working-class rank-and-filers it is indeed a black mark against the name of the central party leadership that no effort was made to establish a Department with the task of assessing the scope of the problem. Only in 1920 was it finally realised that the Secretariat badly needed an Agitation-Propaganda Department to encourage and co-ordinate the explanation of Bolshevik policies to ordinary members. Another sign of the halfheartedness of the reorganisation was to be spotted in the move to abolish the Province-Inspection Department almost as soon as it had been created. No excuse was offered except a vague statement that the original idea had been 'impractical'. There is more than a whiff of suspicion that the real reason was that the other central party offices, notably the Politburo and the Orgburo, remained reluctant to hand over a function of such influence to a mere sub-unit of the Secretariat.[39]

This overriding concern with the acquisition and retention of power was reflected too in the relations between Moscow and the localities in 1919. Central party bodies preserved a measure of decorum in their correspondence. They kept up the habit of 'proposing', 'suggesting' and 'recommending' rather than 'ordering' or 'commanding'. Such a style fooled nobody. There had never been a time in party history when the rights of local committees had been battered around so severely. The Politburo and the Orgburo were beginning to appoint officials to vacant posts in the provinces, both inside and outside the party, without prior consultation with the institutions in question.[40] The increased use of Moscow-chosen plenipotentiaries was an indirect extension of the same development. Special teams of them were sent out to take charge of specific tasks like the conscription of recruits for the Red Army or the requisitioning of grain for the towns; but these tasks were so fundamental to political life in general that local party committees inevitably lost control over much else too. Plenipotentiaries were known to ride roughshod over provincial committees. I. M. Vareikis, always an apologist for local party bodies, said that Bolshevik affairs in the localities were being knocked about by 'punitive expeditions'.[41] The central party leadership, however, took a different view, arguing that the plenipotentiaries did at least get things done. Under Trotski's influence it was therefore decided to set up a fresh hierarchy of political departments', after the fashion of the Red Army, to cope with the urgent problems such as the restoration of a regular network of rail and water transport.[42]

Regional and provincial committees which provoked central displeasure, furthermore, could quickly find themselves in dire straits. The worst mauling was suffered by the Ukrainian Central Committee. In December 1919 a group of leading Bolsheviks working in the Ukraine protested to Moscow on the grounds that they were being edged out of their jobs by the many party officials sent to the Ukraine after the defeat of Denikin. Amongst the newcomers, let it be noted, were Sapronov and other Democratic Centralists who had been causing the All-Russian Central Committee so much trouble in the capital. For the while, however, the Orgburo chose to regard the protesters as envious politickers.[43] Yet its attitude changed when it became known that the Ukrainian Central Committee was allowing a campaign of criticism of official party policies. The critics were not a homogenous bunch. Most Kharkov officials, possibly supported by the Democratic Centralists, wanted a change in attitude to the countryside: they now advocated cutting back on grain requisitionment and giving the peasantry greater opportunity to engage in free trade. At the same time there were other malcontented officials in the Ukraine who attacked the Moscow Central Committee from the opposite point of view and maintained that the party was too mild in its treatment of the 'middle peasant'. Both kinds of criticism were equally anathema in Lenin's eyes. He persuaded the Politburo to redress the situation by appointing a further batch of loyalist activists to postings in the Ukraine.[44]

The ploy did not work. The All-Ukrainian Party Conference which met in Kharkov in March 1920 elected a Central Committee composed predominantly of oppositionists. The Politburo took even sterner measures. It disbanded the new Ukrainian Central Committee and replaced it with a specially selected Temporary Bureau. The excuse given was that Sapronov had cynically overstimulated the influx of rank-and-filers in the 'party week' drive in Kharkov. The result, it was alleged, was that Kharkov oppositionists were vastly over-represented at the All-Ukrainian Conference and were able to get themselves elected to the Ukrainian Central Committee by unfair means. It was even asserted that the Democratic Centralists would be happy to see a split within the party as a whole. This was nasty twaddle. Kharkov's recruiting enthusiasm was fully in accordance with earlier directives from above and was paralleled elsewhere in the country. And to accuse the oppositionists of wanting to divide the party was to ignore explicit public statements to the contrary made by Sapronov himself. Here was a turning-point in Bolshevik affairs. The central party leadership was prepared in the name of discipline to disband any local committee hostile to the political line of the moment.[45]

Yet the Central Committee and its executive offshoots was not omnipotent. Most disbandments, according to Krestinski, had been undertaken solely in order to restore peaceful conditions to lower party bodies whose internal disputes interrupted ordinary daily work. As examples he cited the provincial committees of Bryansk, Kazan, Saratov and Voronezh.[46] It would in fact have been difficult in the circumstances for the Moscow leaders to become more heavy-handed than they already were. Above all the Civil War was too important to allow the Politburo to become unduly bogged down in local controversies. Aside from everything else there was the problem of communications. In mid-1919, after the Central Committee had announced that 20000 Bolshevik

members had just been sent to the front, the Red Army's command
staff retorted that only a fifth of this number appeared to have
arrived. Krestinski continually complained that provincial committees were most grudging in response to pleas for the regular
dispatch of reports and information. He also requested that the
Secretariat should be granted enough hundreds of ancillary
assistants to enable it to keep proper tabs on what was happening in
the localities. Like his colleagues, he based his argument upon the
need to introduce greater rationality to the functions of central
administration.[47] No local official disagreed with him. Nonetheless
it is a matter of historical fact that the consolidation of the Moscow
party apparatus which occurred in following years was most
helpful to the Politburo and the Orgburo in permitting them to do
to further regional and provincial committees what had just been
meted out to the Ukrainian Central Committee.[48]

Local calls for centralisation in 1918 had been evoked mainly by
local hopes for centrally-provided assistance to the provinces; but
now it was evident that the Moscow Central Committee was
interested more in imposing authority than in proffering help.
Thus Kaganovich needed little encouragement to harp on his old
theme that the party ought to be run on the same lines as an army
and that the chairman and secretary of every Bolshevik committee
should henceforward be held personally responsible, like military
officers, for all decisions taken in its name; Sapronov was still
arguing his case for a renewed emphasis upon provincial initiative
and upon clipping the wings of the central leadership's centralising
ambitions.[49] There also remained many functionaries and activists
who, whilst shunning both Kaganovich and Sapronov, nevertheless complained that the Central Committee and its executive
adjuncts had omitted to provide that network of services and
facilities which had been heralded earlier in the year.[50] Yet it must
have comforted the Politburo greatly that the Eighth Party
Conference in December passed without undue trouble. The
Moscow leaders did not escape entirely without hurt; for several
delegates of the various persuasions took the opportunity to hit out
at the drift of events inside the party. But the proceedings seemed
very like a pallid re-run of the controversies of the Eighth Party
Congress itself in March. Nothing new of great significance was
said. The Civil War had yet to be won and, in the main, it was easy
for the Central Committee to ask for a resounding vote of approval
until such time as the military danger was no more.[51]

The situation had changed by April 1920 when the Ninth Party Congress met in Moscow: Denikin was on the run and even his most inveterate supporters gave him little chance of reviving the Whites' fortunes. It was the bitterest debate about organisational affairs since the Second Party Congress of 1903. Sapronov and Osinski made their predictably cutting speeches but it was Maksimovski who led the assault for the Democratic Centralists. He claimed that Bolshevik life was steadily moving away from democratic centralism to bureaucratic centralism. The symptoms picked out by him for denunciation were the Moscow leadership's isolation from the realities of local party problems and its equally irritating insistence upon interfering in the trivia of local affairs. He opposed the increasing transfer of authority from committees to individual officials; he railed against the tendency of the Secretariat's Departments to issue instructions to their local departmental counterparts without consulting the regular party committees. Maksimovski could speak with confidence: he himself had headed the Files-Assignment Department in 1919. For all his personal experience, however, he did not succeed in putting forward highly practical proposals. He called for the 'militarisation of the party apparatus' but avoided explaining how this tallied with his simultaneous request for 'the collective principle' to be observed at all levels. His *bête noire* was the Orgburo; yet all he could suggest was that its composition should be reduced to three members so as to facilitate smooth administration. He also argued that it would greatly help if the respective functions of the Politburo and the Orgburo were demarcated more clearly. But above all it was a new mental attitude that Maksimovski was out to propagate: his viewpoint did not stand or fall by particular proposals.[52]

The central party leaders defended themselves against his onslaught with vigour. They did not have a difficult job on their hands. The Democratic Centralist group was not a highly organised faction. it published only a few special pamphlets and held only a few separate meetings before the opening of the Congress. In fact, it is the devil's own job trying to track down all the delegates who adhered to it. Sapronov, Osinski and Maksimovski had all been Left Communists in 1918 but they never managed to put the Democratic Centralists on the same level of organisation and coordination. Yet it is wrong to regard them simply as would-be party leaders who muffed their chances. The brutal truth, which they were always too dogged and courageous to admit in public, was that they did not represent the feelings and experiences of the vast mass of Bolshevik officials. Their success in mounting a coalition of critics of the Central Committee in the Ukraine was repeated in very few places in the rest of the country. All the prominent figures in the Democratic Centralist group had worked in Moscow for most of the time since the October Revolution and had remained in civilian occupations. Hard as they tried to present themselves as typical local officials, they never fully shook off the suspicion that they were essentially metropolitan theorists who knew nothing of provincial Russia. This was most unfair to them but it was nevertheless a widespread view, especially among Bolsheviks serving in the Red Army. Thus it was no surprise that the Ninth Party Congress decided to refuse to elect a single Democratic Centralist to the new Central Committee.[53]

Yet the effortless trouncing of the Democratic Centralists apparently made the central party leadership reckless of the grievances felt by many other local officials. Only Krestinski seems to have recognised the need for tactful handling. But Trotski would not listen to any censure of the Central Committee. Not only did he denounce all thoughts of effecting a 'decentralisation of party power', but he also rubbed salt in provincial wounds by saying that nobody objected to being re-posted by the Moscow leaders when it involved promotion rather than demotion.[54] Lenin capped this by defending a provocatively narrow interpretation of the party's organisational principles. 'Democratic centralism', he asserted, 'means only that representatives from the localities meet and elect a responsible body which must then govern. But how? That depends on how many suitable people, how many good administrators there are. Democratic centralism consists in the Congress checking on the Central Committee, removing it and electing a new one.'[55] Such a statement must have made many an overworked local official feel that central figures did not give a hoot for provincial problems. Lenin, if he had wanted, could have tuned into the mood of the mass of the delegates by examining a cartoon picture which was in circulation. It depicted Stasova in riding breeches and with spurs on her heels; it was entitled 'The Secretary of the Militarised Party'.[56] Centralisation, in local eyes, was not indeed simply a matter of creating a hierarchy of command stretching out from Moscow to the lowliest party cell; it should also involve central leaders in an endeavour to learn about local problems and to provide the services and facilities to help to solve them.

Evgeni Preobrazhenski, a former Central Committee member working in Ufa, did more than anyone else to dampen this inflammable situation. He took an intermediate position. On the one hand he criticised the present Central Committee for its heavy-handed excesses; on the other hand he criticised provincial committees for being just as heavy-handed in their own approach to lower party bodies. The organisational malaise, he declared, affected all levels of the hierarchy equally. His proposed cure was rather curious. He believed that the best way to secure a desirable 'decentralisation of party power' was to lay more emphasis on the regional tier. To this end he urged that regional committees should be elected freely from below and should be relieved of the interference shown by the central executive bodies since 1918. But the brunt of Preobrazhenski's message was his rousing appeal for all party committees, whatever rung of the hierarchical ladder they happened to occupy, to cease regarding the other rungs with distrust and hostility. The times called for renewed co-operation and mutual understanding.[57] Such a theme was not unattractive to central party leaders since it skirted clear of the much broader programme of the Democratic Centralists. And it pleased those many local delegates who wanted to see the Central Committee doing more in the way of assisting them with their practical problems. Preobrazhenski did not put it in so many words but he was essentially demanding that changes be made in the spirit of the Eighth Party Congress's resolution on the organisational question.[58]

The Central Committee elected by the Ninth Party Congress reflected the atmosphere of compromise. Stasova, it would appear, was chosen as scapegoat: she was the only full member of the previous Central Committee not to be re-elected even as an alternate member. She alone had headed the Secretariat until December 1919 when she was joined by Krestinski; she had been a prominent figure in the Orgburo throughout the year. In her memoirs she claimed that her electoral failure stemmed simply from her desire to introduce new faces to the Moscow leadership and from her consequent decision not to stand as candidate; but it seems too much of a coincidence to deny that her notoriety as a no-nonsense centraliser played a part in her calculations.[59] Be that as it may, the ensuing selection of Krestinski and Preobrazhenski, together with L. P. Serebryakov, to take charge of the Orgburo and the Secretariat, gave the firm impression that a feeling of accommodation and conciliation was in the air. Krestinski had performed like the perfect diplomat in the party controversy over Brest-Litovsk; Preobrazhenski had made his name as a peacemaker at the Ninth Congress. The following year was about to test whether they would be able to run the central apparatus in such a manner as to avoid the tensions and disputes of the past.[60]

Their task was not going to be easy. It already stood in doubt whether the central colleagues of Krestinski, Preobrazhenski and Serebryakov sincerely believed in the desirability of basic altera- tions in the fabric of party life. This was not all. It was also more than likely that leaders at the regional and provincial levels would prove reluctant to release the tight grasp they had acquired upon town committees and lower party bodies. Discipline and obedience had become bywords of Bolshevik consciousness and behaviour. The lurch into internal authoritarianism was given a further push by the increasing investment of single officials with an authority which had once been the prerogative of entire committees. At all odds it was noticeable that most functionaries and activists wishing to change the organisational face of the party talked almost exclusively about the problems of committees and said next to nothing about the rank-and-filers. Not even the Democratic Centralists could be exempted from the charge of negligence in this respect. It was left to that tiny minority of officials who belonged to the nascent Workers' Opposition to raise the alarm. That they were ignored and that the working-class exodus from the party continued was a sign that the Bolsheviks were in for a political shock of enormous dimensions in the rest of 1920. In retrospect the proceedings of the Ninth Party Congress appear astoundingly complacent for a party which sought to base its power upon the active support of the mass of Russian industrial workers.

6 Defeat in Victory
(April 1920–March 1921)

The crises awaiting them after their victory in the Civil War were slow to be fully appreciated by most Bolshevik officials. An excess of confidence was in the air. It was a dangerous mood for a governing party to adopt when its society was exhausted by years of military conflict. That the Politburo was not free from the prevalent optimism was shown by its handling of the border clashes with Polish troops which had been occurring intermittently since 1919. In the following year Josef Pilsudski, then the commander-in-chief of the Polish army, launched an invasion of the Ukraine. It was a most foolhardy step which, as he later recognised, was bound to raise the Ukrainian and Russian populations alike to the boiling-point of nationalist fury. The Red Army quickly recaptured Kiev. The Politburo, eager to drive every foreign soldier off Soviet soil forthwith, ordered its forces into hot pursuit of the hastily retreating invaders. Bolshevik newspapers carried story after story extolling the latest feats of Budenny's cavalry and the other units which had salvaged Moscow's military pride.

This triumph provoked the question whether a full-scale invasion of Poland should be undertaken. A central group led by Lenin, casting aside the doubts expressed by both Stalin and Trotski, felt sure that the Polish lower classes would welcome the Red Army as their liberator and would surge up in revolt against the existing government. Thus, it was expected, the Bolsheviks would lay hold of a political bridgehead from which to set all of Europe ablaze with socialist revolutions. It was the same mistake as had just been made by Pilsudski. Polish nationalism, assisted by the Reds' difficulties with supply lines and with internal disputes about strategy, gathered its strength for a powerful counter-offensive before Warsaw. Now it was the Red Army's turn to speed back towards the frontier and reconstruct Soviet defences as best it could. But the social and economic chaos wreaked by the fighting had by then produced a change of mind in both Pilsudski's government and the Bolshevik Politburo. Neither side saw much point in further conflict. The Red Army particularly needed to enter negotiations since the last White army in Russia, headed by Baron Wrangel in succession to the dispirited Denikin, was exploiting the Polish débâcle by pushing its way northwards into the Ukraine. The Ninth Party Conference in September chewed over the lessons of the failure to 'export' revolution by armed might and announced its support for the search for peace with Poland. The ensuing armistice allowed the Red Army to concentrate its attention upon Wrangel: a brief thrust was all that was required to force him to evacuate the Crimea and flee westwards. The issue of the Russian Civil War was in doubt no longer.[1]

Defeat in the war against Poland, however, had knocked a gaping hole in Bolshevik projections for the future. The fear that the October Revolution might have to endure years of inter- national isolation was strengthened by the observation that neither Germany nor the other highly industrialised countries were im- mediately likely to manufacture their own anti-capitalist upheavals. The Politburo perforce had to limit itself to strengthening and uniting the Communist International. In July 1920 representatives of sympathetic parties from all over the globe convened in Moscow and gave unstinting recognition to the achievements of the Bolsheviks in the previous three years. The prestige of leaders like Lenin, Trotski and Zinoviev enabled them to dominate every debate. The Bolshevik party, it was now decided, should stand as the organisational model for the socialist movement in all the member countries. All the same the Politburo was no longer very sanguine about the immediate prospects of revolutions abroad. It therefore instructed Soviet diplomats to do their utmost to consolidate the foreign trade links forged since the lifting of the Allied Supreme Council's lifting of the economic embargo. Some leading Bolsheviks were uneasy about this. They felt it was inconsistent for a socialist government to strike financial deals with capitalist enterprises at home or in other countries. But the Politburo carried the day. The advance to socialism, declared Lenin, would not be deflected by commercial relations with the Soviet state's ideological opponents.[2]

The destitute condition of the domestic economy bore down upon the Bolshevik party in 1920. Agriculture was in crisis. The grain requisitions carried out by both the Red and the White forces had left the peasantry starving and impoverished. The area under the plough grew smaller not only because rural households saw less incentive to sow all their land but equally because not enough seed-corn was available. The grain harvest of 1920 told its own story. The tonnage reaching the barns was barely five-eighths of the level obtained in 1913, the last full year before military hostilities. Nor was the industrial situation any less depressing. Gross output, it was calculated, had crashed down to a seventh of what it had been prior to the First World War. Numerous factories were derelict; much machinery was rusty, worn out or broken. Railway rolling stock was in dire need of replacement. The factory labour force had taken a terrible battering. Around 60 000 industrial workers are thought to have perished while fighting in the ranks of the Red Army; many hundreds of thousands of townspeople are recorded as having been killed off by the ubiquitous typhoid and malnutrition. Postwar reconstruction was already an awesome prospect.[3]

The Politburo stuck to methods which had served it in the Civil War. Stricter discipline was imposed in the factories; heavier penalties were introduced to deter delinquency. The militaristic spirit was in the ascendant. On Trotski's proposal, it was resolved to suspend the traditional rights of trades unions in key sectors, notably transport and coalmining, and to install 'political depart-ments' on the pattern of the Red Army. Trotski's trust in their efficaciousness found a welcoming audience in the Politburo. With this encouragement he went on to suggest that entire regiments, instead of being demobilised, should be redirected into 'labour armies' which were to set about restoring the factories to full production. Lenin's attitude was just as fierce. In 1920 he was still insisting that forcible large-scale seizures were the most effective way of securing grain for the towns. The Politburo did not demur (although Trotski did momentarily argue that rural discontent could best be mollified by allowing peasants to keep a greater part of the harvest and trade it on the open market). Lenin, taking the bit between his teeth, proceeded to demand that ever tougher measures be applied against peasant households failing to meet their quotas of grain deliveries. As yet no Politburo member seemed to recognise that industrial and agricultural policies were vying with one another in stoking up a massive boilerhouse of social unrest.[4]

The central party leadership's blindness to domestic realities is little short of astounding. Strikes were erupting in all industrial centres, including Petrograd. Bolshevik leaders in the provinces reacted variously: some tried conciliation, others would tolerate no compromise and employed heavy-handed tactics. A production stoppage in the Tula armaments plant induced local officials to imprison the 'troublemakers'.[5] Yet this was as nothing when compared with the treatment meted out to the thousands of peasants who joined the mass insurrections against the Bolsheviks around Tambov and Saratov and in the Ukraine and western Siberia. The rebels found themselves facing regular units of the Red Army just as soon as peace was concluded with the Polish government.[6] But the final straw was yet to come. In late 1920, after a series of minor mutinies elsewhere, it became evident that the Kronstadt naval garrison too was on the brink of revolt. Factory disturbances and peasant uprisings had already given voice to broad demands for political democratisation as well as material improvement. The Kronstadt sailors agreed. Forcible grain requisitionments, they declared, should cease immediately; stern labour discipline should be relaxed in the factories; the other political parties should be allowed to compete freely with the Bolsheviks for popular favour. The Politburo, as the Tenth Party Congress assembled in Moscow in March 1921, knew well that concessions of some kind were needed to secure the October Revolution's survival.[7]

Central party leaders could not escape their share of the blame for the failure to spot the dangers at an earlier stage. Not that that stopped them trying. As usual, they explained to the Party Congress that they had been hugely overburdened by their responsibilities in the previous year. Hardly had the Civil War been won, they maintained, than the Politburo was saddled with the onus of the Polish campaign. Stalin and Trotski were at the war front for lengthy periods and could scarcely ever put in an appearance at Politburo meetings. The old, informal pattern of decision-making had to be retained. To make matters more difficult, the plan to have a triumvirate of Orgburo members at the head of the Secretariat was bedevilled by illnesses afflicting Krestrinski and Serebryakov. Preobrazhenski had to soldier on alone, much like Sverdlov in 1918 and Stasova in 1919. These unforeseeable set-backs were said to have played havoc with the Secretariat's day-to-day operations, making it impossible to establish the long-promised Agitation-Propaganda and Province-Inspection Departments. The picture presented to the rest of the party was that the Central Committee and its executive offshoots were making the best of a bad job in particularly inauspicious circumstances.[8]

This was exaggeration to the point of distortion. Preobrazhenski may have lost his two colleagues for a while; but the Secretariat itself had never been so highly funded and heavily staffed as it became by autumn 1920. The ancillary personnel rose to around 600.[9] The real reason for the failure to install an Agitation-Propaganda Department was that Preobrazhenski's heart was not in the matter. It was an inexcusable attitude. The trouble brewing between party officialdom and working-class rank-and-filers made it acutely necessary to equip a central office to organise facilities to explain Bolshevik ideas and policies to the mass of the party. As regards the Province-Inspection Department, the central leadership was hoist by its own petard. Krestinski himself affirmed that the selection and dispatch of officials to the provinces no longer constituted much of an administrative problem.[10] That being so, why was no Department set up? The answer may well be that the Politburo and the Orgburo remained reluctant to hand over so powerful a function to a mere sub-section of the Secretariat. Hoarding of authority had become almost an obsession. Not content with what had already been done to diminish the Central Committee's influence, Trotski saw that the right to peruse urgent diplomatic correspondence should be restricted to Politburo members. It was a far cry from the 'open diplomacy' of 1917; it was a further step in the direction of enveloping the paramount issues of state with an aura of mystery to which only a handful of initiates was privy.[11]

Preobrazhenski at the Ninth Party Congress had appealed for an improvement in central relations with local committees. Yet this did not come off. The Politburo publicly volunteered the information that it was still sanctioning cross-posting as a means of punishing oppositionists.[12] Krestinski, Preobrazhenski and Serebryakov were later to acquire a reputation for having been 'liberal' and 'gentle' as managers of the central party apparatus. But there is nothing to show that they did anything to protect the Democratic Centralists from the administrative onslaught directed at them in spring 1920. Indeed a thorough investigation was undertaken in the Ukraine, the main refuge of Sapronov's group, to eradicate all active hostility to policies laid down in Moscow. If the Democratic Centralists had drawn comfort from Preobrazhenski's Congress

speeches, they must now have been gravely disappointed: his wish
to mollify the strains between Moscow and the provinces did not
extend to showing indulgence or charity to political adversaries.
He and his central colleagues pointed out that they were acting
completely in accordance with the provisions of the Party Rules.
This was true. Yet many members of the Politburo and the
Orgburo were shortly to rue that they had accepted so extreme an
interpretation of the rights of central executive bodies.[13]

Political conflict was not the only source of trouble. The
Orgburo and the Secretariat also found that most local committees
were chary of complying with orders to release officials to work in
other areas of the country. Smolensk was a case in question. From
the Central Committee's viewpoint it was a 'quiet' province since it
contained no Democratic Centralists. Yet there was an awful fuss
when the Orgburo wanted to recall S. V. Ivanov and V. A.
Smolyaninov to Moscow and to send two recommended officials in
their place. Ivanov was chairman of the Provincial Party Committee, Smolyaninov of the Provincial Soviet Executive Committee.
Smolensk Bolsheviks argued the toss for over a month. In the end a
compromise was reached: Smolyaninov was to set off immediately
for Moscow though Ivanov was allowed to stay put for a while in
order to smooth the transition.[14] The affair had its parallels across
the country. It would be unreasonable to suppose that the central
party leadership would not have been able, had it so desired, to
impose its will upon individual local committees. Such bottlenecks
were irritating to Preobrazhenski, but hardly more than that. In
any case he does in fact appear to have made an effort to be as
tactful as possible in his dealings with lower-echelon party bodies.
Stasova's unpopularity lived on in his memory. No wonder that his
period of administration was soon to be talked about nostalgically
by disgruntled committee members.

Preobrazhenski, moreover, had some reason to feel badly done
by in his attempt to conciliate local interests. Smolensk is again a
good example. At the very meeting where the Provincial Committee protested about the proposed replacement of Ivanov and Smolyaninov it also issued a reprimand to the Yukhnov District Committee for omitting to transfer certain activists to jobs in Smolensk
itself.[15] Hierarchical concerns were on everyone's lips. Many
provincial committees, arguing the need to economise on finances
and manpower, even abolished the district and town committees
based in provincial capitals.[16] Eager to cut an impressive image,

Bolshevik officials not infrequently reported to higher authority that political tension had entirely disappeared from the territory under their tutelage. This was hyperbole: strife in Samara and Tula proved that party life was not as controlled as superficially appeared.[17] Nonetheless the disciplinary trend was no illusion. The campaign against Poland in summer called forth further mobilisations of personnel and left civilian party committees disposing of fewer activists than ever. Chairmen, with what little secretarial assistance they could gather locally, took on still heavier workloads. They were expected to be towers of strength, coordinating party activity in their respective areas and releasing their few remaining colleagues to administer Bolshevik policies in the soviets and other public institutions.[18]

Nobody since 1918 had questioned that wartime required changes to be made in organisational methods. By 1920, however, many officials felt that, at least at the regional level and below, the party's role as the dominant institution of the Soviet state was under threat. Political departments were seen as the culprits. Trotski and his supporters, with their zeal for setting up special agencies to troubleshoot particular economic emergencies, were bit by bit creating a supra-party network of administration. The Donets Provincial Party Committee was more enraged than most. It was being asked to stand idly by while the Donbass Coalmining Political Department supervised the restoration of all local mines and pit-heads. This industry was so much the body and soul of the area that even routine matters of local government were falling to the Political Department. The fear was abroad that such expedients might become permanent features of the institutional scene. What Trotski had not bargained for was the feeling among Bolsheviks that the party, by virtue of its achievements in the October Revolution and the Civil War, had staked an incontrovertible claim as the sole repository of revolutionary energy, wisdom and dependability. In summer 1920 the question taken up most often in the local party press was how to clip the powers of the political departments.[19]

And so it was that an entirely different crisis crept up on party officials across the country, catching all but a few of them unawares and unprepared. Working-class rank-and-file opinion was at last approaching the point of explosion. In midsummer it became a Bolshevik commonplace that a rift existed between 'the top and bottom of the party'. Nobody bothered to define it precisely but all were aware of the main causes: the material privileges and

authoritarian manner of officialdom at every level of the hierarchy
of party committees. Many a rank-and-filer holding a manual job
found it irritating enough to obey the orders of factory managers
and foremen; but this irritation was exacerbated greatly by the
sight of Bolshevik functionaries themselves beginning to ape
middle-class styles of command and living. And there seemed scant
chance of reform. The only alternative, as the malcontents saw it,
was to vote with their feet and allow their party membership to
lapse. The exodus no longer had anything to do with trepidation
about the possibility of a White invasion. It was straightforward
political disenchantment. The number of Bolsheviks in Ivanovo-
Voznesensk province collapsed from 5500 in March 1920 to 2900
in September. The embarrasment was immense. Elsewhere it was
usual for local committees to hush up what was happening and to
stop issuing data about membership. This course was followed in
Moscow too. The Central Committee report to the Ninth Party
Conference in September 1920 omitted all reference, for the first
time in Bolshevik history, to the party's numerical size.[20]

Needless to remark, the departure of so many rank-and-filers did
not restore party life to its former tranquillity. Amongst the first
officials to take up the problem in earnest was Yuri Milonov. Based
in Samara, he had campaigned for organisational reform since
1919. And in January 1920 he had managed to carry off a majority
of delegates at the Provincial Conference. But the majority of the
newly elected Provincial Committee, as it turned out, opposed his
standpoint and blocked discussion of it in Samara newspapers. Not
to be thwarted, Milonov beavered away among lower party bodies
and rank-and-file Bolsheviks. In August he won the debate at the
Samara Town Conference after raising a hue and cry about the
Bolsheviks' degeneration 'from a party of the ruling proletariat
into a party of its administrative stratum, the labour bureaucracy'.
His struggle went from strength to strength. And at the next
Provincial Conference he made no mistake and ensured that a
Provincial Committee was chosen which would lend him the active
support he required. His hope was that fellow oppositionists in
other towns (especially Shlyapnikov and Lutovinov in Moscow,
no doubt) would shortly give his campaign a national importance.[21]

But the going was heavy. Similar ideas canvassed by N. V.
Kopylov in Tula, where strikes in the armaments works had halted
production, got bogged down in controversy from the start.

Kopylov addressed the Provincial Conference in January 1920 but garnered the votes of only a sixth of the delegates. Many local officials regarded Kopylov as little better than the strikers themselves. It was this that lay at the root of the call by Provincial Committee chairman G. N. Kaminski for a battle against 'the petit-bourgeois tendencies and moods in the milieu of the working class, tendencies which are reflected even in the ranks of the party itself'. Kaminski was a hard-liner. Though willing to effect an improvement in workers' food-rations, he persuaded the Provincial Committee to sanction the imprisonment of the working-class militants who had led the strikes. And Kopylov was to be used as a scapegoat. The Tula Provincial Committee announced brazenly that Kopylov's calls for an accommodation to working-class demands were nothing short of Menshevism. Kaminski accused him of aiming to split the Bolshevik party in two. Blindly denying that there was anything to be learnt from rank-and-file complaints, the Provincial Committee was dealing with its crisis simply by applying disciplinary measures against all party members daring to show dissent from its policies.[22]

Other local committees trod more carefully, praying that the problem of rank-and-file discontent would somehow melt away of its own accord. The first non-oppositionist leader to see that repression was no solution was Preobrazhenski. In previous statements on the rank-and-file question he had avoided laying blame upon party officialdom. It does credit to his intellectual honesty that he was willing to change his mind and bring the issue before the Central Committee in July 1920. Without beating about the bush, he declared that the drift towards a system of material privileges and authoritarian discipline inside the party should be halted immediately. The Politburo concurred. It was decided to present a set of reform proposals to the forthcoming Party Conference in September. The first draft was completed by a commission of Preobrazhenski, Krestinski and I. I. Minkov but, upon further consideration, was thought to lack the necessary vividness. Zinoviev was brought in to reword the text and act as Central Committee spokesman. It boded ill for reform. In January 1920 Zinoviev had gone on record in a Petrograd newspaper as saying that the rift between 'the top and the bottom of the party' had been grossly exaggerated and should be ignored. His behaviour at the Ninth Party Conference showed that he had not really changed his mind.[23]

The Conference started with Lenin's report on the Soviet-Polish war and continued with reports by Kamenev and Trotski on diplomatic developments and military strategy. The defeats in Poland infused debate with extremes of emotion. The façade of Politburo unity was shattered when both Lenin and Trotski took the floor to criticise Stalin for contributing to the military débâcle by disobeying strategical orders. Yet the airing of grievances had a cathartic effect. All delegates were in accord that that the Polish defences were too strong and that the war should be quickly terminated. Krestinski's report on the Central Committee's organisational record exhibited the now typical mixture of self-criticism and self-justification. The critics, ranging from Democratic Centralists like Sapronov and Bubnov to non-aligned speakers such as K. G. Pestun and K. G. Zavyalova, mooted the same complaints as had been tossed at the central leadership earlier in the year. Political departments were predictably the bone of greatest contention. It was realised, however, that Zinoviev was shortly to deliver a weighty speech in opening a debate 'On the Immediate Problems of the Party'. Everyone knew that this was to be the liveliest issue before the Conference. Workers' Oppositionists to a man therefore refrained from attacking Krestinski and held their fire until they had heard what Zinoviev had to say.[24]

Zinoviev's report ran true to form: it was slick, superficial and obfuscatory. Absolving the central party leadership of all guilt, he put down rank-and-file troubles to the governing role laid upon the Bolsheviks through the October Revolution and the military role made inevitable by the Civil War. He cited Lenin's remark that internal discontent was conditioned primarily by objective circumstances outside the party's control. Zinoviev then proceeded to attach certain qualifications to his own call for reform. He asserted that no cleavage between 'the top and the bottom of the party' prevailed in Petrograd (which, needless to add, was Zinoviev's location of activity); he defended the central party leaders' practice of appointing officials to jobs in the provinces without worrying about local wishes. Most flagrantly of all, he said that the difficulty of attracting working-class men and women into the party stemmed not from political disenchantment but from their awe and respect for the responsibilities involved in being a Bolshevik. So as to leave no doubts as to his meaning, Zinoviev ended with the words: 'The chief conclusion of the proletarian revolution is the need for an iron, organised and monolithic party.'[25]

This complacent opportunism was torn to shreds by Sapronov. The central leaders, he maintained, had brought the organisational crisis upon their own heads by ignoring warning after warning given in 1919. He denounced the practice of 'exiling' dissentient officials to far-flung localities with the purpose of cutting them off from their political base. He provided the Conference with details about the clean-out of the Democratic Centralists from the Ukraine. His practical proposals were not unlike Preobrazhenski's. Provincial committees should no longer strive to cloak their proceedings in secrecy; party cells should hold open general meetings more frequently; Bolshevik functionaries should arrange 'non-party evenings' to explain governmental policies to all sections of the working population. Obviously Sapronov touched upon the notorious rift between 'the top and the bottom of the party', but his touch was rather light. He believed the way forward, for economic reconstruction as well as for the achievement of socialism, did not lie in acceding to working-class aspirations of the moment. His associate Bubnov took this a stage further by accusing the Workers' Opposition led by Shlyapnikov and Lutovinov of downright 'demagogy'. No love was lost between the Democratic Centralists and the Workers' Opposition. Indeed Sapronov did all he could to emphasise that his group comprised exclusively supporters of the Central Committee's political programme who were simply proffering better organisational methods of implementing it.[26]

This in turn enraged the Workers' Opposition. The charge was tossed at the Democratic Centralists that, in their own localities, they behaved no differently from the common run of party officials. 'Petty satraps' was the phrase used. Calls were made by Workers' Oppositionists like Kollontai and I. I. Kutuzov that Bolshevik leaders should hearken again to the voice of industrial workers and should provide them with an active role inside the party, the soviets and the trade unions. A radical change of attitude was vital. Perks and side-benefits should be abolished, authoritarian modes of behaviour should be eradicated. The Workers' Oppositionists were nothing if not honest about their platform. They admitted that it was not yet as elaborate or as detailed as it might have been; they even conceded that it did not represent a panacea for all the objective problems of economic reconstruction. Their main aim was to convince the Conference that the party's paramount need was to rally the voluntary energy, support and participation of the lower classes. They avoided potentially provocative terms like 'the labour bureaucracy'. Lutovinov and his colleagues felt that the Conference offered a last chance to reform the party before catastrophe ensued.[27]

The Conference's resolution seemed at first sight to give the Workers' Opposition a good deal to feel cheerful about. It called for frank, thorough discussions at open general meetings; rank-and-filers were to be encouraged to participate actively in political affairs; committees and subcommittees were to draw back the veil of mystery surrounding their deliberations; officialdom was to show itself ready to accept criticism from below. There was to be an extensive system of education which would prepare all party members for their civic duties; there was simultaneously to be a purge of all undesirable elements. Political departments were to be phased out. The custom of appointing party functionaries should be abandoned immediately; cross-posting should no longer be exploited as a means of getting rid of awkward officials. It should still be policy to move personnel regularly from one locality to another, but solely in order to root out red tape and routinisation. All public functionaries should make direct contact with workers, peasants and soldiers through non-party mass meetings. And in order to promote the reform's success it was resolved to install a hierarchy of 'control commissions' inside the party, which were to consist of experienced officials, to supervise the activity of the normal party committees.[28]

Yet the Workers' Opposition had failed with its demand that the labour force be given direct influence over industrial and social decisions at the grass-roots level. This failure was predictable. Shlyapnikov and Lutovinov were already giving grounds for the suspicion that they wanted to dismantle the Bolshevik party's monopoly of political power in the Soviet state by transferring substantial rights to the soviets and the trade unions. Thus even Preobrazhenski (who, unlike Zinoviev, aimed to do at least something about the rank-and-file question) excoriated the Workers' Opposition as a 'deviation' from Bolshevik principles.[29] The mood of the Conference, moreover, was a lot less enthusiastic about reform than its resolution implied. Lenin and Zinoviev were astute operators. They saw that political departments and appoint-mentism were the issues which concerned the majority of local leaders most deeply. Concessions on this front, it was felt, would cut the ground from under the feet of the Democratic Centralists. And so it turned out. There was never any doubt but that the delegates would vote overwhelmingly in favour of Zinoviev's resolution, knowing full well that neither Lenin nor Zinoviev was going to compel them to take seriously its radical clauses on the rank-and-file question. Indeed Lenin warned the Workers' Opposition that it would suffer the same disciplinary fate as the Democratic Centralists if it persisted in its attacks on the Central Committee. Some reformer, some reform![30]

Alone of all local party bodies, the Samara Provincial Committee set about implementing the spirit and the letter of the Conference resolution. Milonov worked indefatigably, at mass open meetings and through newspaper editorials, to try to convince his rank-and-filers that the resolution really meant what it said and that a new dawn was about to break in party affairs.[31] Elsewhere the story was very different. Preobrazhenski and Krestinski, to give them their due, refused to be depressed by their own central colleagues' manoeuvrings; they took the trouble of visiting Tula to make sure that there was no repetition of the earlier clashes there.[32] Yet they must have known that the tide of committee opinion was against them. The Petrograd Provincial Committee secretary S. S. Zorin, on returning from the Conference, reported its proceedings as if the main theme had been the need for 'iron discipline and unity'. He complained bitterly about what he described as 'the spiritual weakness' of the rank-and-filers. And Zinoviev, though he had delivered the Central Committee report at the Conference, disdained even to broach the question once back in Petrograd. In Kharkov and Vyatka too it was evidently thought wise to encourage officials to let the sleeping dog of the rank-and-file question lie for a while longer.[33] Even outward support for reform was all too often a total sham. The Smolensk Provincial Committee archives give us a chance to see how much hostility in fact existed to Preobrazhenski's ideas. A certain Latko accused the central leaders of demagogy for allowing the debate to occur in the first place. His associates refrained from so extreme a judgement but nonetheless vociferously corroborated his general attitude.[34]

On the other hand the Politburo and the Orgburo kept their promise to tread more lightly in their relations with local party committees. Appointmentism ceased. Milonov, quite possibly to his own surprise, was left untouched and allowed to go on spreading his ideas in Samara. But in other respects there was little change. The Central Control Commision, hastily established after the Ninth Conference, confessed itself to be unclear about its precise duties and to possess little impact on party affairs.[35] Nor was much progress made towards phasing out the political departments (mainly, be it noted, because Trotski was still struggling behind the scenes, in the Politburo and the Central Committee, for their retention). Yet central executive bodies were not the only ones which were slow to overhaul their activity. Local committees, with extremely few exceptions, did next to nothing to alter the pattern of party life; they took inordinate time about installing control commissions; they temporised when asked to hold public debates more frequently; they gave a firm brush-off to criticisms by lower committees, officials and rank-and-filers. Orderliness and obedience still predominated. The looser approach advocated by Krestinski and Preobrazhenski was not even a weak and helpless baby: it was still-born.[36]

The true direction of developments was to be spotted in a Central Committee decree making a single official personally responsible for the actions of each committee. Kaganovich's arguments had at last been accepted. He had always said that this was the only watertight way to realise a clear division of functions and a clear line of accountability through the hierarchy of party bodies. The decree itself was essentially a formal reinforcement of the wartime emergence of the committee chairman as the ascendant figure in local political life. It was highly popular, as might be expected, among such chairmen. They had already voted for the idea in principle at a semi-official gathering of leading party administrators, local as well as central, during the Ninth Party Conference. The committee leader was now to have the title of secretary. This has led to the erroneous assumption that the functionary who had previously handled only the technical, ancillary side of committee work was suddenly promoted to the pinnacle of local politics. In fact, all that occurred was a change of nomenclature: the chairman was redesignated as secretary.[37] It was probably felt that the new title, sounding less imperious, might make the decree more palatable to those committee members who resented further encroachments on collective decision-making procedures. As it happened, there was little objection. The Simbirsk Provincial Committee was almost alone in arguing that the decree represented the thin end of the wedge. Today, it asserted, the new secretary was solely being made 'responsible' for committee activity; tomorrow he could well become the all-powerful, non-elected local dictator.[38]

An even more disturbing trend after the Ninth Conference was the continuing exodus from the ranks. It is conventionally assumed, on the basis of estimates announced at the Ninth and Tenth Party Congresses, that the number of Bolsheviks rose by 20 per cent between the springtimes of 1920 and 1921. But there are lies, damned lies and statistics. The problem is that the estimate for 1920 does not include those local party organisations unable to send delegates to the Ninth Congress because of wartime difficulties. If we isolate those provinces of European Russia which were in fact represented at both Congresses, we discover a decrease of around 30 per cent in the lists of accredited party members. The industrial areas fared worst. Ivanovo province, recording the greatest decline of all, apparently lost 55 per cent of its numerical strength in those twelve months. Not every region experienced the exodus. Provinces recently recaptured from the Whites in the Ukraine and Siberia reported an incoming wave of recruits to the party as soon as the military crisis had passed. Yet it was the regions which had for some time been under Soviet control which constituted the acid-test of Bolshevik popularity. And there, as Preobrazhenski frankly noted, the persisting symptoms of working-class disenchantment and discontent were observable by all who had eyes to see.[39]

Officialdom, however, still hoped to solve the problem by burying it out of sight. But it was not to be. Trotski let it be known in November to the Central Committee that, if it was still hell-bent on abolishing the civilian political departments, he wanted at least an open debate on the question beforehand. At a stroke he unleashed a dispute called 'the trade union controversy'. All the issues tossed about at the Ninth Party Conference came flooding back: the party's growing alienation from the working class, the rift between rank-and-file Bolsheviks and their officials, the tensions in the hierarchy of party committees, the rivalry between party bodies and other institutions of the Soviet state. The discussion stirred up the ashes of that wide-ranging debate about the future of the October Revolution which had smouldered throughout the middle of 1920. And from Trotski's spark in November it was fanned into a mighty blaze lasting the entire winter and culminating in the Tenth Party Congress in March 1921.

Quick to take issue, Lenin argued that to continue with political departments and labour armies would be to put the survival of the Bolshevik party itself in jeopardy. Bukharin and Zinoviev formed a 'buffer group' to avert an irreparable split between the two leaders. The Central Committee, playing for time, forbade its members to comment on the matter in public and selected a commission to formulate policy afresh. But the commission's composition was transparently stacked in Lenin's favour. By December it seemed to Trotski that he would have to contravene the Central Committee's ban if he wanted to stand any chance of victory. He therefore made his views public. Lenin counter-attacked by declaring it folly to strip trade unions of their right to defend the sectional, material interests of their millions of members. Zinoviev defected to Lenin. Yet the buffer group, now led by Bukharin along with Preobrazhenski and Serebryakov, was still trying to calm the frayed tempers of the central protagonists and keep the controversy away from the local committees; it proposed to put the issue into cold storage until the Tenth Party Congress in 1921. But Trotski would not hear of this. Reluctantly the Central Committee gave its permission for a full-scale, open debate to be joined in late December 1920 at the Eighth Congress of Soviets.[40]

Both the Workers' Opposition and the Democratic Centralists worked feverishly to exploit the reported breach inside the Central Committee. They even combined forces temporarily in November. Their immediate aim, in this rare moment of conciliation, was to propose a motion of censure of official policy before a Moscow Provincial Committee meeting. The plan failed, albeit by a slim margin of votes.[41] Bad as this was for the Workers' Opposition, it was still worse for the Democratic Centralists since it meant the end of their hopes of winning a provincial committee. The Workers' Opposition easily overhauled them in gathering grass-roots support. The Democratic Centralists asked for it. They were pre-occupied by problems in the hierarchy of party committees to the point of regarding the current controversy about industrial workers as a distracting side-issue. Many, outside Moscow, even supported Trotski's views on labour discipline.[42] It is true that the Workers' Opposition could as yet boast only of Samara as a securely held provincial committee. But it was making fast headway elsewhere. Its ideas were finding fertile soil among the workers of places such as Nizhni Novgorod and Tula where discontent with governmental policies was extreme. And Shlyapnikov and Lutovinov in Moscow itself had meanwhile got the Metalworkers' Union Central Executive Committee to declare its espousal of the Workers' Oppositionist platform.[43]

The vast majority of Bolshevik officials, however, were no nearer to supporting the Democratic Centralists or the Workers' Opposition than flying to the moon. The Eighth Congress of Soviets confirmed this. The principal contenders for the votes of the delegates were not Sapronov and Shlyapnikov but Lenin and Trotski. The gloves were off at last. Zinoviev, as spokesman for Lenin's faction, trimmed his sails by saying that the central party machine should desist entirely from appointing functionaries to posts in the provinces without the consent of local party bodies. This was unscrupulous vote-hunting: he had no intention of putting his money where his mouth was. But the debate was restrained and extensive despite all that. Trotski maintained that the Russian working class of 1920 was no longer the highly 'conscious' vanguard of revolution it had been in 1917 and that the Soviet state could no longer afford the luxury of democratic industrial relations. Lenin charged him with dangerous extremism. The troubles with strikes by factory workers would only be aggravated if the party continued to indulge in political departments and labour armies. Lenin's viewpoint won the day. His faction happily recorded victory in the first open confrontation with the faction which was its nearest rival for the favour of Bolshevik officialdom as a whole.[44]

Trotski did not give up the struggle. He travelled the length and breadth of central Russia on a whistle-stop campaign to recover his position. Zinoviev did the same. The buffer group (which still included Bukharin, Preobrazhenski and Serebryakov) at last despaired of effecting a conciliation and came off the fence. It came to an agreement with Trotski: it would support him on condition that he abandoned his advocacy of labour armies. But it did Trotski little good. By early February 1921 even the Urals Regional Committee and the Ekaterinburg Provincial Committee, which had stood by Trotski when others faltered, were adopting Lenin's platform.[45] Trotski could have no complaints. It was assuredly not a calm, gentlemanly debate; its acrimony astonished even hardened polemicists. It was rumoured, though probably maliciously, that Trotski's associate F. F. Raskolnikov had threatened to arrest Zinoviev's adherents in Petrograd and 'put them behind bars'.[46] One way or another, however, the basic arguments got ventilated. Nor was Trotski able to claim that the debate had been manipulated by the central party machine. His own followers Krestinski, Preobrazhenski and Serebryakov ran the Orgburo and the Secretariat. No, the reasons for Trotski's defeat lay in the nature of his proposals. He outraged most officials with his desire to carry on chipping away at the freedom of local party committees; he terrified them with his carelessness about alienating working-class opinion.[47]

With Trotski soundly beaten, Lenin shifted his attention to the Workers' Opposition. Shlyapnikov and Kollontai had by now worked out their programme. In 1920 there had been a certain diffidence among many Workers' Oppositionists when it came to deciding whether to abrogate the party's dominance over the soviets and the trade unions. Milonov held out against such an idea right into 1921.[48] Workers' Oppositionists also found it difficult to determine whether the soviets should be given the right of veto in elections to trade union executive committees. E. N. Ignatov headed a group in Moscow which believed in this as a means of stopping the trade unions being infiltrated by non-revolutionary elements.[49] But eventually it was Shlyapnikov's more radical scheme which carried the day in the Workers' Opposition. Two of his suggestions were of the profoundest importance. First, he wanted to redistribute power inside the Soviet state so that it was shared equally among the party, the soviets and the trade unions; second, he desired to provide the primary producers of society's wealth—that is, the workers and the peasantry—with decisive control over its disposition. Shlyapnikov did not go so far as the Kronstadt mutineers. He had no patience with their calls to permit the Mensheviks and Socialist-Revolutionaries to compete freely again with the Bolsheviks. Yet nobody doubted the fundamental import of his ideas. Of all Bolshevik leaders, he had carried out the deepest reappraisal of his party's ambitions since 1917 and had drawn conclusions which were nearer to lower-class opinions in 1921 than any other Bolshevik programme of the time.[50]

Shlyapnikov, we may be sure, would have achieved greater results if the 'trade union discussion' had been conducted in the same climate of debate as the controversies of April 1917 or even February–March 1918. This is not simply a question of acrimony.

The problem for the Workers' Opposition in so many localities was that officials set their face against consulting rank-and-file opinion until such time as they had haggled the matter out amongst themselves. Samara was an oasis of unimpeded public consideration. Much more typical of contemporary procedures were the attempts made in Petrograd and Vyatka to turn the 'debate' into a ritualistic approbation of a decision already taken by the local committee.[51] What saved the Workers' Opposition from complete muzzlement in many a town was the fact that Lenin and Trotski failed to settle their own disagreement behind closed doors. Shlyapnikov went down to defeat because his radical programme incurred the wrath of nearly all Bolshevik functionaries and activists. Few officials took his ideas at all seriously. Most of his critics either condemned him out of hand as a pernicious renegade or declared that his programme would simply produce more anarchy and chaos than already existed. Lenin was able to wrap up an easy victory over the Workers' Opposition in February 1921.

The Tenth Party Congress, delayed by the course of the controversy, finally met in Moscow in March. The mutiny on Kronstadt overshadowed all its proceedings. Brooding over the current wave of social and economic unrest, Lenin had by then sketched out the bare bones of an overall plan to retrieve the party's fortunes. The economic centrepiece was to be the replacement of foodstuffs requisitionment by a fixed, graduated tax in kind. This was designed both to mollify peasant feelings and to facilitate the delivery of sufficient grain to appease working-class demands. He was enough of a realist to see that the trouncing of the Workers' Oppositionists in the controversy belied the socialist favour which might well accrue to them if working-class rank-and-filers were given a free chance to express their views. Lenin therefore planned to criticise Shlyapnikov's programme in no uncertain terms at the Congress. He took the view that the party, if it was to accomplish an orderly retreat from the economy of War Communism, could well do without the potentially unsettling factor of Workers' Oppositionist propaganda. As the news from Kronstadt worsened it seemed to Lenin that his darkest fears were being realised.[52]

His political report to the Congress examined these themes in greater detail. Taking up the refrain audible in official circles since mid-1920, he mounted a blistering attack upon the Workers'

Opposition and for the first time denounced its programme as a 'deviation' from Bolshevism. His denunciation was accompanied, however, by a plea for collaboration. He dressed down those speakers who objected to Workers' Oppositionists being included in the list of officers handling the day-to-day management of the Congress. It made more sense, in Lenin's mind, to allow a few individuals like Shlyapnikov to be elected to the party's leading executive bodies than to aggravate tensions by excluding them. Shlyapnikov's own reaction to this characteristic blend of aggressiveness and conciliation is not known. But it was probably not very favourable. Shlyapnikov was well past the stage of being taken in by mere gestures.[53]

Krestinski's organisational report dwelled upon the effort expended by the Orgburo and the Secretariat in following up the Ninth Party Conference. He scarcely mentioned the disputes of the winter. Aaron Solts, a Central Control Commission member who took Lenin's side, asserted that the Central Committee had badly let the party down by permitting the controversy to become bitter and divisive; I. I. Skvortsov-Stepanov, another of Lenin's faction, claimed that the public argy-bargy had assisted the growth of anti-Bolshevik 'banditry' across the country. Lenin did not want Krestinski's report to get its usual vote of unconditional approval. He let his associate E. M. Yaroslavski proffer a resolution reprimanding the Central Committee for giving the go-ahead for a debate before agreeing on its own viewpoint and being able to 'instruct' the local committees accordingly. Such an interpretation was extremely provocative. Workers' Oppositionists enumerated the many abuses suffered by them in the previous year. So did the Democratic Centralists (although they joined Lenin in deploring the 'syndicalist tendencies' of Shlyapnikov's platform). Trotski's faction said remarkably little about organisational life but expressed disquiet that the party was paying too much attention to the peasantry and not enough to factory workers—an attitude which took a bit of swallowing after three months of disputation about trade unions.[54]

Once Yaroslavski's resolution was given its expected sanction by the Congress it was left to Lenin and his confederates to formulate their plan of campaign. Fifteen of them gathered privately. Lenin proposed that his group should see to it that they filled two thirds of the places in the line-up of the new central executive bodies of the party. This would mean that opponents such as Trotski and

Shlyapnikov could also be offered seats without undue risk. But the velvet glove covered a mailed fist. Lenin had by now decided to introduce a last-minute motion, entitled 'On the Unity of the Party', which called for an end to all factionalism and threatened future delinquents with expulsion from the ranks if they persistently disobeyed. Individual leaders were even to be ejected from the Central Committee in the event of non-compliance with official directives. In order to make his intentions as clear as crystal, Lenin proceeded to suggest a further motion aimed at the Workers' Opposition and called, provocatively, 'On the Anarcho-Syndicalist Deviation'. Nobody knows precisely why he chose this moment to come down so heavily upon Shlyapnikov's faction. Perhaps it was the potential danger posed by the Workers' Opposition if they should go away from the Congress with the aim of proselytising further thousands of discontented rank-and-filers; perhaps it was the sudden boiling up of the sailors' mutiny on Kronstadt. Whatever may have been the motivation, Lenin was given the full support of the group of fifteen.[55]

He must also have felt cheered by the turn of events in the ensuing proceedings of the Congress. The next debate was about the nationalities question and was settled with very little fuss. But then came a discussion devoted to 'Questions on the Building-Up of the Party'. The Central Committee had chosen Bukharin as its spokesman since, despite their disagreements in the 'trade union controversy', both he and Lenin were striving to give the public impression that democratic practices should be reintroduced to party life. The Democratic Centralists and the Workers' Opposition, as expected, used the opportunity to denounce the whole affair as hypocritical window dressing.[56] But Ivan Smilga, who had recently returned from active military service, took an entirely different tack. Contemptuously dismissing all the erstwhile talk of organisational reform at the Ninth Party Conference in September 1920, he argued that the slightest sign of political relaxation in the present crisis could only give comfort and succour to such party members who were not really communists and who did not really espouse the party's ideals. He would have nothing to do with what he regarded as 'rosy liberal' points of view. Like Kaganovich in 1918–19, he reckoned that political democracy both inside and outside the party would have to remain a dead letter in the foreseeable future. The Democratic Centralists, in his judgement, were just as bad as the Workers' Opposition and should be expelled from the party altogether if they continued their 'wrecking, anti-Marxist and anti-Communist work'. Forty-three delegates signed Smilga's motion (which was a much greater number than could be mustered by either the Democratic Centralists or the Workers' Opposition).[57]

So extreme an analysis was rejected by Lenin as being bereft of both tactical sophistication and political practicality; he resolved to keep to his own salami-style approach. Bukharin's motion went on to win support from a majority of delegates. But the episode had shown to the Congress audience that the party possessed in its fold a strong, energetic minority of officials with a penchant for authoritarian, administrative techniques extending far beyond what was presently found acceptable by the ascendant central leadership. The recognition that Lenin was not the wildest of the wild men of Bolshevik officialdom stood him in good stead in the following elections to the Central Committee. He alone was voted into office unanimously. All the other leaders involved in the 'trade union controversy'—including Trotski, Stalin and Zinoviev—witnessed a fall-off in the ease with which they secured re-election.[58] It was Lenin's peculiar, almost brazen mixture of conciliatory and uncompromising behaviour which probably consolidated his position in so striking a fashion. In later years those who had known him were to claim that only he had been capable of knitting together the various warring factions of the Bolshevik party. This was hyperbole; for he had hardly done much to endear himself to the Workers' Opposition. Yet his rise in stature in the eyes of the overwhelming mass of the party's officials was real enough for all that.

As it turned out, the Congress debate on the trade union question was not so disruptive as had once seemed likely. The calm with which it was conducted made a contrast with the recent furore in most localities and allowed matters to be discussed with a degree of clarity hitherto so lamentably absent. Zinoviev put the case for Lenin's group. Trotski replied in person, claiming that the pressure of events would compel the party to adopt his policies willy-nilly in the year ahead. Unrepentant as ever, he called upon the Congress to stop beating about the bush and to commit itself openly to a 'dictatorship of the party'. This was strong stuff, strong enough to have come out of the mouth of the die-hard authoritarian, Ivan Smilga. But Trotski knew already that he had lost the day. Nor can Shlyapnikov, deputed by the Workers' Opposition to put forward its recommendations, have had any illusions about his own chances. Yet his speech was a far more sustained piece of criticism than anything elicited from the Democratic Centralists. Their main speaker, a certain Drobnis, still took the view that the 'trade union controversy' had been an unnecessary, unwelcome distraction from the major issues of the moment. Lenin must have rubbed his hands with glee at such myopia. Nobody can have been at all surprised when Zinoviev's motion was given an impressive sanction by the floor of the Congress.[59]

The remaining debates were dealt with at breakneck speed; three were introduced by Lenin, one by Kamenev and another by Zinoviev. They covered questions of crucial interest to the October Revolution's survival. Lenin, revealing just how much he had swapped horses about agrarian policy since midsummer 1920, carried a proposal to scrap forcible methods of grain collection in favour of a less rapacious, graduated tax in kind. Peasant opinion was to be enthusiastically courted in the years ahead. Kamenev backed this up with a speech on the international situation revolving round the theme of the Soviet republic's political and economic isolation. For the time being, he suggested, the party would have to content itself with struggling for 'communism in a single country'. Zinoviev then reported on the Communist International. His growing doubts about the immediate prospect of socialist revolution reinforced the idea that the Bolsheviks would have to accept a much slower rate of advance to the achievement of their ultimate goals. The introduction of the New Economic Policy, as it shortly became called, involved concessions to private enterprise in industry and agriculture which did not come easily to the central party leadership. Everyone knew it represented an ideological retreat, however temporary it was meant to be. It was also widely felt that such a retreat could get out of hand unless carefully monitored and controlled. Lenin consequently had no great trouble in getting the Congress to confirm the need for cohesion and discipline embodied in his motions entitled 'On the Unity of the Party' and 'On the Anarcho-Syndicalist Deviation'.[60]

The Democratic Centralists refused to allow this to go through without a fight. A. Z. Kamenski waxed greatly indignant at the authoritarian excess portended by the 'Unity of the Party' motion; he was incensed especially by the threat to expel oppositionist groups from the party. Yet he had no comment to make whatsoever about the other motion. His silence eloquently confirmed that the Democratic Centralists did in fact believe that the Workers' Opposition, through their rejection of the party's monopolistic claim to be the 'vanguard' of the revolution, had strayed far away from the original tenets of Bolshevism. In the event all three Democratic Centralists with voting rights raised their hands in favour of condemning Shlyapnikov's group as an anarcho-syndicalist deviation.[61] Thus did the very proponents of democracy inside the party make their own contribution to the crudification of Bolshevik life. There was indeed some truth in the charge that the Workers' Opposition had radically revised traditional ideas about the party's role; but there was just as much in the Workers' Oppositionist counter-charge that the ascendant central leadership had trampled on that wealth of notions about working-class initiative and enthusiasm which had pervaded Bolshevik proclamations during 1917. The question at stake was who was to be allowed to define Bolshevism. Shrugging off the appeals by both Shlyapnikov and Medvedev, the Congress put the issue beyond doubt by voting overpoweringly in Lenin's favour.[62]

Well might Karl Radek, though himself not an oppositionist, voice the fear that the new regulations might one day be turned against its own proposers.[63] Organisationally the party had never before been so taken up with discipline and order. Those who had hoped to see the Ninth Party Conference's decisions lead to an all-round efflorescence of democratic procedures were bitterly disappointed by the time of the Tenth Party Congress. Only the aim of abolishing civilian political departments was taken seriously by most officials. In all other respects the wartime internal regime was consolidated. It was not just the central party apparatus which was seen to go on augmenting its authority at the expense of lower committees. There was hardly a regional, provincial or town party body which did not move vigorously to reinforce its control over political, economic and social affairs in its territorial domain and to clamp down heavily on the slightest sign of dissidence. Dramatic as they were, the Tenth Party Congress's proceedings did not amount to a sudden turnabout in the interior operation of the Bolshevik party. A steady, though often imperceptible, movement towards internal heavy-handedness had been occurring all through 1920. Thus it happened in November that a central decree was issued to strengthen rather than weaken the practices of single leadership inside local committees. So much for the Ninth Party Conference's call to re-establish collective methods of discussion and decision. Under such an organisational framework it is no surprise that the exodus of working-class rank-and-filers from the party continued apace.

7 The Bolsheviks Retreat (March 1921– December 1922)

The New Economic Policy was something of a misnomer since it had political as well as economic ramifications. No Bolshevik leader, at least in the first few months of its operation, pretended that it did not constitute an ideological retreat. The party was perfectly aware of the hazards involved in permitting the free trading of agricultural products and the denationalisation of the smaller factories, but rightly calculated that the hazards of refusing such concessions would be even greater. The inspiring hope was that these measures would guarantee the speedy recovery of Soviet society and its economy from the devastation of the Civil War. After the Tenth Party Congress it was decided by the Politburo to extend the scope of its accommodation to private enterprise. Fixed-term contracts were to be signed with numerous foreign firms ready and willing to operate in the Baku oilfields and other traditional areas of the country's industry. Care was always taken to retain 'the commanding heights' of the economy in governmental hands; large-scale factories, banking and foreign trade were kept outside the private sector. The results were impressive. Factory output is reckoned to have risen by over 40 per cent between 1920 and 1921, and by a further 30 per cent between 1921 and 1922. It is true that gross industrial production in 1922 was still little more than a quarter of what it had been in 1913, but definite progress had been made since the end of hostilities.

Agriculture too made remarkable strides forward. The harvest of 1920 had been abysmally poor and badly affected the springtime sowing of 1921 since the peasantry was so hungry that it used much seed-corn for its own consumption instead of planting it. Governmental surveys, however, revealed grounds for optimism. Rural households were found to be enthusiastic about the replacement of forcible requisitioning by a level of taxation designed to leave them an annual surplus to dispose of on the free market. Confidence returned to the countryside. Steadily the peasants clawed their way back from the wartime ruin and expanded the area of land under cultivation. By 1923 it was being boasted that the sown acreage was already nine tenths of what it had been in the economically happier days of 1913. Naturally it took longer for actual output to return to its former dimensions. Soil which had fallen fallow in the Civil War and which had run wild with weeds and grasses could not be expected to be satisfactorily productive again without a lengthy period of intensive attention. Indeed the famine of 1921 saw the authorities hard pressed to rush the vitally needed relief supplies to the starving regions of the Volga and the Ukraine. Typhoid carried off thousands of victims. Yet an agricultural recovery was under way despite all the difficulties. The grain harvest of 1923 was still only two thirds that of 1913 but the prospects of further progress, so long as the government persevered with its New Economic Policy, seemed reasonably bright.[1]

The Bolshevik party was constantly nervous that its programme of concessions to private enterprise, both in the towns and in the countryside, might get out of hand. Its most nagging fear was that the Mensheviks and Socialist-Revolutionaries, few though they were in number at the time, might manage to make political capital out of the situation. Intermittent and not entirely whole-hearted attempts to stamp out these two sources of trouble had been undertaken in 1920. Undisguised repression shortly followed. Menshevik and Socialist-Revolutionary leaders who declined to abandon active opposition were either shoved out into emigration or locked up by the Cheka. It was made absolutely clear that the Bolsheviks were henceforward to be the only political party allowed to contest the elections to local soviets and other public institutions. Small clutches of Mensheviks and Socialist-Revolutionaries succeeded in maintaining their underground connections for a while but the government, though shrilly denouncing their counter-revolutionary capabilities, did not encounter great obstacles in rounding them up. The Bolshevik triumph was consummated in the show-trial of Socialist-Revolutionary Central Committee members in 1922. The defendants were accused of giving encouragement and assistance to the White generals in the Civil War and were sentenced to death after being found guilty by the Revolutionary Tribunal. The international furore kicked up by the blatant injustice of much of the prosecution's case led to the commutation of the sentences to long terms of imprisonment. Despite the last-minute reprieve, however, it was obvious to all the former adherents of the Socialist-Revolutionaries and the Mensheviks that the Bolsheviks were in a strong position to monopolise the political arena in the foreseeable future.[2]

Foreign policy could scarcely be disposed of with such self-confidence. Lenin had uplifted the Tenth Party Congress with the hope that investment capital could soon be attracted from abroad to resuscitate the prostrate economy of the Soviet republic. The collapse of negotiations with capitalist countries at the Genoa Conference of 1922 made a mockery of his optimism. The governments of Britain, France and the USA had resolved to keep up the pressure on the Bolshevik state and now saw economic ostracism as the most effective method of achieving this. The fact that Sovnarkom was able to sign a treaty of mutual aid with Germany, the other black sheep of Europe in the eyes of the Allies, was some solace to the Bolsheviks but hardly enough to cheer their flagging spirits. The Politburo was tormented by disputes about how to cope with what had occurred. Its uncustomary indecision was aggravated by the crippling illness which temporarily put Lenin out of action in 1921, laid him low again in the following year and made a helpless invalid of him in 1923. The critical issue was the running discussion about the possibility of socialist seizures of power in the rest of Europe. The Tenth Party Congress, for all its mood of reappraisal, had not tilted at the article of faith that the German working class was not far from the brink of revolution. The question was: how far? Bukharin and Stalin felt the immediate chances were highly unfavourable and that the Bolshevik party should therefore aim to avoid offering the slightest pretext to Britain and France for intervening militarily in Soviet affairs; Trotski and Preobrazhenski argued that the October Revolution could not long survive in isolation and that a more active commitment should be given to stirring up the working masses abroad. As late as mid-1923 it was still not clear which of the two judgements was the more realistic.[3]

Besides, the Politburo was once again having to confront a serious tide of social unrest at home. The peasantry, whose various revolts against the Bolsheviks had been put down with bloody ruthlessness in Tambov province and elsewhere in 1921, no longer constituted much of a problem. The New Economic Policy had taken the steam out of its material discontent. The memory of the behaviour of the punitive detachments at the end of the Civil War still rankled but was not sufficiently provocative to sustain the hopes of those who still wanted to mount a guerrilla war against the Bolsheviks. Most rural households were much more interested in getting a good price for their wheat, potatoes or milk than in contemplating armed insurrection. As was to be expected, some peasants fared better than others. Many a poor family had to sell its labour to its richer neighbours in order to survive the rigours of postwar reconstruction. Social differentiation of this kind was not to the party's liking, of course, but had to be tolerated so long as the concessions given to private enterprise in the countryside still seemed unavoidable. For the time being, however, the idea of an all-out drive towards equalisation was recognised as impracticable even by those leaders, such as Trotski and Preobrazhenski, who felt that the state should considerably increase its fiscal pressure upon the better-off sections of the peasantry.[4]

To the party's intense embarrassment, it was amongst the industrial workers that anti-governmental feelings were strongest. Almost universally they had welcomed the end to grain requisitionments, knowing that this was the quickest way to get the peasantry to expedite the passage of food supplies to the towns. But disenchantment speedily returned. The urban areas teemed with the influx of vagrant peasants and demobilised soldiers in search of factory jobs after 1920; yet as late as 1923 there were still only a million and a half workers in paid employment. The swift rise in industrial output in these years was achieved less by a numerical expansion of the work force than by success in raising productivity. Unemployment was a chronic sore. Its presence indirectly damaged the ranks of the employed too since it weakened their bargaining position as regards private factory owners. Worse still, the Politburo transparently had no wonder-working answer to the problem. The factories in the nationalised sector experienced grave difficulties in gearing their production to the demands of the peasant market. There was a crisis of investment. At the end of 1922 it was thought temporarily necessary to lay off skilled as well as unskilled workers from such enterprises as could not find a sufficiently regular mass clientele for their products.[5]

This most sensitive issue opened wider the political chasm already dividing the central party leaders. The group headed by Trotski and Preobrazhenski desired a short-term policy of concentrating resources in the industrial areas of highest productivity (even at the cost of increasing unemployment) together with a long-term policy of further nationalisations, faster industrial growth and greater scope for control by governmental planning agencies. Such a programme, in the absence of foreign assistance, could be financed only through schemes to siphon off more taxes and savings from the mass of the peasantry. Kamenev, Zinoviev and Stalin consequently stepped forward as the arch priests of social stability and urged that nothing should be done to jeopardise the existence of the New Economic Policy. Their view prevailed within the Politburo and the other central party bodies. Yet the radical problems of the revolution—how to look after workers in the immediate future and how to ensure the further expansion of the industrial economy—remained. Strikes broke out in factories all over the country. Most ominous of all was the news that many Bolshevik activists and rank-and-filers who had walked out of the party on political grounds were joining new parties in the underground. Their names—such as 'Workers' Truth', 'Workers' Group' and 'Workers' and Peasants' Socialist Party'—served to emphasise their commitment to getting rid of the Bolshevik party altogether and installing a government more in line with the feelings of the mass of the working class and the peasantry. Not for the first time, the Politburo was obliged to go out and meet a head-on threat to its political supremacy.[6]

The central party leaders, whatever other disagreements kept them apart, were unanimously determined not to surrender to working-class demands. It had already been decided at the Tenth Party Congress that a purge should be conducted of local members of the Workers' Opposition if they persisted in opposing official policies. And now the growth of rival parties such as 'Workers' Truth' gave a further fillip to those diehards who maintained that the Moscow leadership had been careless to the point of irresponsibility in not launching a serious campaign to protect the ideological 'purity' of the party. That campaign was quickly organised in 1921. It was done covertly in some places, it was done with all sorts of self-exculpatory remarks in others. But it was done. *Pravda* announced in June 1921 that the Central Committee had resolved that the party should be cleaned out of all undesirable elements.[7] A list was given of the grounds thought to justify expulsion. Moral reasons were prominent, notably drunkenness, careerism, religious belief, laziness and corruption; but tucked in at the end of the list was a clause calling for the removal of all Bolsheviks who had failed to carry out party instructions. Only the dullest officials in the provinces could not see that the purge was meant to be conducted on the political as well as the moral plane. Expulsions began in earnest in August. By the end of 1921, it was later revealed, fully a quarter of the total membership of the Bolshevik party had been ejected from the ranks.[8]

The Central Committee's discomfiture was such that it chose to stress that most ejections were motivated on moral grounds. And undoubtedly it would be ludicrous to suggest that the purge was an exlusively political affair. It was now accepted by the leadership in Moscow that many party and soviet officials had abused their positions of hierarchical authority and material privilege in the Civil War; it was also feared, with sound reasoning, that such abuses would become still more extensive under the corrupting influences of the New Economic Policy. Let us be clear about this. No central leader was calling for the whole-scale abolition of the perks deriving from the tenure of party membership and official posts. But immorality, as described in the decree on the purge, was an entirely different matter and was to be punished severely. Bolshevik officials throughout the country were ordered to be vigilant. Offenders would be summoned to a summary hearing and drummed out of the party. Elsewhere it was often a prolonged affair. Indeed a minor agricultural official in Smolensk province, Lyakhovski by name, succeeded in dragging out the proceedings for several weeks before the local committee finally resolved to expel him.[9] Not everyone was as adroit as he. Yet it was obviously in the local committee's own interest to avoid the miscarriage of party justice in questions of a moral nature. Otherwise it would have to operate with a lot fewer ordinary party members in its locality than was required.

The Secretariat claimed that only 11 per cent of the purge had to do with men and women charged with failing to carry out party instructions.[10] It will not be possible to check the accuracy of this percentage until all the archives are opened to public gaze. And even then it will be no easy topic of research. The main difficulty is that a multitude of Bolshevik sins were tacked together under such a clause. No doubt there were numerous rank-and-filers and activists who were kicked out simply because they were too lazy or careless to do as they had been bidden by higher authority; but there must also have been a sizeable bunch of party members who fell out of favour for no other reason than that they disagreed with official policies. The main collective victim was the Workers' Opposition. Until recently it was hard for scholars to give a confident judgement on what really happened. All the witnesses were either leading Workers' Oppositionists or close sympathisers. Yet the memoirs of Anastas Mikoyan, who worked at that time in Nizhni Novgorod and was notorious as being no lover of any kind of opposition, come as near as is now thought seemly in the Soviet Union to admitting that the purge was indeed directed against Shlyapnikov's supporters. The central party leadership, moreover, must now be convicted of complicity. Three teams of investigators were sent out from Moscow to examine complaints made by local Workers' Oppositionists against the Nizhni Provincial Committee. All to no avail. In the end, as might have been expected, the Orgburo ruled that the Provincial Committee had acted perfectly fairly and that nothing untoward had occurred. The only remarkable aspect of these events was that the Central Committee, after making its unambiguous threats against the Workers' Opposition at the Tenth Party Congress, continued to evince so much embarrassment in putting them into effect.[11]

Deliberate expulsions were in any case only one way whereby the party lost many rank-and-filers. The voluntary exodus was still in full spate. It was noticed that the torrent was particularly strong in provinces like Samara where the Workers' Opposition had been solidly ensconced before March 1921. Samara appears to have lost 35 per cent of all its members even before the arrival of the orders to start the purge.[12] Official spokesmen, as was by now traditional, liked to argue that most absentees were persons who had been physically exhausted by the exertions of wartime, had been rendered too tired to cope with the burdens of political activity. But this will not do. Even three years later, in 1924, it was still being reported by occasional secretaries that political disenchantment remained a cause of rank-and-file members leaving the party.[13] As if this was not bad enough, a number of departing Bolsheviks refused to content themselves with inactivity. The underground cells of 'Workers' Truth', 'Workers' Group' and the 'Workers' and Peasants' Socialist Party' were composed predominantly of ex-communist members who now loudly proclaimed that the New Economic Policy was essentially a New Exploitation of the Proletariat.[14]

The Bolshevik leadership in Moscow was not unmoved by

events. It issued a spurt of decrees designed to facilitate the recruitment of party members from the working class. Yet the infusion of industrial workers to the ranks fell to little more than a trickle by late 1921. The Eleventh Party Congress in April 1922 resorted to drawing up discriminatory rules to make it easier for workers than for other social groups to enter the party. When this did not work out very well it was resolved by the Twelfth Party Congress to make the discriminations yet more extensive.[15] Again the results were disappointing, to put it mildly. Bolsheviks of working-class origin made up only 44 per cent of the party by the last month of 1923. It was a merely marginal increase over 1921. The Politburo hoped to save face by asserting that the quality of rank-and-filers mattered ineffably more than their number. It is doubtful that anyone was taken in by this. In fact it was admitted in mid-1923 that only 15 per cent of all party members currently held manual occupations whereas it had been around 60 per cent in 1917.[16] It is even possible that the Secretariat was fiddling the records. Certainly I. N. Morozov, leader of the Samara Provincial Committee, confessed to being unable to explain why the central party apparatus had been capable of discovering more working-class party members in the province of Samara than he and his local colleagues could. He concluded sarcastically that the source of the discrepancy probably lay in the fact that the central apparatus had chosen 'special account-clerks' to conduct the local surveys.[17]

In the meantime it was freely confessed that white-collar employees were steadily increasing their proportion of the party's membership. This was extremely depressing. Everybody knew that many recruits were still managing to conceal their middle-class background. In addition the percentage of members currently doing non-manual jobs, regardless of their social origins, was increasing unchecked. By 1923, it was downheartedly revealed, nearly two thirds of all Bolsheviks held down administrative posts of some kind or other.[18] All this was fuel to the flames of the critics' argument that the party was turning into a horde of bureaucrats dominating the very workers who were meant to be served by them. It was also said that a growing section of those Bolsheviks with manual occupations tended to be the more submissive and less skilled kinds of industrial worker. According to Sarkis, the Petrograd Provincial Committee secretary, the factory labourers inside the party were 'culturally' less capable than their fellow labourers outside its ranks. It was quite a change from the heady days of 1917 when the working-class Bolshevik of Petrograd was looked upon as glory and flower of the October Revolution.[19]

Most officials, both central and local, saw the situation as beyond their control. They pointed out that numerous skilled workers still belonged to the party but had left the factories upon being given jobs in the soviets and other state institutions. The Bolshevik party's need to bring order back to the economy, moreover, was said to have made clashes with working-class sentiments an unfortunate inevitability: the departure of faint-hearted or discontented rank-and-filers was seen as a price which had to be paid for political survival. It was also vital to attract newcomers from regions of the country like the Trans-caucasus and the western Ukraine where the Bolsheviks had traditionally received little support before seizing power; and this too was bound to involve recruiting non-workers since such regions had experienced less industrial development than central Russia. And throughout the country it was vital to encourage the peasantry to enter the party; for it would otherwise be quite an administrative problem to keep an eye on developments in the countryside, not to mention the goal of proselytising the rural population in the name of socialism.[20] Other social factors too limited the Politburo's freedom of action in recruitment policy. Women had rapidly constituted an ever larger section of the party in the Civil War; but by 1922, when their menfolk had returned from the Red Army and were clamouring for jobs in the factories, the women tended to leave the Bolsheviks and resume their traditional role of political inactivity.[21] When all due allowance is made, however, it is hard to see how the Politburo can duck the charge of having made matters greatly worse by its own actions. Above all the persecution of Workers' Oppositionist rank-and-filers and other dissentients was a paramount blunder, to put it charitably, which could not fail to have counter-productive results among the mass of industrial workers.[22]

A more indirect, but no less insidious, form of organisational degeneration was to be beheld in the internal affairs of party cells. Every trick in the bureaucratic book was used to put obstacles in the way of rank-and-filers wanting to voice their own personal point of view. In many places, so it was reported, the agenda would not be announced in advance of each cell meeting.[23] Hardly any true discussion occurred. What usually happened was that the official speaker, typically the cell secretary, would deliver a report and would see that the rest of the meeting was spent in formally ratifying his proposals.[24] By 1922 the habit had become ingrained. Thus confusion abounded whenever the secretary omitted to supply his cell members with a clause-by-clause resolution which allowed a vote to be taken without further ado.[25] Such a ritual reinforced the contempt felt by numerous officials towards their rank-and-filers. It was claimed that many a speaker would turn up at the cell meeting and confess to his fellow activists: 'God knows I haven't got round to making preparations. . . . Well, never mind, it will turn out alright in any case.'[26] Carelessness of this sort was frowned upon by higher authority. Yet punishment was unlikely to be countenanced unless there also happened to be evidence that the speaker in question had shown hostility to the orthodox political line of the moment. The overriding aim, as a Tula official put it, was to secure the formal consent of rank-and-file members and to expedite party business 'at a cavalry gallop'. The military metaphor was not inappropriate.[27]

The authorities, on those few occasions when they addressed themselves to such issues, threw up their hands and gave out the excuse that the average Bolshevik lacked all political and cultural sophistication.[28] At best this was ideological paternalism; at worst it was naked authoritarianism. 'The level of consciousness', to quote the phrase of the day, had tumbled down a long way since the end of the Civil War (just as it was said to have done immediately after the October Revolution). A survey conducted by a suburb committee in Petrograd concluded, with arithmetical precision, that 60 per cent of rank-and-filers were 'politically illiterate' and that a mere 8 per cent were conversant with Marxism.[29] Away from the metropolitan areas, it was widely affirmed, the state of affairs was still more depressing. An activist in Vyatka wrote that, at least in his experience, most local Bolsheviks hardly differed in their outlook upon the world from the bulk of the Russian peasantry.[30] This may well have been so. But what is more doubtful is that the condition of the working class's so-called consciousness had undergone remarkable change since 1919, or even since 1917. In short, party officials before the seizure of power had mistaken the generally anarchistic and populistic attitudes of industrial workers for a specific commitment to a Bolshevik programme. Yet most spokesmen were too imperceptive, too craven or too cynical to admit to this; they shied away from explaining why those same rank-and-filers who in 1917 had been seen as repositories of class awareness could now be described as political illiterates. A few functionaries, it is true, essayed to attribute the alleged change to the exhaustion of rank-and-filers in the Civil War and to their consequent 'spirit of demobilisation'.[31] But such reasoning, though it was not entirely without foundation, had an increasingly hollow ring about it as the months and years wore on.

The cure for all ills was thought to be the establishment of schooling facilities inside the party. Evening clubs and discussion circles were set up with enthusiasm and with a range of subjects which could extend from basic reading skills to Engels or Esperanto. Staggeringly good results were occasionally claimed. Party teachers and lecturers evidently felt that their achievements would not be accorded fair recognition unless presented in quantified terms. And so it came about that the Smolensk Provincial Committee could, without a trace of self-parody, boast in 1924 that 'the political level' of party members had risen by 12 per cent in the previous twelve months.[32] Besides, it was far more usual to hear of the disappointingly low figures of attendance at party clubs. The suggestion was made that meetings could best be enlivened by the introduction of some articles by Lenin to the staple fare of education; but it is doubtful that this would have made much difference since not even his greatest admirers ever saw him as a coruscating exponent of Russian prose style.[33] A further suggestion, which got closer to the heart of the matter, was that teachers should make sure that they had fully prepared the lessons before tackling their pupils.[34] Such problems did not affect the party schools in large industrial centres like Moscow and Petrograd, where high-flying young Bolsheviks, being groomed for official posts, had the benefit of lectures from the most prestigious pedagogues and theorists available. Yet rank-and-filers elsewhere could not count upon their teachers' providing them with a carefully planned, carefully delivered course of instruction. It was therefore sheer hypocrisy for certain local officials to declare that the difficulties of party schooling lay exclusively with the intellectual inadequacies of the mass of ordinary members.

This brings us back to the original sticking-point that Bolshevik life was now being directed by an administrative stratum which had little sympathy with the immediate aspirations of the working-class membership. Cell secretaries were all-important to the hierarchy of party committees in seeing that no rank-and-filer could step out of line with impunity. Accolades were showered upon them. The leader of a Bolshevik factory group in Tula was accorded the following glowing tribute in the provincial newspaper: 'A surge of work has been observable in the past two months since the cell entrusted its activity to cell secretary V. Zubov. The workers love cell secretary Zubov and have turned to him with all kinds of questions and requirements.'[35] The editorial did not describe, however, whether these same workers were able to get satisfaction from their leader. Their chances were very slim unless they were lucky enough to be given an exceptionally responsive leader. And that depended in turn upon decisions taken by higher authority; for the selection of cell secretaries was no longer a matter deemed to necessitate consulting the feelings of ordinary members. Appointment had by 1922 replaced election nearly everywhere (even though the outward ceremonies of democratic procedure were maintained). Woe betide any appointee, moreover, who was suspected of giving undue latitude to the expression of complaints from the factory bench. Most cell secretaries, it is true, were themselves of working-class origin and had joined the party in the difficult days of the Civil War.[36] Nonetheless they had to obey directives from above to the letter if they wanted to keep their jobs. Long gone were the days of 1918 and 1919 when cell members could collectively register a decisive impact upon the general affairs of their factory or enterprise. Nowadays the behaviour of managers could be modified but not subjected to fundamental change by party pressure. In any case it was the cell secretary, not the rank-and-filers, who was expected to undertake what little pressurising was permissible.

Obedience and discipline were imposed upon the cells all the more easily as the result of the patterns of subordination introduced to the hierarchy of local committees. The star of the regional and provincial bodies was in the ascendant. Samara, of all provinces, was most troubled by wrangles inside the party in mid-1921; yet in the following year it was brazenly announced that its Provincial Committee had been 'unanimously' elected by delegates from lower committees at the Provincial Conference.[37] Probably the voting was indeed unanimous but it is less than certain that it was freely obtained. Town and suburb committees, while superficially appearing to take their own decisions, had in reality to accept memoranda from on high which 'suggested' that they put particular topics on their agenda and pass preordained resolutions.[38] A Bryansk functionary said that his own town committee's actual functions amounted to little more than agitation and propaganda work.[39] He was exaggerating, but not all that much. Regional and provincial bodies were now so sure of themselves that they took to issuing uniform instructions to party organs and officials at all lower levels; but while this simplified the tasks of administration, it also led to a greater neglect of specifically local conditions than ever before. Nor did lower officialdom always cope with the duties assigned to them. In such contingencies it was usually decided to launch a kind of organisational *Blitzkrieg*. A town committee would be picked out, amidst much publicity, for its unsatisfactory conduct and would be compelled to set its house in order as an example to all other party bodies in the vicinity. This technique helped with policies of high priority but scarcely facilitated the methodical implementation of the entire party programme.[40]

The internal workings of each local committee changed accordingly. Officials could still criticise the orthodox party line of the moment in private, in informal discussions; yet it now seldom happened that these criticisms were given an airing in formal sessions. Immense importance was attached to selecting suitable functionaries. In 1922, in fact, the Samara Provincial Committee reported unashamedly that its principal job in recent months consisted in choosing persons to act as district secretaries.[41] This was again a hyperbole. The Provincial Committee had not suddenly ceased promoting society's economic recovery from the Civil War. Nor was it any less thorough than its counterparts elsewhere in subjecting all governmental institutions in their locality, right down to the bottom level, to the closest scrutiny. Beyond that point, however, the emphasis fell upon the appointment of personnel; for the typical response to incidents of insubordination was the immediate withdrawal of the offending official and the substitution of a new one.[42]

Secretaries ruled the roost in local committees. The idea of single leadership was not to everyone's liking: Gomel and Tambov insisted on keeping two provincial secretaries each for some months after the Tenth Party Congress; and Tver had three. The Simbirsk Provincial Committee asserted, with more principle than sense of self-protection, that the demise of collective practices represented a lurch into 'Bonapartist' tendencies.[43] These early tremors, however, quickly died away and in any case had always been few in number. Local party bodies were obliged to resign themselves to acquiring and losing their secretaries with bewildering frequency. The high turnover of officials caused by the mobilisations of 1918 was now followed by the high turnover caused by demobilisations.[44] Political commissars who had held leading civilian posts before the Civil War or had made a name for themselves during it were clamouring to be given party appointments commensurate with their proven organisational abilities. And their demands were met. It was an unsettling period; and Simbirsk was apparently not alone in experiencing a succession of three provincial secretaries in 1921 alone. Nonetheless the central party leadership saw some benefit in it. Swift, regular transfers of functionaries not only lent flexibility to the handling of postwar reconstruction; it also helped combat the growth of 'localist' cliques which might stymie instructions sent from above.[45]

Every party secretary was made to understand that his duties covered every aspect of political, economic and social affairs in his geographical area. But who were the party secretaries? Let us begin by examining the backgrounds of the men, for men they all were, who headed both the regional committees throughout the country and the more important provincial committees of central Russia in autumn 1923: twenty-nine officials all told.[46] It is not the simplest of exercises since the sources tell us next to nothing about the incumbents of office in Ryazan, Saratov and Tsaritsyn. On the face of it this would appear to confirm that regional and provincial secretaries had been nonentities inside the party in earlier times. It has even been maintained that they had been mere pen-pushers during the October Revolution and the Civil War. In fact only two out of our sample, Kharitonov of the Urals and Kviring of the Ukraine, had been party secretaries in 1917 (when secretaries still performed mainly technical functions). Furthermore, Kharitonov had combined his secretaryship of a suburb committee with a prominent role in the Petersburg City Committee and in no way limited himself to 'pen-pushing'. And Kviring, whilst acting as secretary of the Kiev City Committee, had also been elected chairman of the Kiev City Soviet—hardly a back-room sinecure. Similarly, only two in the sample had been party secretaries in 1918 or 1919. And again the couple in question, Vareikis of Central

Asia and Zorin of Ivanovo-Voznesensk, had already risen to prominence: Vareikis was a Peoples' Commissar in the short-lived Donbass Soviet Republic and later became Simbirsk Provincial Committee chairman; Zorin had been Petrograd City Committee secretary in the Civil War but was obliged, in the frequent absence of colleagues like Zinoviev himself, to deal with matters which went far beyond technical administration.[47]

Most of our officials, then, were leaders of at least local distinction in the October Revolution and the Civil War. Fourteen out of twenty served in the Red Army, mostly as political commissars (though some like Osmov of Vladimir were military commanders).[48] The remainder occupied posts of local prominence in the civilian sector. They characteristically worked as chairmen of party or soviet committees, mainly but not exclusively at the provincial level of the hierarchy. All but two of our twenty-six, moreover, had joined the Bolsheviks before 1917. The exceptions were Meerzon of Tula and Zorin of Ivanovo-Voznesensk: the first had been a well-known figure in the Jewish Bund, the second a founder member of the American Socialist Party. Very few regional or provincial secretaries, it would seem, had ever lived abroad or had acquired extensive interests of an intellectual kind. Most were sons of working-class or peasant stock.[49] To their jobs under the post-revolutionary order they brought a hard-headed practicality produced by a lifetime of anti-capitalist embitterment and frustration. Commentators who looked upon them as revolution-shy, battle-shirking incompetents seriously under-estimated their capacities.[50]

How representative the twenty-six officials were of Bolshevik secretaries in general, it is hard to be sure. Useful clues can be found. The central party apparatus, aware that its files contained only the sparsest information about functionaries below the provincial level, was worried that all sorts of ideologically undesirable interlopers might be running the party in the localities. Decrees were issued to give preference, when appointments were being made, to candidates of working-class origin who had belonged to the party for some years. It was a rough-and-ready measure. And obviously it was not designed to be applied at the highest echelons or else nearly every Politburo member would have had to resign his position! Nevertheless what little may be guessed about the secretaries at town, district and suburb levels suggests that all but a majority of them were of lower-class backgrounds. Their average date of joining the Bolsheviks is obscure. It would not be greatly surprising if a good proportion, perhaps even a majority, were not party members of pre-revolutionary vintage.[51] However that may be, it would seem quite out of joint with other current trends if these same secretaries had taken 'back-seat' roles during the Civil War. Looking at this from a sightly different angle, we can see that only a tiny proportion of local party secretaries of late 1919, when their job was still a primarily technical affair, retained secretaryships in late 1923. [52] With the change in the nature of the post had come a change in the kind of qualifications expected of its incumbents.[53]

The bias towards choosing functionaries with an eye mainly upon their administrative ability reinforced other shifts in the style of party life. Secretaries tended to avoid the public gaze; they would append their names to directives and editorials but, increasingly, would steer clear of direct contact with rank-and-file members. Even fellow members of local committees could no longer bank upon being taken seriously by their appointed leader. The 'comradely togetherness' of an earlier epoch was fading, and fading fast.[54] Not all secretaries, of course, strove to be as faceless as possible; but many who tried to cut an approachable image among their subordinates were seen to be falling into the opposite trap of encouraging their own minor cults of personality. The worst case was Mark Minkov of Vyatka. Not only did he publish autobiographical extracts in the local newspaper but he also allowed the editor to print an ode which was addressed to him and which began as follows:[55]

> There is no need for beautiful words
> When thousands of people are talking. . . .
> Today your own image, Minkov,
> Is imprinted in the Komsomol member's heart.
>
> Everyone in our ranks knows
> That there are not a few such as you
> Who have built the world of labour
> And laid bridges to the new land.

Faceless administrators or self-lauding heroes, the local party secretaries left no doubt that they considered themselves a breed apart.

A small number of them, indeed, were already seen to be comporting themselves with a crudity and vulgarity of the worst kind. A horrified Bukharin commented upon this at the Twelfth Party Congress in April 1923. In a casual conversation he had asked a fellow delegate what he had been up to lately, and had received the reply: 'Nothing much. We're throttling the nationalities.'[56] Lenin too picked up early warnings about the problem; he knew that Russian chauvinism was not confined to local officials but could be traced to central leaders such as M. P. Tomski as well.[57] Yet his worst shock occurred when he discovered that G. K. Ordzhonikidze, on a mission from Moscow to Georgia on behalf of the Central Committee, had not only applied excessive repression to the Georgian population at large but had personally used physical violence upon Georgian Bolshevik leaders who had disagreed with him. Lenin, to his credit, called for disciplinary sanctions to be brought to bear in redressal; but his own health was broken and he was unable to mount a successful struggle against Ordzhonikidze.[58] Another official found to have acted with brutality against non-Russians was N. I. Ezhov, then a local party secretary and later to attain infamy as the head of the Soviet secret police in the 1930s. In his case an enquiry was indeed set afoot and he was found guilty; but this did not stop him re-entering the secretarial hierarchy after a short period of suspension.[59] Dark, subterranean forces were gathering inside the Bolshevik party by 1923. For all its pronouncements against nationalistic arrogance, the Politburo cannot escape the charge of having acted ineffectually to initiate a radical improvement.

1921 and 1922 were also years when changes were taking shape inside the party machine in Moscow. Trotski's defeat at the Tenth Party Congress led to his high-placed supporters being removed from both the Politburo and the Orgburo after failing to secure re-election to the Central Committee.[60] Zinoviev stepped into Krestinski's shoes as Politburo full member and vacated his own alternate membership to Vsyacheslav Molotov, the new chief of the Secretariat. Krestinski, Preobrazhenski and Serebryakov lost their places in the Orgburo to a bevy of Lenin's adherents. Molotov was joined in the Secretariat by two further critics of Trotski in the trade union controversy: V. M. Mikhailov, who had gained some prominence as the Moscow City Committee secretary; E. M. Yaroslavski, who had long been established as one of the party's leading orators and propagandists. Such a bunch was unlikely to waver in maintaining the collective dominance of the Politburo, Orgburo and Secretariat over the Central Committee as a whole. To have done so would have supplied Trotski (and Shlyapnikov, come to mention it) with an even broader forum wherein to canvass his ideas than he already had in the Politburo. The demise of the Central Committee was accelerated; the expectation of the Politburo was to run the party as it saw fit. Why this was allowed to pass with so little challenge is a mystery. Perhaps it derived from the force of organisational inertia or from the unparalleled prestige of figures like Lenin; perhaps it also had to do with the general lack of interest amongst Bolsheviks against building institutional checks against the hyper-concentration of power in a few hands.

The Politburo's supremacy, however, did not last in every way. The immediate reason was Lenin. His physical fitness had never come back fully to normal since the assassination attempt on him in mid-1918. In late 1921 he suffered the first of his serious relapses which eventually killed him. The task of co-ordinating all the various subcommittees and adjuncts of the Central Committee had been growing steadily more complicated. Of no body was this truer than of the Secretariat. The opinion was gaining ground that Molotov was not the man to handle the much-needed reorganisation and consolidation of its Departments. Certainly Lenin was less than happy with him.[61] There was hardly the barest minimum of co-operation and co-operativeness among the several subdepartments of the Organisational Department; there was the scandal that the Files-Assignment Department director often failed to attend its meetings and constantly omitted to assemble complete records about leading officials.[62] Lenin himself has unfairly been blamed for this: it has been said that he was inherently incapable of operating a highly complex apparatus of administration; but such criticism does not square well with the known facts of his direction of the Red effort in the Civil War. There is no pressing reason to doubt that had his health held out he would have been able to bring the central party machine to a high pitch of smooth-working order.

In his absence it was Stalin who was asked to take on the role of central co-ordinator of party administration. In 1921 he was already taking a hand in the running of the Agitation-Propaganda Department after it had become obvious that Molotov and his colleagues were not making much of a job of it. At the same time he was expanding the Orgburo's sphere of influence. The Orgburo, prodded by the Politburo, was steadily pushing its way into controlling ever further aspects of administration connected with the provinces. Selection of personnel became a particular concern of the Orgburo's (even though the Politburo had still not resigned itself to inactivity in this matter).[63] Lenin, while convalescent, owned himself out of touch with changes in the party machine: he expressed ignorance about the precise division of functions between the Orgburo and the Secretariat; he confessed to knowing little about the scale of the Orgburo's involvement in appointing officials.[64] Yet this does not constitute proof that Lenin was extraordinarily incompetent or naive in things organisational. Rather it betokens the extent to which it had already proved possible, with the prior agreement of the central leadership as a whole, to demarcate the activities of the various subcommittees of the Central Committee. To this agreement Lenin too had been party: only ill-health prevented his supervising its implementation more closely. Ever since 1919 the Bolshevik party had been seriously trying to establish itself as the Soviet state's paramount organ of administration. It was no surprise, then, that an attempt was at last being made, now that the Civil War was at an end, to reorganise and re-equip the central party apparatus in such a way as it could run the business of the complicated network of the central soviet machine.

Not that Stalin was slow to take personal advantage of the situation. He did this, according to Trotski's memoirs, despite the fact that Lenin had initially demurred at his appointment as General Secretary to the Central Committee.[65] Once appointed, however, Stalin pressed on regardless. He wanted there to be no doubt whatsoever in the public mind that he had been put in charge of party administration in general and the Secretariat in particular. It is doubtful that the Central Committee thereafter felt unavoidably obliged to comply with Stalin's wishes; but it is a matter of historical fact that it did comply with them. His partners, moreover, were political allies of his: Vsyacheslav Molotov and Valeri Kuibyshev. Molotov's demotion (for that was what it was despite official denials issued at the time) signified the feeling that the highest office in the organisational field should in future be occupied by a proven administrator belonging already to the top rank of the party's leadership. Whether all this power would have been granted so easily to Stalin if Lenin had not been ill is another issue altogether; but it is hard to conceive of a Lenin in charge of all his political faculties and skills being totally outmanoeuvred by Stalin in the years ahead. Be that as it may, there was no sign in early 1922 that Lenin yet felt like campaigning to oppose the decision to invest his colleague Stalin with the tasks of co-ordinating and streamlining the work of the Orgburo and Secretariat. Other measures, of course, were taken at the Eleventh Party Congress or immediately afterwards. The Central Committee was expanded so as to include twenty-seven full and nineteen alternate members; the Politburo's composition was allowed to stand unchanged and the Orgburo's was slightly altered, notably through the introduction of Kuibyshev. Yet in retrospect it is obviously the appointment of Stalin as General Secretary which was much the most decisive consequence.[66]

The Politburo meanwhile continued to dominate the soviet administrative framework. Lenin's lengthy absences led to many kinds of lesser affairs which would usually have been handled by Sovnarkom being transferred to the Politburo; for leaders such as A. I. Rykov, who deputised for Lenin in Sovnarkom, were not thought to be of sufficient standing to deal with all his duties. The Politburo was also continuing to distance itself from the rest of the Central Committee. Osinski, himself a Central Committee member, attempted to call attention to the situation before it was too late to curb the Politburo. To his dismay, he found that he was often prevented from discovering even the topics on the Politburo's agenda sheet; to his greater dismay, he found that his Central Committee colleagues were not prepared to stick their necks out far enough to rectify the problem.[67] The Secretariat too scarcely gave a fig about the Central Committee. The Politburo, desiring to devolve some of its power over administrative business, invested the Secretariat with sweeping rights in the choice of local party personnel up to the level of the provincial committees. It was revealed that the Files-Assignment Department exercised its new authority forty-four times in the year after the Eleventh Party Congress.[68] What was thought of this by the Orgburo members is conjectural. We know neither the names of all those who attended it most regularly nor the exact subjects of its discussions. Whatever separation of duties was decided between the Orgburo and the Secretariat, however, we may rest assured that Trotski would have been only too grateful to have been able to tell us in his memoirs about any acrimonious exchanges between the two central bodies, if such exchanges had ever taken place. So careful and astute a politician as Stalin, with a seat in both the Orgburo and the Secretariat, would naturally see his own interests as lying in keeping relations as amicable as possible.

Yet the image of all central leaders working co-operatively together was illusory. Lenin's debilitating stroke in May 1922 had provoked the thought, perhaps for the first time, that his return to a fully active career could no longer be banked on. The struggle for 'the succession' had begun. Trotski had retained his own place in the Politburo even though he had been thrashed so overwhelmingly in the 'trade union controversy' of 1920. Lenin, furthermore, had never allowed disagreements with Trotski to be used as a pretext for excluding him from high-level discussions. In Lenin's absence, however, a different attitude prevailed. Kamenev, Stalin and Zinoviev set themselves up as an informal triumvirate (or 'troika' as they were more popularly called) and concerted themselves to submit Trotski to political ostracism. Lenin had further grounds for worrying about Stalin. Ordzhonikidze's physical assault upon Georgian Central Committee members was at first officially claimed never to have taken place; but Lenin, though taken in for a time, gradually realised what had really happened. He learnt too that Stalin had played a major role in covering up the affair. To add to Lenin's worries, it now transpired that Stalin had allied himself with Bukharin and Kamenev to call for what to Lenin seemed an intolerable extension of the concessions to private enterprise in the form of a lifting of the governmental monopoly over foreign trade. Casting round for support, Lenin felt himself drawn closer to Trotski. A compromise was being worked out between Lenin's desire to keep the New Economic Policy as it currently stood and Trotski's to go for a faster rate of industrial growth and for greater authority to be granted to central planning agencies.[69]

A political and organisational shake-up was on the horizon. Quite how far-reaching it would have been, had Lenin's health held out, can only be guessed at. It would be wrong to assume that Lenin looked upon Trotski with unqualified faith and admiration. Knowing that he was about to die, he had jotted down his assessment of the character and capability of his erstwhile leading colleagues in a series of notes which came to be known as his last testament. None of them emerged without piercing criticism. As

Lenin saw it, the likelihood of factional struggle in the near future was strong; he also foresaw that Trotski and Stalin would probably be the most dynamic leaders of the rival factions. Trotski he praised for his brilliance and competence but called to task for his inordinate penchant for seeking merely 'administrative' solutions to complex social problems. Stalin came in for sterner words. He not only exhibited a highly administrative bias but also had already concentrated enormous power in his hands and, in Lenin's view, could not be trusted to use it impartially in the interests of the party as a whole. Stalin's behaviour in 1922 strengthened these doubts, particularly after reports that he had comported himself insultingly in conversation with Lenin's wife, Nadezhda Krupskaya. The upshot was that Lenin came to the firm conclusion that Stalin should be sacked from his post as General Secretary forthwith. By early 1923, then, the position of the central party leadership was in a state of flux.[70]

Political cosmetics, however, were used by the Politburo to disguise the cracking surface of the face it showed to the world. The central leaders, despite all the disputes and animosities amongst themselves, agreed that the party in the provinces needed governing with a firm, heavy hand. Not a single one of them lifted pen or voice in protest at the repression of the Workers' Opposition. Milonov, not unexpectedly, was among the early victims. Quickly after the Tenth Party Congress he and his supporters were unceremoniously transferred from Samara and bundled off individually to places where it was thought they would have less opportunity to rock the official boat.[71] The next object of attention was the central executive body of the Metalworkers' Union. Here too the tactic adopted was to pull the offenders away to other jobs and scout round for more pliable functionaries to take their place.[72] Thereafter it was not unduly difficult to scoop up the pockets of Workers' Oppositionist groupings elsewhere. The Nizhni Novgorod Provincial Committee, as we have seen, was given all the backing it required to deal with its own local Workers' Opposition. And when the Archangel Provincial Committee's leaders themselves were found to have sympathised with Shlyapnikov's ideas it was not long before the central party apparatus, by way of a general deterrent, had them banned from holding responsible official positions for two years.[73]

The Workers' Opposition was far from being supine. In Odessa the dissidents even resorted to blocking mention in the local press of aspects of the New Economic Policy of which they disapproved.[74] Samara was still a melting-pot of oppositionist sentiments. After the Central Control Commission had failed to bring all the officials into line it was decided in autumn 1921 to send down V. A. Antonov-Ovseenko, Trotski's confederate in the trade union controversy of 1920, to sort matters out there.[75] Shlyapnikov himself refused to lie low. Not mincing words and unafraid about whoever might be listening to him, he denounced the Politburo's policies as being essentially 'anti-worker'. Lenin wanted the Tenth Party Congress's secret clause to be applied and Shlyapnikov expelled from the Central Committee. But the Central Committee, on one of those increasingly rare occasions when its collective view was allowed to triumph unchallenged by its own subcommittees, let Shlyapnikov off with a severe reprimand. Shlyapnikov fought on. In February 1922 he and twenty-one Workers' Oppositionist leaders petitioned the Communist International's leadership with a complaint about the bout of repression unleashed upon them. It was a sign of desperation as much as of courage. The Bolshevik Politburo had nearly always managed to get its way with the Communist International. Trotski and Zinoviev were chosen to explain and justify the orthodox party line before the massed members of the Executive Committee. The Communist International, after a brief debate, came down on Lenin's side and berated the contents of Shlyapnikov's luckless petition.[76]

The campaign of attrition against the Democratic Centralists too was maintained in 1921. They seem to have got off more lightly than the Workers' Opposition inasmuch as none of their rank-and-file supporters suffered expulsion from the party; yet their leading figures, such as Maksimovski and Sapronov, were being hounded off into minor posts in precisely the same way as Shlyapnikov and Lutovinov. The repression achieved its desired results. The Democratic Centralists no longer held on to any local committee, not even to any local party newspaper. Only Osinski, battling away as their sole representative in the Central Committee, was able to keep the light of their ideas flickering wanly in the public eye. He must have known by now that the chances of mounting a remotely damaging attack upon the Politburo were slim. Stalin, it would seem, made sure of this by covertly sending emissaries round the provinces to warn leading local officials to avoid having dissentient figures elected to the Eleventh Party Congress in April 1922. Among such emissaries was a young Armenian Bolshevik who had already been the butt of Workers' Oppositionist criticism in Nizhni Novgorod, Anastas Mikoyan. He was told by Stalin that Trotski's provincial supporters should be edged out of the Congress delegation lists equally as firmly as Sapronov's; he was also given to understand that this secret plan had Lenin's full blessing. Whether Lenin really knew anything about it can never be ascertained: Mikoyan is careful to mention that he spoke not a word to Lenin about the matter. That Stalin and his adherents truly were indulging in a piece of Trotski-bashing as well as Sapronov-bashing, however, there is no needful reason to question.[77]

It was not just the oppositionist section of officialdom which had to endure organisational pillage at the hands of the rampant apparatus in Moscow. Run-of-the-mill committees too in the provinces—committees which had gone out of their way to avoid the Politburo's displeasure—constantly felt harried by centrally-ordered transfers of their personnel and centrally-directed intervention in the trivia of local party administration. The Secretariat, first under Molotov and then under Stalin, kept an aquiline eye on all that went on and vetted lower-level functionaries accordingly. The pretence was made that there was a 'lively exchange' of information, experience and viewpoints between Moscow and the provinces.[78] But this kidded nobody. As Preobrazhenski sardonically revealed, the Politburo's mania for centralisation carried over into holding prolonged discussions about setting local prices for jam and other household products.[79] The only self-protection available to subordinate party bodies was that of 'office mice' in all places and at all times: to compose excessively optimistic reports to higher authority and pray that this would stave off the day of inspection from above. The central party apparatus's reaction was to impress an even tighter control over the localities. The Politburo, still worried that the regional committees might subvert its authority, decreed that they should keep their noses out of the business of selecting the office-holders at the provincial level.[80] No oppositionist raised the steam to criticise the decree. It was all the same to Democratic Centralists and the Workers' Opposition whether the central or the regional party leadership made lower-echelon appointments.

Cabalistic centralism ruled. The party leaders in Moscow got up to every trick in the book to keep their deliberations mysterious and secret until they were ready to announce clear-cut, irreversible decisions. And so the Bolsheviks of mid-Siberia, who in 1918 had taken it as their natural right to be kept fully informed about Soviet diplomatic developments, now complained—weakly, perforce—about being left in the dark even in matters such as relations with Japan, which directly affected them.[81] Local party bodies were expected to know their place. Take the Saratov Provincial Committee: in earlier days it would not have shrunk from offering advice to Moscow on the gamut of political and economic crises of the hour; but by mid-1922, cutting its cloth more modestly, it professed to find questions of agitation and propaganda 'the most interesting' of all.[82] The isolation of provincial officials from behind-the-scenes goings-on in the capital could produce episodes worthy of the pen of Dickens or Gogol. A panic occurred in Bolshevik circles in the small township of Dukhovshchina after a rumour had been spread about that the Politburo was on the point of conscripting all party activists into the Red Army for immediate active service in Germany in 1923. The ensuing enquiry did not conclude that such fiascos could be prevented if more information was allowed to become generally available. Instead, in a fit of male-chauvinistic pique, it blamed the rumour on gossiping wives and urged that even more stringent measures be taken towards keeping party affairs secret.[83] And the Politburo came down like a ton of bricks on all who strove to pull down the curtains from its discussional sanctum. To administrative sanctions against un-orthodox officials were added all the refinements of organised innuendoes and smear campaigns. Alexandra Kollontai quipped mordantly to an Italian communist friend that if he should read in the papers back home that she had been arrested for pilfering the Kremlin's silverware he should infer that she had fallen out with Lenin on some basic aspect of ideology.[84]

Such an atmosphere was a small but significant indicator of the organisational transformation undergone by the Bolshevik party in that small, crowded space of time between 1917 and 1923. A political movement which had once been known, at least by informed observers, for its internal anarchy was now the paragon of control, discipline and orderliness. Comradely persuasion had given way to administrative fiat. Party life, below the heady stratum of the central executive offices in the capital, was steadily being reduced to the technical business of implementing commands from above. Local secretaries' job-tenure depended directly upon their success in seeing that none of their own subordinates stepped out of line. Revolt at the nether levels of party structure was becoming increasingly unlikely as the central party apparatus grasped more and more power. Independently-minded rank-and-filers, activists and officials either turned in their membership cards or learnt to keep their mouths shut tight in public. Factionalism and unorthodoxy, it is true, had still not disappeared entirely. But disputes could nowadays be triggered off only if a leader of central status was ready and determined enough to flout the Politburo majority and appeal for support in the provinces. Except in such contingencies, the organisational lid was placed down upon the system and was likely to remain firmly sealed. Rigid and disciplined, the Bolshevik party bore little resemblance to the mass organism which had made its advancement after the February Revolution through an internal flexibility allowing it to remain constantly sensitive to the current demands of the working class and the peasantry. Now it ruled society with a stern, unbending arm of political control.

8 The Winds of Bureaucracy (January 1923– January 1924)

The Bolshevik Politburo met a spring and summer of crisis in 1923. The economic symptoms were a slow-down in the rate of industrial growth and a fall-off in the amounts of grain reaching the towns from the countryside. The peasantry felt it was getting a raw deal. The prices of industrial goods had risen, in real terms, three times as quickly as the prices of agricultural products in the decade since the start of the First World War. Rural households perceived less and less incentive to trade in the urban market. Quite apart from the mounting difficulty of feeding the population of the towns, it was becoming no easy task to keep the factories at anything near full operating capacity. Peasants refused to pay so much for their industrial purchases. The Politburo, in a bid to balance its financial books, concluded that a cut-back in factory production was inevitable. This was a drastic measure. Not only did it mean the consignment of valuable machinery to temporary disuse; it also involved the lay-off of thousands of members of the work force. Strikes burst out across the country. The underground groups led by ex-Bolsheviks, despite all the dangers they were running in defying the government, took up the cause of the strikers. A more embarrassing situation was scarcely conceivable for a political party which had ridden to power on its promises to the working class.

Shlyapnikov, Sapronov and Trotski were a motley band of opponents of the New Economic Policy; but they agreed that a large part of the country's problems lay in the Politburo's refusal to draw up an overall industrial plan and initiate a faster rate of industrial growth. All of them, in addition, felt constricted by the regime inside the Bolshevik party which prevented them from freely speaking their minds and canvassing for support. It may well have been of some comfort to them that the dying Lenin was moving to a not dissimilar viewpoint. As part of his attempt to effect a rapprochement with Trotski, he had already indicated his readiness to contemplate greater scope for centralised economic planning than had previously seemed advisable to him. He was also hoping to reform party life. In particular, he wanted both Ordzhonikidze punished for his behaviour in Georgia and Stalin sacked for abusing his position of power. In broader terms he had come round to thinking that the most effective way to reorder the central apparatus was to introduce ordinary industrial workers among its membership. Yet Stalin got off the hook. Lenin's absence from the Twelfth Party Congress in April 1923 placed Trotski in the invidious position of seeming to be making a bid for 'the succession' if he criticised any of his central colleagues. Kamenev, Stalin and Zinoviev were easily able to fudge all issues under contention. More than that: they consolidated themselves by packing the expanded membership of the Central Committee with their own supporters (who, though mainly of working-class origin, were not currently engaged in factory jobs).[1]

Yet the 'troika' was worried. Politicking alone could not wash away the rising current of feeling that both economic and organisational affairs were being mishandled. The 'troika' did something to ease things by lowering industrial prices and thereby tempting the peasantry back to the market. Concern, however, was not immediately allayed. The Central Committee shortly set up three commissions of enquiry into the interrelated subjects of the governmental budgetary system, the widespread outbreak of strikes and the party's internal troubles. The first two commissions took some time over their deliberations; but the third, which was headed by Dzerzhinski, got through its work rapidly and the early signs were that it sympathised with much of the criticism levelled at the 'troika'.[2] But Dzerzhinski's report, when delivered in October, turned out to be a whitewash job. Worse still, it recommended the enforcement of still stricter forms of party discipline, even to the point of enjoining all Bolsheviks to pass on any evidence of clandestine, factional 'groupings' not only to the Central Committee but also to the secret police. This was too much for Trotski and on 8 October he complained to the Central Control Commission about the report. He described a large range of organisational trends which, taken together, pointed to 'the bureaucratisation of the party'. The practice of appointing committee secretaries from above attracted his fiercest ire. He dwelt little upon the causes of the process, perhaps because he had not yet had time to reflect upon them at leisure; but he did mention that he had first recognised the problem around the period of the Eleventh Party Congress in April 1922. This was therefore hardly a case of early observation. But that was only the smallest crumb of comfort to the 'troika'; for Trotski's newly urgent tone, together with his expressed intention of carrying his views to all Bolsheviks whom he regarded as 'sufficiently prepared, mature and self-restrained', clearly presaged a battle royal for the party's general approval.[3]

The 'troika' at this stage evidently considered its own interests to lie in gagging comment on the affair. The precaution was taken of getting both the Central Control Commission and the Moscow City Committee Bureau to pass resolutions, which were not to be made public immediately, condemning Trotski's action.[4] There the matter rested for a day or so. It appears to have come as a shock to the 'troika' to learn on 15 October that a further document of oppositionist content had arrived at the Central Committee's offices. This was what came to be known as the Declaration of the Forty-Six (after the number of its signatories). Evgeni Preobrazhenski, Lev Serebryakov and Boris Breslav had collected the signatures and were straightaway accused of having done the deed in cahoots with Trotski since they had supported him in 1920. But such a conspiracy was probably a figment of Stalin's imagination. Preobrazhenski, though he may well have had access to Trotski's letter, had almost certainly not hatched a plot. Many signatories had had nothing to do with Trotski in previous years; some such as the Democratic Centralists had been ranged against him in earlier disputes about internal organisation. In any case the Declaration of the Forty-Six was much more sophisticated and far-reaching than Trotski's hastily penned missive. Firstly, Preobrazhenski traced the party's troubles not just to the spring of 1922 but right back to the end of the Civil War; secondly, he claimed that the central leadership's excess of hierarchicism had effects far beyond the organisational field alone and was also to be blamed for the failure to take a flexible, dynamic approach to economic policy.[5]

Both Trotski and the Forty-Six presented themselves as loyal critics. They refrained from calling for the party's ascendant leadership to be sacked; they suggested that internal reform could be effected by due process of the party regulations and without recourse to extraordinary measures of administration. Indeed their practical proposals in certain respects resembled the organisational resolution officially accepted at the Ninth Party Congress in September 1920. Central executive bodies, they said, should release their fierce grip on local party life and should become responsive to demands from below; the local committees themselves should be chosen by means of genuine elections and should likewise desist from the heavy-handed methods currently used by them in their dealings with lower bodies; committee secretaries should no longer lord it over their colleagues; activists and rank-and-filers should be encouraged to call their representatives to account and participate more actively in true politics. Despite the innocuous terminology of this platform, however, the 'troika' would have been amazingly idiotic not to see that such ideas, if consistently put into effect, would shake the organisational condition of the party to its foundations and perhaps sweep away the ascendant leadership in the process.[6]

The 'troika' acted accordingly. On 19 October it sent a strongly worded letter to both the Central Committee and the Central Control Commission condemning the oppositionists out of hand. A joint session of the Central Committee and the Central Control Commission was called for 25 October. Its deliberations lasted full three days but the issue was never in serious doubt. The handful of oppositionists invited along to state their case were unable to sway their audience. By 110 votes to 2, with 10 abstentions, it was decided to denounce Trotski's letter and the Declaration of the Forty-Six as a concerted 'factional outburst', incapable of solving the party's difficulties and pervaded by utter hypocrisy. Illness prevented Trotski's attendance so that it fell to Preobrazhenski to present the case for the signatories. Both men were singled out for censure in the final resolution. The 'troika' was obviously more than a little keen to make sure that there would be no repetition of the 'trade union controversy' and that no leeway would be proffered to oppositionists wishing to stir up the ashes of past disputes.[7]

A few days later, on 7 November, Zinoviev reappeared in his former role as keeper of the party's conscience in organisational matters. He admitted that the Bolsheviks stood in danger of stumbling down the road of degeneration mapped out by the German Social-Democratic Party before 1914; he conceded that 'a section of comrades assigned exclusively to party work have not always been adequate to the immense new tasks being made for them by the growing needs of the masses'. He called for reform. He asserted that the chances of success were better than ever now that industrial output was returning to prewar levels and industrial workers were taking up their old jobs in the factories.[8] It was a crafty tactic. Trotski and Preobrazhenski had been put in the awkward position of confronting an opponent who professed allegiance to their very own cause. Zinoviev was therefore able to demand that all discussion should be directed away from the 'negative' business of criticising the ascendant leadership and towards the 'positive' task of devising commonly accepted remedies. Of course, Trotski was no duffer. Seeing the trap being laid for him, he spun out the rest of November insisting that the 'troika' should spell out more concretely what organisational changes it intended to implement or allow. But this tactic could not last forever. Finally, on 5 December, Trotski agreed to a compromise resolution which was entitled 'On the Construction of the Party' and which was delivered to the press on the same day. For the moment it looked as if Zinoviev's manoeuvring had won the day: not only had he managed to keep local party bodies from plunging into an all-in controversy, but he had also succeeded in putting a political gag on the person whom he regarded as his most dangerous adversary.[9]

To the hook he was using to pull in Trotski, Zinoviev had had the audacity to attach a concealed barb which he must have hoped would damage Stalin too. O, Byzantium! It was some time in the summer of 1923 that Zinoviev apparently first noted Stalin's amassment of personal power with alarm. Whilst on vacation, he arranged a semi-conspiratorial meeting with Bukharin and others in a cave outside the spa resort of Kislovodsk. Here the proposal was made to curb Stalin's domination of the Secretariat by making Trotski and Zinoviev (or Bukharin or Kamenev) members of it as well. Stalin, on hearing this, adroitly suggested an alternative scheme which would permit all the leading figures in the Politburo to occupy places in the Orgburo. His idea was accepted; his sway inside the Secretariat remained unchallenged. Anyway, it would have mattered little if Trotski and Zinoviev had indeed been appointed to the Secretariat; for their record of ill-attendance at subsequent sessions of the Orgburo shows just how much they continued to underestimate the importance of mundane organisational chores. Nonetheless Zinoviev had not yet given up the chase. His newspaper article of 7 November, with its glancing references to the shortcomings of 'a section of comrades assigned exclusively to party work', was almost certainly designed to be construed as a warning to Stalin not to overstep the mark. Zinoviev's softly-softly methods of defeating Trotski were thus the preliminary blast in the coming battle inside the 'troika' itself.[10]

On 8 December, however, Trotski's sudden, unexpected counter-offensive compelled Zinoviev and Stalin to close ranks tightly again. The immediate cause was his series of short articles known as 'The New Course'. From Trotski's viewpoint, the positive side of the compromise resolution of 5 December was that the 'troika' had put their hands to the promise of a reform which was at least as far-reaching as had been demanded by the Declaration of the Forty-Six; but the price he had had to pay for this was the addition of a paragraph which detailed the Tenth Party Congress's blistering attack upon factionalism in the resolution 'On the Unity of the Party'. Now, in 'The New Course', Trotski cast aside all equivocation. The debilitating malaise of Bolshevik life, he declared, was not the chimera of factionalism but the unchecked growth of bureaucratic practices, a growth which was being fertilised and tended by the assiduous efforts of the entire secretarial hierarchy. He maintained that the party apparatus had broken clear of democratic constraints, that the older Bolshevik cadres were barring the path of advancement to the younger generation, and that the true barometer of feeling inside the party was embodied in those thousands of idealistic university students who were champing at the bit of administrative red tape and interference. The deeper causes of this transformation, according to Trotski, were the country's economic and cultural 'backwardness' together with its international isolation. But the weight of his analysis fell elsewhere. He tracked the beginning of bureaucratisation back to the start of the New Economic Policy and argued that a change of the organisational regime should go hand in hand with a change in the industrial programme. This was the analysis not of a scholastic observer but of a leader calling followers to the fray.[11]

The circulation of 'The New Course' was especially cheering for Preobrazhenski and Sapronov. Based in Moscow, they had spent most of November stumping for support for their ideas and could point to particular success in university circles. But that was never enough to trouble the 'troika'. In the provinces it had been noticed that local party bodies, when invited to discuss the comments made by Zinoviev in his article, were most loathe to risk criticising the central party machine in any way. Chelyabinsk was later to become known as a nest of oppositionist sympathies; and yet, if its party newspaper reports are to be believed, its deliberations about the spread of bureaucracy were confined to examining exclusively local manifestations.[12] Most places took caution to greater lengths. Indeed the characteristic reaction was a masquerade of formal approval of Zinoviev's verbalising and a barely disguised complacency about the issues under examination. The Nizhni Novgorod Provincial Committee and their secretary preened themselves for having raised the subject of reform as early as summer 1923; but their practical efforts to alter the internal situation were less than nugatory.[13] Yet the real hard-liners would not stoop to this. Officials in towns like Saratov and Semipalatinsk avoided discussing the Zinoviev article like the plague, omitting even to make the usual approbatory noises in the direction of Moscow. No wonder the signatories of the Declaration were restless and despondent in November 1923.[14]

Trotski's action changed all that. On 11 December a mass party meeting was convoked for all Moscow Bolsheviks to thrash out a decision about the organisational question. Preobrazhenski and Sapronov, still filling in for the bed-ridden Trotski, argued the oppositionist viewpoint; Kamenev and Zinoviev, with Stalin keeping himself in the background, replied on behalf of the ascendant leadership. The political atmosphere was vilified by the smears and distortions used by the 'troika' to blacken the Declaration. The ascendant leadership won its expected victory, but only after a lengthy debate and only then by a far from crushing majority. Further effort was required of the central party machine if the oppositionists were to be routed for good. Bukharin felt compelled to come off the fence in public and on 15 December he published an editorial in *Pravda* excoriating Trotski and Preobrazhenski for stirring up a storm even though they had already been granted everything they had asked for in the compromise of 5 December. So heightened was Bukharin's sense of the need to keep the New Economic Policy as it stood that he was ready to support the 'troika' come what may. Party cells across Moscow were bombarded throughout December by canvassers for both sides in the controversy. The minority support for Trotski and Preobrazhenski was remorselessly whittled away so that by the end of the month they were back where they had started: student circles were again the only places where they hung on to solid followings in the capital.[15]

Contemporary observers who read only the central party press might be forgiven for assuming that the 'troika' had the debate in the provinces much more securely under wraps in December than in Moscow.[16] And this, no doubt, was precisely what the 'troika' wanted people to believe. Why bother giving succour to local oppositionists by telling them how their confederates elsewhere in the country were progressing with their campaign? Kamenev, Stalin and Zinoviev clearly still wanted to keep the debate within limits as narrow as was politically possible. In fact, a handful of places stood aside entirely from the dispute. N. I. Ezhov, who was secretary to the Semipalatinsk Provincial Committee, had the gall to dismiss the need for discussion by claiming that the avowed purpose of the Zinoviev 'reform' was to reinforce and streamline the party apparatus.[17] He would not have got away with this sort of rubbish outside areas like Semipalatinsk, which had only very recently acquired party organisations. This was discovered to their intense embarrassment by many committee secretaries—notably in Bryansk, Nizhni Novgorod and Saratov—who, in a fit of administrative zeal, opted to put a complete damper on all serious airing of the issues.[18] There was scarcely a province in central Russia or any other traditional region of Bolshevik activity where some official or other did not kick over the hierarchical traces and stampede his colleagues, willy-nilly, into a turbulent, virulent dispute.

It was against this background that the 'troika' set out to marshal its organisational forces, successfully as it turned out, to secure a victory at the forthcoming Thirteenth Party Conference in January 1924. The oppositionists could nevertheless point to quite a few local triumphs. Chelyabinsk, Cherepovets, the Crimea, Kaluga, Khabarovsk, Kiev, Odessa, Penza, Ryazan, Simbirsk and Vyatka were all provinces where the ascendant leadership went down to humiliating defeats.[19] And there were disturbing tremors in other towns too. Sergei Minin reported bitterly to his superiors that Pskov was the sole province in the entire northern region that had not given sign of 'vacillations'.[20] The central party machine was speedy in its reaction to such tendencies. Trusted, prestigious orators like Anatoli Lunacharski, the Peoples' Commissar for Enlightenment and a former member of the Central Committee, were sent out in posses to track down local dissent and cajole party audiences into accepting the orthodox line. Occasionally, though by no means always, resort would be had to crossposting particularly able and active supporters of Trotski to out-of-the-way jobs. One way or the other, however, the 'troika' pressurised most 'oppositionist' provinces into submission; only a minority of recalcitrant strongholds continued their resistance into late January. Trotski's rout was completed well in advance of the Thirteenth Party Conference.[21]

The Conference was therefore a predictable affair. In order to guarantee that there would be no last-minute upsets, moreover, Stalin had arranged for most of the 128 delegates with voting rights to be party committee secretaries.[22] Rykov kicked off the proceedings with an official report on economic policies, ridiculing the Opposition for its belief that the drawing up of a national industrial plan was yet a practicable proposition. Molotov and G. E. Evdokimov described, in a sinister light, the past association of prominent oppositionists with highly centralist attitudes; they too maintained that only the official leadership possessed truly practicable proposals. And so it went on. Kamenev said that the left Opposition's suggestions would breed intolerable manifestations of centralisation; Mikoyan could see nothing but insincerity in an oppositionist programme which called for both fast industrialisation and organisational democratisation. Preobrazhenski and his supporters—again Trotski was absent through ill-health—tried to staunch the flow of their wounds. Their replies to the 'troika' were replete with dire warnings about the dangers inherent in the New Economic Policy for a political party which claimed to be in pursuit of a socialist revolution. But the tone of their remarks, at once strident and desperate, gave the game away that everyone realised that the vote on the economic debate was a foregone conclusion.[23]

Stalin gave the report on the organisational question. At open mass meetings prior to the Conference he had used Zinoviev's tactical ploy of hamming it up as the convinced democrat. But now he took off his mask, or at least one of them. In the semi-privacy of the Conference, whose proceedings were reported somewhat sketchily in the party press and whose minutes were to be published in a limited-circulation edition, he made clear his doubts about reforming party life.[24] The Bolsheviks, he said, had never 'made a fetish' of democracy. The survival of the October

Revolution depended in his opinion upon a developed condition of industrial production, a comfortable material environment for the working class, a high level of cultural attainment throughout society and the absence of the threat of foreign intervention. To these great obstacles in the way of democratisation he added three further hurdles: the widespread habituation to militaristic techniques produced in the Civil War, the untoward influence of the soviet apparatus upon the party apparatus and the low 'cultural level' of many party organisations, especially in the country's peripheral regions. Such difficulties, Stalin emphasised, would persist into the foreseeable future. And then, wanting to have his cake and eat it too, he rounded off his speech with the throwaway line that he supported the full and immediate implementation of the organisational reform.[25]

Stalin had pulled no punches in what he had to say about leading oppositionists. Trotski, he exclaimed, had tried to set himself on high above his colleagues and behave as though he were a 'superman'. Going into details, Stalin denounced his absent adversary on the grounds that he had failed to criticise the Declaration of the Forty-Six, had drawn a false contrast between the Bolshevik party and its organisational apparatus, had mischievously distinguished between the younger and the older generations of party officials, had improperly represented the student population as the 'barometer' of social change and had advocated allowing like-minded Bolsheviks to form their own 'groupings' solely in order to create a tightly organised faction of his own. Stalin went on to call for the publication of the Tenth Party Congress's hitherto secret clause on the expulsion from the Central Committee of anyone found to have indulged in factional activity.[26] Nor was this the end of Trotski's travail by proxy. V. Lominadze argued that the democratisation of Bolshevik life would have the undesirable consequence of handing influence on a platter to that considerable segment of the party ranks with a background which was not only not working-class but was even ex-Menshevik or nationalistic; E. M. Yaroslavski harped on the same theme by mocking Trotski for his inability to attract support outside the agricultural provinces and by questioning whether he and his adherents had really ditched their known penchant for extreme centralism for good and all.[27]

Preobrazhenski prefaced his reply with the statement, evidently provoked by Stalin's expressed view of industrialisation as a long-term problem, that the industrial recovery from the Civil War had in fact proceeded much faster than most leaders had anticipated. He bemoaned the smear tactics employed against the Opposition in general and Trotski in particular; he censured the growing cult of quoting phrases from old speeches and articles by Lenin in order to fabricate charges against opponents. Widening the scope of his analysis, Preobrazhenski took the high incidence of factory strikes in mid-1923 to be a general sign that the ascendant party leadership, far from being at the helm of events and developments, was in fact lagging far behind and trailing in their wake. A clutch of delegates spoke up for him. S. Vrachev said that the chaos of party life had reached the point where a mass of decisions and resolutions about local affairs would be taken centrally and yet nobody in the provinces would hear a word about them. The top storey, in his words, did not communicate adequately with the bottom storey of the house. Sapronov said that the Left Opposition's lack of success in industrial regions stemmed wholly from the central party apparatus's transfer of prominent dissenters to jobs in agricultural provinces. But it was Karl Radek who made the most cutting quip of the day. Why was it, he enquired, that Stalin supported organisational reform if he thought the road ahead was really as obstacle-strewn as he had described it?[28]

The organisational issue was the centre-piece of the Conference. Zinoviev's official report on the international scene, full of self-exculpation for his own part in the fiasco of the attempt at socialist revolution in Germany in November 1923, passed almost without comment.[29] The crowning humiliation for the Opposition was a tendentious resolution which went under the title 'On the Results of the Discussion and on the Petit-Bourgeois Deviation in the Party'. It retailed a highly distortive history of the course of the recent controversy; it offered up all the various criticisms already directed at Trotski during the proceedings; and it condemned the Opposition as embodying a fundamental break with the traditions of Bolshevism. The practical proposals had sinister overtones. The resolution demanded the publication of the Tenth Party Congress's expulsion clause; it heralded a campaign to propagate the tenets of 'Leninism' and to explain and publicise the original split between the Bolsheviks and the Mensheviks; it strictly banned the circulation of forbidden documents (without, it may be noted, specifying what literature came into this category); it requested that special attention be paid to those local committees which had not seen fit to back up the ascendant leadership in the previous month. With a fanfare of enthusiasm it also announced that efforts were to be made to recruit a hundred thousand new party members from the working class without delay. But any hopes being harboured that this marked a change of heart inside the central party machine were dissipated by the proviso that 'freedom of deliberation' did not involve 'freedom to break party discipline'. The Thirteenth Party Conference ended on 18 January 1924, three days before Lenin's pain-racked body at last gave up the unequal struggle.[30]

Amongst the immediate reasons for the Opposition's demise it would be fatuous to discount the control of the central party machine by the 'troika'. It put Trotski at a disadvantage from the very start by leaving him short of organisational resources and exposed to administrative onslaughts. No one had ever challenged Stalin's talent for placement politics. In fact he had done his job so well before autumn 1923, judiciously shuffling the personnel pack to put the oppositionist knaves out of play, that he seldom needed to insist on many sackings during the controversy itself. The most notorious last-minute demotion was V. A. Antonov-Ovseenko's loss of his post as chief political commissar in the Red Army. Less well known, however, is that the oppositionist committee secretaries of the provinces of Kaluga, Vyatka and the Crimea were allowed to keep their jobs until after the Thirteenth Party Conference. And the Crimean official avoided the boot altogether by agreeing to a public recanting of his 'heretical' views.[31] This was caution at work, not magnanimity. Indeed the 'troika', though already off to a head start by virtue of holding the party offices which counted, distinguished itself by grubbing round unashamedly in the filthiest gutters of Bolshevik life. All manner of rumour, slander and libel was put about. Stalin and his central buddies were not the only culprits. A distraught oppositionist in Saratov gives us some idea of the texture of the debate there: 'Even at official meetings of party organisations you can hear a pile of "witty cracks" about the "idiotic" speeches of Sapronov, the "mistakes" of Trotski, and a certain praising of Stalin for "having unseated Trotski so cleverly".'[32]

The Opposition nonetheless made the ascendant leadership's task greatly easier by tactical ineptitude. Trotski and Preobrazhenski, though on the best of terms personally and politically, failed by a long chalk to achieve that degree of co-ordination and solidarity which would have lent greater clout to their attempt on the 'troika'. It would have been better for them, surely, if they really had got together conspiratorially in September 1923; it would have been still better if they had done so even earlier. Trotski was later to affirm that he could easily have done down Stalin in the winter of 1922 by agreeing to the ill-fated pact with Lenin.[33] This is fair comment (even though Trotski's troubles would have been far from over since he still had lots of other bitter adversaries in the party leadership). By playing the match according to rules composed by the 'troika', and with the 'troika' as both referee and opposing team, Trotski and Preobrazhenski had forfeited their chances before taking to the field. Stalin, moreover, was engaged in a deep game of his own. Anastas Mikoyan, arriving in the capital from Rostov-upon-Don in November 1923, was aghast at the stir kicked up by the Opposition in Moscow student circles; it seemed to him that Trotski and Preobrazhenski had been allowed far too much rope to lasso a political following. But Stalin took him aside and reassured him that the same rope would be used as a noose for the Opposition. And sure enough in December, when Trotski had made his compromise with the 'troika', it was possible for Stalin to ask rhetorically why his opponents were making all their noise when no point of disagreement separated the two sides.[34]

For those officials who had ears to hear the undertones of the debate, furthermore, there was much in Stalin's arguments which was not entirely demagogic. Democratising the Bolshevik party was nowhere near as simple and straightforward an endeavour as proposed by the Opposition. A census of rank-and-filers in 1922 suggested that at least one in every fifteen was a former Menshevik.[35] It stood to reason that there were many from other parties who had so far managed to escape detection and who had stood a good deal to the right of the socialist camp in 1917. A risk was posed also by the large numbers of Bolsheviks who made no secret of their non-Bolshevik past. In order to consolidate its power it was hardly avoidable that the party should seek to attract recruits from the rural depths of peasant Russia as well as from the non-Russian regions. Nobody could pretend that all these newcomers were distinguished by a whole-hearted commitment to the Politburo's long-term objectives. Besides, the strike movement of 1923 had shown that the party was still at odds with disgruntled sections of the working class. To open the gates of the political arena to untrammelled, uncurtailed democracy would therefore present an invitation to every so-called Bolshevik who did not share his party's philosophy to cause whatever havoc he wished. Further bands of infiltrators, Stalin suggested, would be queuing up to become party members if they heard that Trotski's organisational reform had been carried through.[36]

In such circumstances, it was widely held, the oppositionist leaders would be as fiercely repressive as anyone. They were judged and found wanting on the basis of their past behaviour. Trotski and his faction in 1920 had advocated a series of measures to restore the economy which were nothing if not excessively brutal and authoritarian. In the following year it was V. A. Antonov-Ovseenko, then as now a close associate of Trotski's, who had directed organisational operations against the Workers' Opposition in Samara.[37] Nor was Sapronov as pure as the undriven snow. He had signally omitted to do very much to help stop the persecution of Shlyapnikov's group.[38] And so it came about that not a single Workers' Oppositionist leader would agree to put his pen to the Declaration of the Forty-Six. This was not just a case of old memories dying hard. The small print of both the Declaration and 'The New Course' envisaged democratic reform of a much narrower order than had been demanded by the Workers' Opposition since 1920. Scarcely a word was spent on the theme of cutting back the material privileges enjoyed by party officialdom. Trotski, Preobrazhenski and Sapronov were alike in their failure to take seriously the widespread resentment felt by working-class rank-and-filers who saw egalitarianism in economic as well as organisational terms.[39]

The Declaration's signatories were in fact a faction divided against itself. A dozen of the Forty-Six, though agreeing to go along with its general analysis, insisted upon adding the reservation that they thought its criticisms of the party's organisational condition to be exaggerated. With reformers of this ilk, Stalin might have concluded, who needed conservative allies? But other signatories went further still. Five centralist oppositionists signed whilst attaching the proviso that, in their view, 'any weakening of the political dictatorship' at that time would be most dangerous. Evidently it was not organisational reform which attracted such people to Trotski and Preobrazhenski, but rather the economic side of their programme.[40] The self-admitted authoritarianists in the Left Opposition's ranks gave additional fuel to the official leadership's argument that Bolshevik life would be a good deal tougher and stricter under Trotski. The 'troika' also made political capital out of the social composition of the Declaration's followers in the party cells. Trotski found it much easier to get support among administrative personnel, both in the Red Army and in the soviet institutions, than amidst other groups in society.[41] There are hints that the 'troika' was momentarily worried that the Opposition would also make headway in the secret police.[42] Yet industrial workers by contrast gave little grounds for Stalin to be afraid. Trotski believed that party cells in the factories had simply been cowed by threats of administrative sanctions. But that was only part of the story. Of equal importance, very probably, was the lack of enthusiasm in the working class for the rigours which might be involved in an all-out bid for fast industrialisation.[43]

Knowing that victory was there in his grasp, Stalin began to come out of his shell towards the end of the controversy. He had detected a current of restlessness among many otherwise loyal party officials. It was widely touted that the 'troika' had been excessively gentle, not to say indulgent, in its treatment of the Opposition; it was widely held that there had been no need whatsoever to sound a note of apology when discussing the organisational question. The militarised party had already become a positive goal in not a few Bolshevik functionaries' minds. A certain Panfilov of Vyatka urged unequivocally that the party should 'place a wager upon the trained committee secretary' as the surest guarantor of the achievement of a socialist programme of action—in much the same terms as Stolypin had bet on the 'strong, sober peasant' to secure the survival of the Romanov autocracy.[44] Stalin echoed such attitudes. He spoke of the party as if it were a 'caste' of mediaeval knights; he delivered a funeral oration to Lenin as if he was some form of demi-god to whom to render unflinching, unthinking devotion. The Secretariat, under his aegis, started printing pamphlets and articles which purported to prove that 'What Is To Be Done?' had always been intended to stand as a practical guide to organisational activity in all times, in all places and under all conditions. The drive towards 'the monolithic party' was under way.[45]

Conclusions

Why did it happen?

All mass organisations in industrial society, if they want to flourish, need to make internal arrangements for the swift exchange of information, formulation of decisions and implementation of plans. Therein lies officialdom's chance to exploit its administrative position to its own advantage. Karl Marx, so successful in putting other aspects of human activity under his microscope, gave scarcely a second glance to this particular problem. It was left to his later critics, Robert Michels and Max Weber, to indicate how a political party's functionaries may easily become so accustomed to a higher standard of living as well as to the exercise of power that they see their own interests as being divergent from those of the rank-and-file members. Democratic procedures fall to the depths of ritualistic mockery. Formal rules to preserve accountability from below are turned into a mask disguising the manipulatory solidarity of officials who impose strict control over party life and head off every movement of opposition. Michels and Weber saw themselves as demythologisers; they were out to show that socialist parties were bound to follow precisely the same path of organisational development as their liberal and conservative rivals.

They overstated their case enormously. The German Social-Democratic Party, whence they drew their real-life examples, was never as centralist and authoritarian as they liked to believe. The Bolsheviks too, for all their regimentation, did not follow the paradigm to the letter. Michels had said that officials would generally act as a corporate group and eschew conflicts among themselves; yet officials of the Russian Communist Party can hardly have shown much active solidarity if nearly all who held office under the New Economic Policy perished so docilely at the hands of Stalin's clique in the 1930s. Weber took a slightly different tack, arguing that officials would generally enjoy secure employment so long as they obeyed prescribed, bureaucratic routines. But again the Bolshevik experience was different. Mere adherence to the written regulations did not guarantee job-tenure even in the 1920s; the central party apparatus remorselessly judged local secretaries by their practical achievements and sacked anyone found to have lacked gusto in implementing vital policies. The studies by Michels and Weber commit the same error of presuming that a revolutionary party's leadership, come hell or high water, will always ditch its original zeal to turn society upside down. Nothing could be further from the truth in the early history of the USSR. Bolshevik officials in Moscow and the provinces regarded the New Economic Policy's concessions to private enterprise as a temporary expedient. They proved this in 1928. Then it was that the majority of them were brought to give support to the intensive programme of nationalisation and collectivisation called for by Stalin. Such a programme did not lead to the flowering of socialism (and indeed its appalling excesses did much to turn the Soviet population away from socialist ideals), but it scarcely betokened a party leadership eager to speak the comfortable language of compromise.

It is a little unfair to Michels and Weber to test their ideas over so narrow a time-span. And developments in the Communist Party of the Soviet Union under Leonid Brezhnev exhibit a steady growth of professional solidarity and social accommodation: it requires spectacles of a more than ordinarily rose-tinted hue to see the current gerontocracy of the Politburo as thrusting, undauntable revolutionaries. But it still remains to be explained why it took over forty years for such a situation to come to fruition. This question cannot be wished away simply by invoking universal bureaucratic pressures or some 'iron law of oligarchy' and leaving the matter at that. Michels and Weber were right in stating that democratic practices inside every political party are limited and conditioned by requirements in communications, decision-making and administration; but they failed to prove that all attempts to construct barriers against extravagances of centralist authoritarianism are doomed to be utterly futile. At the base of their philosophy they harboured a profound pessimism. By the end of their days both Michels and Weber came to believe that the only way to stave off the approach of a completely grey, mediocre, bureaucratised world was to confer supreme power upon an individual leader of such dynamism and charisma as could cut through all the obstructions of the massed phalanxes of officials and functionaries everywhere. With such an outlook it is not surprising that they propounded the surely mistaken idea that the dissimilarities in the organisational lives of political parties are trivial and negligible in comparison with their similarities.

The odds on Bolshevik affairs taking the turn they did were much shortened by the environment inherited from the Russian past. The Soviet Union of the 1920s was still a country at an early stage of industrial expansion. Its large-scale factories, mining enterprises and railway networks, while impressive in themselves, called upon only a small portion of the total sum of endeavour in the economy. The USSR had to make up for much lost time if it was to catch up with the industrial and military power of foreign states like the USA and Great Britain. The first problem was cultural. The lower classes in society, especially the peasantry, needed to be persuaded to break with centuries-old habits and customs; they required an education which would equip them with the literacy skills essential to a modern economy. Greater still, however, was the difficulty of securing industrial investment. The options were few. A government might try to attract capital from abroad in the form of direct loans or of concessions offered to foreign companies; it would also very probably endeavour to augment its own revenues by increasing its fiscal pressure on the domestic population. And even if the financial wherewithal could be obtained, there would yet remain the enormous task of marshalling it effectively.

Such an inheritance was primed for a ruling political party to resort to authoritarian measures. Most workers and peasants were unlikely to take very enthusiastically to invocations that they should accept a lengthy period of material self-sacrifice. A good deal of non-co-operation at best and of opposition at worst was in prospect. Quite aside from this, the Romanov autocracy had bequeathed to its successors a society bitterly divided by political and social rivalries. A socialist government was bound to run into obstacles put in its way by conservative and reactionary groups refusing to recognise its right to govern; but it would also have to contend with an upsurge of separatist strivings by those non-Russian nationalities as yet unreconciled to being associated with a Moscow-centred state. Indeed the possibility of the Bolshevik leadership plumping for highly coercive techniques of administration, inside and outside the party, was strengthened by the tsarist traditions themselves. All revolutionary activists before 1917 had lived and breathed an atmosphere of police persecution and suppression. It would have been astounding if some of the imperial government's heavy-handedness in dealing with society had not rubbed off on to many Bolsheviks too.

Yet the Politburo was not entirely the victim of circumstances. Not even the most hard-bitten defamer of working-class culture could deny that it had given birth to a sturdy variety of grass-roots organisations of self-protection. The health-insurance schemes of the 1890s developed into the trade unions of the twentieth century. The February Revolution demolished the political walls constricting such endeavours and led to hitherto unimagined manifestations of mass self-organisation by Russian industrial workers. The Bolshevik leadership itself in 1917 testified to this. In that extraordinary year there was no feature of the country's social, economic or political life unaffected directly by the intervention of the chosen representatives of the working class. Anarchy there certainly was. But beneath all the chaos lay a discernible pattern of factory-level activity inspired by a belief that representative democracy was the guarantee that all the inequalities and sufferings of the past would soon be eradicated forever. Thousands of independently-minded and industrially-experienced workers did in fact join the Bolsheviks before the October Revolution. Their number was not great; they formed the firm heart of talent and enthusiasm within the body of a more volatile and unsophisticated factory work force. The party leaders, local as well as central, made use of their support after 1917, but seldom as comprehensively and wholeheartedly as they might have done.

Bolshevik apologiae try to justify this by pointing to all the unpredicted volte-faces in conditions following the seizure of power. The speedy overthrow of capitalism's global mastery did not occur. At home the Soviet government confronted both a rapid deepening of the economic crisis and the threat of imminent invasion by the armed might of the German and Austro-Hungarian empires. Social discontent mounted in town and countryside. The signature of the Brest-Litovsk treaty led to a rupture of the governmental coalition and a walk-out by the Left Socialist-Revolutionaries. At that very moment the Civil War was on the brink of exploding. White armies, which had devoted the winter of 1917–18 to military preparations, hurled themselves into central Russia and, with the backing of anti-revolutionary states abroad, fought out a bitter but unsuccessful struggle for supremacy over the next two years. And then in the middle of 1920 came the war with Poland, hastily engaged in and then humiliatingly terminated. The Bolshevik party had steadily to accustom itself to a lengthy period of international isolation. Foreign socialist revolutions failed to follow the expected timetable; foreign investment capital failed to flow into the coffers in the manner predicted. The Soviet state had barely announced its existence to the world when it was pulled up short by the necessities of dealing with a society in the extremes of economic destitution and social dislocation.

This unanticipated outcome could not help but be reflected in Bolshevik life. The party had consistently laid claim to legislative control over the state's activity ever since the October Revolution; but until 1918 there had been great reluctance to saddle the party with the additional responsibility of acting as the paramount organ of governmental administration. The Civil War fuelled a powerful spurt of organisational proliferation. Central and local party bodies fast started acquiring funds, offices and staffs—and the methods to match—already possessed by the soviets and other public institutions. Bolshevik officials were adopting patterns of attitude and behaviour which distinguished them from the rest of the party. It became difficult to resist the call to give high wages to party functionaries, especially when their counterparts in soviet posts had long ago obtained them. And temporary expedients quickly took on the force and sanction of custom. That stern corpus of Bolshevik officials who had proved their administrative mettle in the rigours of the Civil War was most unlikely to take enthusiastically to suggestions that the edifice of its hard-won privileges should be torn down.

When all is said and done, however, an exceedingly large amount of sugar would be required to help to swallow the argument that internal party affairs would have been greatly different if a socialist revolution had occurred in Germany or if the Civil War had been avoided in the Soviet republic. The German economy was in a bad way, to put it mildly, in the early 1920s and would surely have been incapable of performing the prodigy of securing the restoration of Soviet industrial output. A communist government in Germany, moreover, would not necessarily have been a strong enough bulwark against British and French interference in eastern Europe. Indeed social upheaval in that part of the world would almost certainly have strengthened, not weakened, the hands of those politicians in Britain and France calling for a full-scale anti-revolutionary crusade. In any case the Bolsheviks recognised even before the start of their own Civil War at home that they had hugely over-inflated their hopes of promoting the advance of domestic industrial production. The White armies aggravated but did not create political divisiveness, economic ruin and social unrest. Evidently the particular swirl of events after 1917 did in fact occupy a large role in shaping the party's organisational condition; but even if the Bolshevik leadership had enjoyed happier circumstances it is still hard to imagine that party life would have easily been anywhere near to attaining a condition of internal democracy.

At all events the 'objective' nature of the international and domestic environment was not alone in influencing the organisational metamorphosis. Ideas mattered too. There really was something in the Menshevik accusation that Bolshevism from its inception had been geared to driving the engine of social change at an excessive velocity. Lenin and his supporters wanted action. They ridiculed the Mensheviks as being passive observers with no serious intention of overthrowing the *status quo* either before or during 1917; they prided themselves as the sole unflagging graspers of revolutionary opportunity whether under Nicholas II or the Provisional Government. The achievement of a socialist society, they were saying, was both simpler and easier than had ever been dreamt of in the philosophies of their rivals and opponents. Alongside this relentless impatience stood a degree of suspiciousness bordering on paranoia as regards political opposition from within as well as from without the Bolshevik faction. The party was schooled never to take popular opinion automatically as its lodestar. The duty of a Bolshevik was constantly represented as being to mould events, to struggle unremittingly against any tide of social hostility (or indeed social apathy). It was but a short distance hence to rigid intolerance. The hounding of the Workers' Opposition in 1921 was assuredly not the inexorable result of pre-revolutionary ideology, but neither was it unrelated to it. Bolshevik leaders regarded gentleness with adversaries as the thief of time and the eroder of goals.

Bolshevik organisational theory, such as it was, pushed in the same authoritarian direction. Yet it was a sin more of omission than of direct intent. 'What Is To Be Done?' and other such writings before 1917 were intended as proposals about the internal arrangements required for the extension of the party's impact upon society while yet managing to evade the clutches of the imperial police. They said scarcely anything serious about how to go about constructing a mass social-democratic party in the post-autocratic future when parliamentary democracy had at last been established; they said absolutely nothing about what further organisational adjustments might have to be made in the event that the Bolsheviks should emerge as the governing party. Worldly-wise though they were in so much of their thinking, Lenin and his colleagues were supremely naive when it came to ideas about administration. The undesired possibilities spelled out by Michels and Weber fell off them like water from a duck's back; the unattractive features of the German Social-Democratic Party were laughed away by them, at least until 1914, as being a fiction concocted by socialism's enemies. This carelessness, whilst probably being unconscious, was far from being accidental. It had its origins in the Bolshevik belief that the ends justify the means, that what is done utterly dwarfs how it is done in political and moral value.

On the other hand the leaders of the Bolshevik faction cannot be written off as a freakish collection of demons and idiots. They themselves constantly and rightly pointed out that their strategy of revolution was not uniformly distrustful of the working class's creative potentiality and that it was not they but the Mensheviks who looked to the bourgeoisie as the battering-ram which would bring down the gates of the Romanov autocracy. In 1905 and again in 1914 it was the Bolsheviks, not the Mensheviks, who stirred the urban crowds with appeals to have the confidence to cast down the authorities. Bolshevik ideas before 1917, and for some time thereafter too, manifest a tension between their 'authoritarian' and 'democratic' polarities. Indeed there were times, notably after the February Revolution, when almost the entire faction gave itself over to far-reaching, generous faith in grass-roots self-reliance and initiative. The Bolsheviks were certainly not plaster saints but most of them were not unalloyed megalomaniacs either: the particular course of their internal development after they had seized power was always likely, even highly probable, never entirely inevitable.

Many organisational considerations in Bolshevik minds after

February 1917 were anyway of a practical nature and had nothing
to do with theoretical abstractions. All Russian mass political
parties suffered likewise. They could brag of apparently un-
questionable successes: they were operating freely and without the
threat of police harassment, they were building up countrywide
networks of regional and town committees, they were attracting—
almost without having to move a muscle—thousands upon
thousands of new rank-and-file members. Yet the years of tsarist
suppressions still cast a long shadow. Bolsheviks, Mensheviks and
Socialist-Revolutionaries alike were plagued by the shortage of
experienced ex-undergrounders they could lay their hands on to
staff and run their local organisations. There was no immediate
solution except to overwork and overload all available manpower
with administrative responsibility. The need to supply representatives to the soviets and other public institutions was a further heavy
burden; and it was a need which suddenly became yet more acute
for the Bolsheviks in late October when they became the ruling
party. Worse was to come. The outbreak of the Civil War in 1918
necessitated a still greater dilution of the party's human resources
in the towns as droves of activists were siphoned off into the armed
forces. In such conditions it is not surprising that Bolshevik
functionaries, when asked to shoulder ever increasing workloads,
demanded in return that they should be allowed to get on with the
job without having to submit each and every decision, major or
minor, to scrutiny and debate by lower party bodies.

Such pressures also shoved local functionaries into accepting the
need to establish truly hierarchical order and discipline throughout the countrywide network of party committees. The seeds of
organisational change were already sprouting in 1917. Bolshevik
life after the February Revolution was as contentious, divisive and
anarchic (or nearly so) as the next party's; there was scarcely a
Bolshevik committee anywhere which did not at some time or
other become locked in furious combat with either higher
authority or its subordinates. All the same this could not last
indefinitely after the seizure of power. Even very large party
organisations before the October Revolution were pleading for
central assistance in the form of additional manpower. They
wanted better information services too. Indeed, many a small
group or committee of Bolsheviks asked the central party
apparatus to send them detailed directives about the problems of
the day in their locality. Governmental responsibilities were bound

to strengthen these tendencies. Party bodies in the provinces began to learn, often through bitter experience, that the technical difficulties of economic restoration and social administration could not be solved unless the leadership in the capital were given greater scope to act decisively. Again it was the Civil War which did the trick. Almost overnight it was witnessed that nearly all those dyed-in-the-wool defenders of local rights in 1917 were now ready, however reluctantly, to recognise that the military crisis called for the introduction of stern internal discipline if the party was ever to stay in power.

This is the point. The early stages of the organisational metamorphosis did not occur simply at the behest of the Central Committee or upon the proposal of its local stooges and toadies. Nearly all Bolshevik officials were directly or indirectly involved. Never before had party functionaries at every level so fully appreciated the positive potentiality of that chain of interdependence binding together all the links from the central executive bodies through the regional, provincial, town and suburb committees down to the basic party cells. The hierarchical side of democratic centralism had been little more than highfalutin scrawls on paper. Yet if any officials in 1918–19 seriously expected a return to the erstwhile looseness in organisational affairs just as soon as the Civil War was over, they must have been cruelly disillusioned in 1920. The mountain of social, economic and political troubles of 1917 had not been miraculously washed away: it now bulked even larger on the horizon. And the human and material resources at the party's disposal were more limited than ever. The price paid for the victory over the Whites were the deaths of thousands of valuable activists and rank-and-filers and the ruination of industrial and agricultural production. The technical burdens of administration alone were enough to daunt the bravest spirit. Pragmatic considerations in such a vein were usually relegated to the back pages of Bolshevik newspapers and only seldom hit the headlines; yet they wielded no negligible influence over the party's internal transformation in the half-decade after the October Revolution.

Individual Moscow-based leaders certainly hastened the process, but it is wishful thinking to believe that their oft-mentioned machinations were the decisive factor. In fact, the most extreme arch-centralisers in the critical years of 1918 and 1920 were to be found outside the capital. Both Kaganovich in the early months of the Civil War and Smilga at its end headed groups of local officials who felt that the central party apparatus was culpably indulgent to criticism from below. Not that Lenin and his close colleagues needed much prodding to stiffen the regime inside the party. They eagerly exploited the chances offered to them; they gave short shrift to all who sought to reverse the direction of change. But it is not as if they had to exert themselves unduly to achieve what they wanted. Lenin scarcely opened his mouth in the vital debates about the organisational question at the Eighth Party Congress and the Ninth Party Conference. He knew things were already running his way without his intervention. In addition, the early succession of Central Committee secretaries—Sverdlov, Stasova, Krestinski and Molotov—were certainly, like Lenin, highly adequate directors of centralising policies. But they were not much more than that. They could never have succeeded in bringing about so rapid a turnabout in Bolshevik life unless they had been assured of active collaboration from lower echelons of the party hierarchy. Even Stalin, without a doubt the most ruthless and devious of the central party organisers, had much less impact upon the metamorphosis than his critics imagined. Not only did his military postings severely restrict his Orgburo work between 1919 and 1921, but also his appointment as General Secretary in April 1922 occurred after, not before, the broad pattern of the party's internal administration had been settled.

It is a moot point whether those factions in favour of a democratic reform of party life would have radically altered the situation even if they had won the disputes of 1918-23. The Democratic Centralists fought long and hard for their idea of inner-party democracy, constantly lambasting the central party machine for its neglect of lower-echelon opinions and its clamp-down upon collective decision-making procedures. Yet they were not as thorough-going democrats as is sometimes supposed. The Workers' Oppositionist call for ordinary workers and peasants to be given a direct say in discussions about the production and distribution of society's goods left Sapronov cold. And so, when matters came to a head, the Democratic Centralists did not raise much of a fuss in order to protect the Workers' Opposition in 1921. Nor had their view changed in 1923 when they linked up with Trotski, Preobrazhenski and their supporters to form the Left Opposition. The chances of a democratically run political party under Trotski's leadership were anyhow not too bright. The Left

Opposition in 1923 remained unrepentant about the hounding of the Workers' Opposition; it disapproved too of proposals to strike at the party's monopoly of state power; it said nothing about the financial privileges currently enjoyed by party and other public officials. Not a few of his associates, moreover, made no secret that they did not really sympathise with his organisational recommendations.

Accordingly the Workers' Opposition was the sole group of internal critics who looked the party's problems squarely in the face. They alone truly believed, deep in their marrow, that the working and living conditions of the mass of factory employees not belonging to the Bolsheviks had an immense indirect effect upon the interior affairs of the party itself. Their plans would surely have run into huge obstacles. Their desire to dismantle the party's domination of all the other institutions of the Soviet state was all very well but it would in practice have produced a great deal of administrative chaos. And such a situation would once again have allowed the more bureaucratically-inclined Bolshevik officials to exercise a malignant influence on party life. Yet Shlyapnikov's instincts were correct in the debates of 1920–21. All the profounder was the pity that the Workers' Opposition represented so insubstantial a section of Bolshevik officialdom. A huge dose of hypothetical argumentation is called for if we are to go about asking what would have happened if Shlyapnikov had won the day in the dispute. In reality he was politically outgunned even before he had shown his head above the turret.

This is not to say that the Bolshevik party of the mid-1920s was yet the regimented grotesquerie it was to appear in the 1930s. To many a contemporary commentator, indeed, it seemed that Soviet politics had never before been so tumultuous, so uncontrolled from above, so ready to tear the fabric of state and society asunder. In 1925 the 'troika' of Kamenev, Zinoviev and Stalin openly started fighting among themselves. Stalin's victory pushed Kamenev and Zinoviev ever closer to Trotski and led them shortly, in 1926, to form the United Opposition with him. But it was too little and too late. Stalin's faction annihilated its enemies politically and compelled them to recant their views or else suffer expulsion from the ranks. It was Bukharin's turn at the end of the decade. Stalin was by then almost ready to abandon the New Economic Policy lock, stock and barrel and to condemn its proponents as constituting a Right Opposition. With all these controversies raging throughout the 1920s it would be ludicrous to maintain that the stuffing had been completely knocked out of Bolshevik life not long after the Civil War. Yet it would be no less silly to deny that under the regime of the New Economic Policy it took politicians of the stamp and eminence of Trotski, Kamenev, Zinoviev and Bukharin to keep the flame of wide-ranging, public discussion alive. Long gone were the days when local oppositionists could independently anathematise the central party leadership and expect to escape being sacked.

At first sight it is hard to imagine a more depressing saga. Here, it would seem, was a social revolution bound from its very beginning to lurch down a road leading to political iniquities more oppressive than had existed even under the government of Nicholas II, against whom the struggle had been launched in the first place. So deterministic an outlook is unjustified. The degeneration from the unhealthy but by no means moribund party organism of 1923 to the rotten, deathly hulk of the late 1930s was not unavoidable. The Great Terror need not and ought not to have happened. Preventive measures could have been taken if only a majority within the ascendant party leadership had possessed a keener awareness of the moral and practical dangers of permitting excesses of coercive administrative techniques. Stalin could easily have been caught. But first he and his appalling clique had to be recognised for what they really were or had become: the representatives of the unacceptable, inhuman face of socialism. The lasting harm they did to the socialist idea is incalculable. Inside and outside the Soviet Union it became widely believed that any and every large-scale enterprise to build a new society, a new world on non-capitalist principles would give birth to a social nightmare worse than anything endured under capitalism.

The organisational metamorphosis of the Bolshevik party in the first half-decade after the October Revolution was only one among many political, social and economic circumstances facilitating the events of the late 1930s. It was a crucial process in itself nonetheless. The Bolshevik officials of the early 1920s had implemented revolutionary changes in the structure of ownership in the industrial and agricultural economy. They had survived a most vicious, bloody Civil War. They were beginning to cope with a welter of social and cultural problems which had existed since the pre-revolutionary period and had been aggravated by the years of military conflict. But the party's undoubted achievements were made at the cost of a steady drift away from its pre-October commitment to tapping the wellsprings of working-class enthusiasm and initiative to realise its objectives. This drift was not without its bitter ironies. That same generation of officials who had promoted the initial changes in party life was itself to become the mass victim of the Stalinist purges before the Second World War. Such officials had all along thought of themselves as acute, realistic observers of their environment; but the truth was that they saw the world through a glass darkly. And, in the end, they paid the ultimate price for their failure.

MAP 1a: EUROPEAN RUSSIA BEFORE 1917

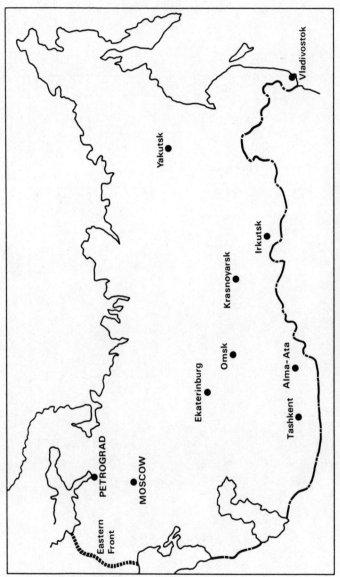

MAP 1b: THE RUSSIAN EMPIRE BEFORE 1917

Notes and References

The system of transliteration used in the rest of this work is modified in the notes and references inasmuch as titles of books (though not the names of their authors) are now given as recommended by the journal *Soviet Studies*.

Chapter 1

1. G. V. Rimlinger, 'The Expansion of the Labour Market in Capitalist Russia, 1861–1917', *Journal Of Economic History*, June 1961, pp.208–15; T. von Laue, 'Russian Peasants in the Factory, 1892–1903', *Californian Slavic Studies*, 1964–5, no.3; R. E. Zelnik, 'The Peasant and the Factory', in W.Vucinich, *The Peasant in Nineteenth-Century Russia* (Stanford, 1968); J. H. Bater, *St. Petersburg: Industrialization and Change* (London, 1976).

2. See this Chapter, note 1.

3. M. Perrie, *The Agrarian Policy of the Russian Socialist-Revolutionary Party, from its Origins Through the Revolution of 1905–1907* (Cambridge, 1976), Part 1.

4. A. K. Wildman, *The Making of a Workers' Revolution: Russian Social-Democracy, 1891–1903* (Chicago, 1967), Chapters 1 and 2.

5. S. P. Baron, *Plekhanov, the Father of Russian Marxism* (London, 1963), Chapters 5 and 6.

6. S. P. Baron, *Plekhanov*, Chapters 6 and 7.

7. S. P. Baron, *Plekhanov*, Chapter 8; A. K. Wildman, *The Making of a Workers' Revolution*, Chapter 2.

8. A. K. Wildman, *The Making of a Workers' Revolution*, Chapters 2 and 3.

9. S. P. Baron, *Plekhanov*, pp.164–7.

10. A. K. Wildman, *The Making of a Workers' Revolution*, Chapters 6 and 7.

11. N. Harding, *Lenin's Political Thought*, Volume 1: *Theory and Practice in the Democratic Revolution* (London, 1977), Chapter 6.

12. P. I. Lyashchenko, *Istoriya narodnogo khozyaistva SSSR*, Volume 2 (4th edition: Moscow, 1956), Chapter 8.

13. V. I. Lenin,'Chto Delat?' in *Polnoe Sobranie Sochinenii* (5th edition: Moscow, 1959–68), Volume 6, pp.1–192.

14. V. I. Lenin, 'Chto Delat'?

15. L. H. Haimson, *The Russian Marxists and the Origins of Bolshevism* (Massachusetts, 1955), Chapters 7–9.

16. L. H. Haimson, *The Russian Marxists*, Chapter 9; N. Harding, *Lenin's Political Thought*, Chapter 7.

17. L. H. Haimson, *The Russian Marxists*, Chapters 10 and 11.

18. D. Lane, *The Roots of Russian Communism: A Social and Historical Study of Russian Social-Democracy, 1898-1907* (Assen, 1964), Part 2.

19. D. Lane, *The Roots of Russian Communism*, Chapter 1.

20. Not that this has stopped scholars from trying. Notable examples are D. Lane, *The Roots of Russian Communism*, Chapter 1, and S. G. Strumilin, *Sostav kommunisticheskoi partii*, pp.32-3, which was reprinted in E. Smitten, *Sostav vsesoyuznoi kommunisticheskoi partii (bol'shevikov)* (Moscow-Leningrad, 1927).

I have used Lane's method of computing the total number of Russian social-democrats (though our respective answers differ by 2000 members): *The Roots of Russian Communism*, pp.13-15.

21. P. I. Lyashchenko, *Istoriya narodnogo khozyaistva*, Volume 2, Chapter 9.

22. S. Schwartz, *The Russian Revolution of 1905* (London, 1975).

23. S. Schwartz, *The Russian Revolution of 1905*.

24. M. N. Lyadov, *Londonskii s"ezd RSDR Partii v tsifrakh* in *Itogo londonskogo s"ezda* (St Petersburg, 1907), p.84; R. V. Daniels, *The Conscience of the Revolution: Communist Opposition* (Massachusetts, 1960), Chapter 1.

25. D. Lane, *The Roots of Russian Communism*, Part 2.

26. G. Hosking, *The Russian Constitutional Experiment: Government and Duma, 1907-1914* (Cambridge, 1973).

27. G. T. Robinson, *Rural Russia under the Old Regime* (New York, 1932), Chapters 11-12.

28. Stalin commented on this in 1920: *Sochineniya* (Moscow, 1946-51), Volume 4, pp.316-17.

29. R. V. Daniels, *The Conscience of The Revolution*, Chapter 1.

30. L. Valiani, 'La Storia della Socialdemocrazia Tedesca, 1863-1914', *Rivista Storica Italiana*, 1968, fascicolo 1; L. B. Schapiro, *The The Communist Party of the Soviet Union* (2nd edition: London, 1970), Chapter 4.

31. V. I. Lenin, 'Chto Delat?' in *Polnoe Sobranie*, Volume 6, pp.121-2; I. V. Stalin, 'August Bebel' in *Sochineniya*, Volume 2, pp.201-8; G. E. Zinoviev, 'Vybory v Germanii' in *Sochineniya* (Leningrad, 1924-6), Volume 2, p.157.

The only contemporary Bolshevik leader known not to have espoused the SPD as a future organisational model was S. G. Shaumyan (who held somewhat syndicalist ideas): *Pis'ma, 1896-1918* (Erevan, 1958), pp.149-50.

32. R. V. Daniels, *The Conscience Of The Revolution*, Chapter 1.

33. J. P. Nettl, *Rosa Luxemburg* (London, 1966), Volume 1, Chapters 3-4; S. P. Baron, *Plekhanov*, Chapters 6, 7 and 9.

34. R. C. Elwood, *Russian Social-Democracy in the Underground: A Study of the RSDRP in the Ukraine, 1907-1914* (Assen, 1974), pp.36-87.

35. P. I. Lyashchenko, *Istoriya narodnogo khozyaistva*, Volume 2, Chapter 13; L. H. Haimson, 'The Problem of Urban Stability in Urban Russia, 1905-1917', *Slavic Review*, 1964 (no.4, pp.619-42) and 1965 (no.1, pp.1-22).

36. M. A. Tsyavlovski (editor), *Bol'sheviki: dokumenty po istorii bol'shevizma s 1903 po 1916 god byush, moskovskago okhrannago otdeleniya* (Moscow, 1918), p.92; G. E. Zinoviev, 'Chto Delat'? (Uroki isklyuchitel'nogo zakona)' in *Sochineniya*, Volume 1, pp.189-205; *Kommunisticheskaya Partiya Sovetskogo Soyuza v rezolyuziyakh i resheniyakh s" ezdov, konferentsii i plenumov TsK*, Volume 1 (8th Edition: Moscow, 1970), pp.328 and 334.

37. L. H. Haimson, 'The Problem of Urban Stability'.

38. P. I. Lyashchenko, *Istoriya narodnogo khozyaistva*, Volume 2, Chapter 13; L. H.

Haimson, 'The Problem of Urban Stability'; Robinson, *Rural Russia Under The Old Regime* Chapters 13–14.

39. G. Katkov, *Russia 1917: The February Revolution* (London, 1967), Chapters 1–2.
40. Nearly all the basic criticisms levelled at the SPD by Russian social-democrats were composed after rather than before the First World War.
41. R. Luxemburg, *Massenstreik, Partei und Gewerkschaften* (Hamburg, 1906) which is reprinted in *Gesammelte Werke* (Berlin, 1925), Volume 4, pp.410–79; R. Hilferding, *Das Finanzkapital* (Vienna, 1910); R. Michels, *Zur Soziologie des Parteiwesens in der Modernen Demokratie* (Leipzig, 1911); M. Weber, *From Max Weber: Essays in Sociology* (edited and translated by H. H. Gerth and C. W. Mills: London, 1967); G. Schmoller, *Schmollers Jahrbuch*, 1915, no.1.
42. V. I. Lenin, 'Chto Delat'?, ' in *Polnoe Sobranie Sochinenii*, Volume 6, pp.121–2; and *Shag vpered, dva shaga nazad*, Volume 8, pp.385–92.
43. V. I. Lenin, *Pod chuzhim flagom*, which was published after censorship cuts in 1915 and reprinted in full in 1917, and again in *Polnoe Sobranie Sochinenii*, Volume 26 (see especially pp.148–9); *Krakh Vtorogo Internatsionala*, which is reprinted in *Polnoe Sobranie Sochinenii*, Volume 26, pp.258–62. G. E. Zinoviev, *Rossiiskaya sotsial-demokratiya i russkii sotsial-shovinizm*, first published in 1915 and reprinted in *Sochineniya*, Volume 5 (see especially pp.136–48); *Esche o grazhdanskoi voine*, first published in 1916 and reprinted in *Sochineniya*, Volume 5, pp.243–50. N. I. Bukharin, *Imperializm i mirovoe khozyaistvo*, which has been translated as *Imperialism and the World Economy* (London, 1972): see especially pp.165–7. Y. M. Sverdlov, *Raskol v germanskoi sotsial-demokratii*, written in 1916, first published in 1917 and reprinted in *Izbrannye proizvedeniya* (Moscow, 1957), Volume 1.
44. A. G. Shlyapnikov, *Kanun semnadtsatogo goda: vospominaniya i dokumenty o rabochem dvizhenii v revolyutsionnom podpol'e za 1914–1916 gg.* (Part 1, 2nd edition and Part 2, 3rd edition: Moscow-Petrograd, 1923); T. Sapronov, *Iz istorii rabochego dvizheniya (po lichnym vospominaniyam)* (Moscow-Leningrad, 1925), Chapters 2–4.

Chapter 2

1. L. S. Gaponenko, *Rabochii klass Rossii v 1917 godu* (Moscow, 1970), pp.34–79; L. E. Mints, *Otkhod krest'yan za zarabotki* (Moscow, 1926); A. G. Rashin, *Formirovanie rabochego klassa Rossii: istorikoekonomicheskie ocherki* (Moscow, 1958); S. G. Strumilin, *Problemy ekonomiki truda* (Moscow, 1957); P. V. Volobuev, *Proletariat i burzhuaziya Rossii v 1917 godu* (Moscow, 1967).
2. S. M. Dubrovski, *Stolypinskaya zemel'naya reforma* (Moscow, 1963), p.518; L. S. Gaponenko, *Rabochii klass Rossii*, pp.75–6; L. E. Mints, *Otkhod krest'yan za zarabotki*; P. V. Volobuev, *Ekonomicheskaya politika Vremennogo pravitel'stva* (Moscow, 1972); M. Ferro, 'The Aspirations of Russian Society' in *Revolutionary Russia* (edited by R. Pipes: London, 1968).
3. P. V. Volobuev, *Ekonomicheskaya politika Vremennogo pravitel'stva*; R. A. Wade, *The Russian Search for Peace, February–October 1917* (Stanford, 1969).
4. *Sed'maya (aprel'skaya) vserossiiskaya konferentsiya RSDRP (bol'shevikov): protokoly*, pp.241–60 (which contain the official resolutions); D. A. Longley, 'The Divisions in the Bolshevik Party in March 1917', *Soviet Studies*, 1972–3, no.4.
5. A. Rabinowitch, *Prelude to Revolution: The Petrograd Bolsheviks and the July 1917 Uprising* (Indiana, 1968); R. A. Wade, *The Russian Search for Peace*, Chapters 5–7.
6. P. H. Avrich, *The Russian Revolution and the Factory Committees* (Columbia University Ph.D., 1961); M. Ferro, 'Le soldat russe', *Annales: Economie, Société,*

Civilisation, 1971, no.1, pp.14-39; L. S. Gaponenko, *Rabochii klass Rossii*, pp.68-9 and 182-200; D. G. P. Koenker, *Moscow Workers in 1917* (Ph.D. thesis, University of Michigan, 1976); S. F. Naida and N. F. Pudovkin, 'Bol'shevistskaya partiya v bor'be za krest'yanskie massy v 1917 godu', *Voprosy Istorii KPSS*, 1957, no.3, pp.40-7; L. A. Owen, *The Russian Peasant Movement, 1906-17* (London, 1937).

7. J. Keep, *The Russian Revolution: A Study in Mass Mobilisation* (London, 1976), Chapters 8-11.

8. P. H. Avrich, *The Russian Revolution and the Factory Committees*; J. Keep, *The Russian Revolution*, Chapters 6-8; Koenker, Chapters 6 and 7.

9. D. A. Chugaev, *Triumfal'noe shestvie sovetskoi vlasti* (Moscow, 1963); J. Keep, 'October In The Provinces' in R. Pipes, *Revolutionary Russia*; A. Rabinowitch, *The Bolsheviks Come to Power: The Revolution of 1917 in Petrograd* (New York, 1976).

10. T. Sapronov, *Iz istorii rabochego dvizheniya*, p.126.

11. S. G. Strumilin, *Vserossiiskaya perepis' chlenov RKP(b)* in *Statistiko-ekonomicheskie ocherki* (Moscow, 1958); V. V. Anikeev, 'Svedeniya o bol'shevistskikh organizatsiyakh s marta po dekabr' 1917 goda, *Voprosy Istorii KPSS*, 1958, no.2.

12. Y. M. Sverdlov, *Shestoi s"ezd RSDRP (bol'shevikov): avgust 1917 goda; protokoly*, pp.36-7.

13. G. I. Bokii, *Sed'maya (aprel'skaya) konferentsiya*, p.149; A. S. Bubnov, *Bol'shaya Sovetskaya Entsiklopediya* (1st edition: Moscow, 1930), Volume 11, column 531.

14. Y. M. Sverdlov, *Shestoi s"ezd*, pp.36-7. T. H. Rigby discusses exaggerations in *Communist Party Membership in the Soviet Union* (London, 1968), pp.61-2.

15. *Protokoly Tsentral'nogo Komiteta RSDRP(b): avgust 1917-fevral' 1918* (Moscow, 1958), p.94; *Sed'moi (ekstrennii) s"ezd RKP(b): mart 1918 goda; stenograficheskii otchet*, pp.3-4.

16. The Central Committee handed out a questionnaire to local delegates to the Sixth Party Congress: *Shestoi s"ezd*, pp.319-90. If we excise those reports which duplicate material to be found in others, we are left with forty-seven reports containing an answer to the question on the party's numerical strength. Forty-one revealed no drop in membership after the July Days.

Of the six answers reporting such a drop, two specified the number: Serpukhov lost 135, Kuznetsovo lost 15. The questionnaire reports must obviously be taken with a pinch of salt (see this Chapter, note 14), but they probably indicate at least broad trends in this particular instance.

17. S. G. Strumilin, *Vserossiiskaya perepis' chlenov RKP(b)*.

18. Sverdlov gave the geographical distribution in *Shestoi s"ezd*, pp.36-7. The Sixth Party Congress questionnaire reports have 39 per cent of local organisations working exclusively amongst the working class and 83 per cent working amongst both workers and other social groups.

19. For a Menshevik comment see Izmailov, *Chrezvychainoe sobranie upolnomochennykh fabrik i zavodov g. Petrograda*, no. 1-2, 18 March 1918 (which has been reprinted in *Kontinent*, no.2: see p.395).

Bolshevik comments on their peasant lad recruits are discussed in Chapter 3, pp.70-1.

20. Chapter 3, pp.71-2.

21. S. G. Strumilin, *Vserossiiskaya perepis' chlenov RKP(b)*.

22. Official resolution, *Shestoi s"ezd*, p.268.

23. Chapter 4, p.103.

24. Y. M. Sverdlov, *Shestoi s"ezd*, pp.36-7.

25. Central Committee questionnaire, *Shestoi s"ezd*, pp.319-90.
26. T. Sapronov, *Iz istorii rabochego dvizheniya*, p.126.
27. Nor was it seriously taken up for some years: Chapter 6, pp.137-8.
28. D. A. Longley, 'The Divisions in the Bolshevik Party in March 1917'; T. Sapronov, *Iz istorii rabochego dvizheniya*, Chapter 5; V. P. Antonov-Saratovski, 'Saratov s fevralya po oktyabr', *Proletarskaya Revolyutsiya*, 1924, no.4/27.
29. D. A. Longley, 'The Divisions in the the Bolshevik Party in March 1917'
30. The influence exerted by rank-and-file opinion is discussed in this Chapter, pp.53-4.
31. M. Frumkin on Krasnoyarsk, 'Fevral'-oktyabr' 1917 g. v Krasnoyarske', *Proletarskaya Revolyutsiya*, 1923, no.9/21, pp.145-6; V. P. Antonov-Saratovski on Saratov, 'Saratov c fevralya po oktyabr', p.178.
32. Y. M. Sverdlov, *Shestoi s"ezd*, p.38; *Perepiska sekretariata TsK RSDRP(b) s mestnymi partiinymi organizatsiyami: mart-oktyabr' 1917 g.; sbornik dokumentov* (Moscow, 1957), docs, 30, 33, 66, 88, 92, 132, 140, 155, 156 and 165.
33. *Protokoly Tsentral'nogo Komiteta*, p.15 (on the Interdistricters); N. Sukhanov, *Zapiski o revolyutsii* (Berlin, 1923), Volume 6, pp.42-3.
34. This is the impression given by *Protokoly vtoroi moskovskoi oblastnoi konferentsii RSDRP(b) 1917 goda, Proletarskaya Revolyutsiya*, 1929, no.12/95, 144-5; *Shestoi s"ezd*, p.55; *Perepiska sekretariata*, Volume 1, docs. 213, 231, 260, 264, 337, 361 and 367.
35. The Sixth Party Congress questionnaire reports have only five party organisations with over 750 members claiming to possess no intellectuals: Baku, Saratov, Makeevka-Yuzovka-Petrovsk, Gorlovka-Shcherbinovka and Orekhovo-Zuevo. The Baku and Saratov claims were flagrant fabrications. The other three organisations were situated in relatively non-urbanised areas of the country.
36. The Central Committee sanctioned a survey of Sixth Party Congress delegates and collected information about 171 of the 264 delegates (whether with voting or consultative rights). The results (in *Shestoi s"ezd*, pp.294-300) point to the considerable importance of intellectuals in local and central party bodies.
37. Soviet salaries are discussed by J. Jeep, in *The Russian Revolution*, pp.67-89 and 138.
38. *Shestoi s"ezd*, pp.294-300.
39. *Shestoi s"ezd*, pp.294-300.
40. See V. P. Nogin's remarks in *Sed'maya (aprel'skaya) konferentsiya*, pp. 322-5.
41. *Shestoi s"ezd*, pp.294-300.
42. *Shestoi s"ezd*, pp.294-300.
43. V. V. Anikeev, 'Svedeniya o bol'shevistskikh organizatsiyakh'.
44. Tashkent was one of the few social-democratic centres not undergoing an organisational split before the October Revolution: P. T. Alekseenkova in the preface to *Materialy i dokumenty pervogo s"ezda kompartii Turkestana* (Tashkent, 1934).
45. For example, V. P. Antonov-Saratovski, 'Saratov s fevralya po oktyabr', pp.164-7.
46. Not that decisions were not often subverted, nor that uproars were not often provoked; but the Petersburg Committee minutes indicate just how carefully officials scrutinised each other's behaviour: *Pervyi legal'nyi Petersburgskii komitet bol'shevikov v 1917 godu: sbornik materialov i protokolov zasedanii* (edited by P. Kudelli: Moscow-Leningrad, 1927).
47. *Shestoi s"ezd*, pp.37-8.

48. *Pervyi legal'nyi Petersburgskii komitet* supplies valuable data here.

49. For Vyborg see the detailed account by D. A. Longley, in 'The Divisions In The Bolshevik Party In March 1917'; for Saratov see V. P. Antonov-Saratovski, 'Saratov s fevralya po oktyabr', pp.169-70.

50. M. Frumkin, 'Fevral'-oktyabr' 1917 g. v Krasnoyarske', pp.145-6. Sverdlov described the general problem in *Shestoi s"ezd*, p.38.

51. V. P. Antonov-Saratovski, 'Saratov s fevralya po oktyabr' 1917 g.', pp.185-6.

52. The events of 1918 were yet to show that committees could move a very long way adrift from rank-and-file opinion: Chapter 3, pp.79-83.

53. V. P. Antonov-Saratovski, 'Saratov s fevralya po oktyabr'', pp.193-5 gives useful information on this phenomenon.

54. D. Longley, 'The Divisions In The Bolshevik Party In March 1917'.

55. The delegate lists are given in L. Trotski, *Stalinskaya shkola falsifikatsii* (Berlin, 1932) and *Sed'maya (aprel'skaya) konferentsiya.*

56. This estimate is put forward, amidst other organisational data, in F. G. Zaikina, 'Organizatsionnaya perestroika kommunisticheskoi partii posle Oktyabrya (Oktyabr' 1917-1918 gg.)' *Voprosy Istorii KPSS*, 1966, no.11, p.52. The dubiety of Zaikina's study is suggested by the fact that neither Smolensk nor Ekaterinoslav, which are included in her list, for late summer, claimed to have provincial committees at the time of the Sixth Party Congress.

57. Y. Grunt, 'Oktyabr' v Kolomne', *Proletarskaya Revolyutsiya*, 1922, no.10, pp.323-4.

58. *Perepiska sekretariata*, Volume 1, p.379; 'Iz protokolov zasedanii Moskovskogo oblastnogo byuro 1917 goda', *Proletarskaya Revolyutsiya*, 1928, no.10/81, p.186; *Shestoi s"ezd*, p.172.

59. *Perepiska sekretariata*, Volume 1, doc.236.

60. V. P. Antonov-Saratovski, 'Saratov s fevralya po oktyabr' 1917 goda', Part 2, p.184.

61. *Perepiska sekretariata*, Volume 1, docs.270, 282 and 435; *Protokoly pervoi moskovskoi oblastnoi konferentsii tsentral'nogo-promyshlennogo raiona* in *Proletarskaya Revolyutsiya* 1929, no.10/93, pp.205-6.

62. On the role played by the Moscow Regional Bureau's *Sotsial-Demokrat* see *Shestoi s"ezd*, pp.330, 334, and 340-1.

63. *Ural'skii Rabochii* (Ekaterinburg), no.3, 5 January 1918 (as well as L. Elenskii, 'Oktyabr' na Urale', *Proletarskaya Revolyutsiya*, 1922, no.10, pp.513-14); *Perepiska sekretariata*, Volume 1, docs.105 and 131.

64. *Shestoi s"ezd*, p.347; E. V. Bosh, 'Oblastnoi partiinyi komitet yugo-zapadnogo kraya sotsial-demokratov (bol'shevikov)', *Proletarskaya Revolyutsiya*, 1924, no.2/25, p.133; *Perepiska sekretariata*, Volume 1, doc.213.

65. A. S. Bubnov and V. N. Yakovleva in *Protokoly zasedanii Moskovskogo oblastnogo byuro: mai-iyun' 1917 g.* in *Proletarskaya Revolyutsiya*, 1927, no.4/63, pp.240-3; E. V. Bosh, 'Oblastnoi partiinyi komitet yugo-zapadnogo kraya', pp.128-9.

66. E. V. Bosh, 'Oblastnoi partiinyi komitet yugo-zapadnogo krzya', pp.141-3; *Moskovskoe oblastnoe byuro pered oktyabr'skimi dnyami* in *Proletarskaya Revolyutsiya*, 1922, no.10, p.473. Ivan Morozov described suburb-level political activity in October in *Kommuna* (Samara), no.1170, 7 November 1922.

67. *Protokoly i rezolyutsii Byuro TsK RSDRP(b): mart 1917 g.* in *Voprosy Istorii KPSS*, 1962, no.3, pp.136-47.

68. *Sed'maya (aprel'skaya) konferentsiya*, pp.228 and 322-5.

69. *Shestoi s"ezd*, pp.266 and 439. Y. K. Milonov was the author of the motion to include regional representatives: *Shestoi s"ezd*, pp.20-1 and 174.
70. The end of the inner subcommittee is deducible from *Protokoly Tsentral'nogo Komiteta*, pp.3-121.
71. *Protokoly i rezolyutsii Byuro TsK*, pp.149-50; K. T. Sverdlova, *Yakov Mikhailovich Sverdlov* (Moscow, 1957), pp.334-5; *Protokoly Tsentral'nogo Komiteta*, pp.115-16.
72. On Sverdlov's mathematics see this Chapter, p.43.
73. *Rabochii Put'*, no.41, 20 October 1917; *Protokoly Tsentral'nogo Komiteta*, pp. 106-8.
74. M. I. Akhun and V. A. Petrov, *Bol'sheviki i armiya v 1905-1917 gg.* (Leningrad, 1929); A. Rabinowitch, *Prelude to Revolution*; *Protokoly Tsentral'nogo Komiteta*, pp.20-5.
75. *Protokoly Tsentral'nogo Komiteta*, pp.3-121; *Shestoi s"ezd*, pp.147-50; *Perepiska sekretariata*, Volume 1, p.vi.
76. Not that the seizure of power was highly co-ordinated across the country. On the contrary, most local committees were not given advance notice of the precise timing of the Petrograd uprising: J. Keep, 'October In The Provinces'.
77. Removal from party posts was a measure contemplated by Lenin upon hearing the rumour that Moscow Bolshevik leaders had been co-operating with the Mensheviks: *Polnoe Sobranie Sochinenii*, Volume 34, pp.73-8.
78. Y. M. Sverdlov, *Shestoi s"ezd*, p.37.
79. Y. M. Sverdlov, *Shestoi s"ezd*, p.38.
80. On Kronstadt see A. Rabinowitch, *Prelude to Revolution*, Chapters 5-8; on Moscow as well as Kiev see the references in this Chapter, note 66.
81. *Perepiska sekretariata*, Volume 1, docs.328, 364 and 389.
82. On the Far-East Regional Bureau: *Perepiska sekretariata*, Volume 1, doc.436 and Volume 2, doc.44; on the Moscow Regional Bureau: *Protokoly Tsentral'nogo Komiteta*, doc.2 and *Protokoly vtoroi moskovskoi oblastnoi konferentsii*, pp.136-40.
83. See in particular his 'Gosudarstvo i revolyutsiya' in *Polnoe Sobranie Sochinenii*, Volume 33, pp.1-120.
84. On requests for manpower: *Perepiska sekretariata*, Volume 1, docs.202, 213, 222, 226, 263, 264, 266, 272, 279, 286, 307, 309, 316, 329, 337, 362, 390, 391, 396, 402, 403, 414, 446 and 460. On requests for newspapers and the like: *Perepiska sekretariata*, Volume 1, docs.174, 175, 183, 185, 187, 188, 190, 201, 219, 235, 238, 239, 250, 263, 269, 284, 289, 321, 336, 339 and 405. On requests for detailed guidance: *Perepiska sekretariata*, Volume 1, docs.236, 239, 260, 270, 274, 284, 323, 337, 358 and 405.
85. *Perepiska sekretariata*, Volume 2, doc.1.
86. *Perepiska sekretariata*, Volume 2, doc.21.

Chapter 3
1. D. A. Chugaev, *Triumfal'noe shestvie sovetskoi vlasti*; J. Keep, 'October in the Provinces'.
2. E. H. Carr, *The Bolshevik Revolution*, Volume 2 (London, 1952), Chapter 15 and Volume 3 (London, 1953), Chapter 21.
3. M. P. Iroshnikov, *Sozdanie sovetskogo tsentral'nogo gosudarstvennogo apparata: Sovet Narodnykh Komissarov i narodnye komissariaty, oktyabr' 1917 g.-yanvar' 1918 g.* (Moscow-Leningrad, 1966); K. G. Federov, *VTsIK v pervye gody sovetskoi vlasti, 1917-1920 gg.* (Moscow, 1957); T. H. Rigby, 'The First Proletarian Government', *British Journal of Political Science*, January 1974, pp.37-52.

4. M. Vladimirski gave a rueful contemporary description in *Osnovnye polozheniya ustanovleniya granits administrativno-khozyaistvennykh raionov: doklad na vtoroi sessii VTsIK 8-go sozyna* (Moscow, 1920), pp.52-4.

5. *Chrezvychainoe sobranie upolnomochennykh fabrik i zavodov g. Petrograda;* V. Z. Drobizhev, *Rabochii klass sovetskoi Rossii v pervyi god proletarskoi diktatury* (Moscow, 1975), pp.38, 101-2, 107-8 and 118; E. G. Gimpel'son, *Sovetskii rabochii klass, 1918-1920 gg.: sotsialno-politicheskie izmeneniya* (Moscow, 1974), pp.27-9 and 76-86.

6. D. J. Male, *Russian Peasant Organisation Before Collectivisation: A Study of Commune and Gathering, 1925-1930* (Cambridge, 1971), pp.18-23; Y. Taniuchi, *The Village Gathering in Russia in the Mid-Twenties* (Birmingham, 1968), pp.8-13.

7. O. H. Radkey, *The Election to the Russian Constituent Assembly of 1917* (Massachussetts, 1950).

8. I. Deutscher, *Trotsky: The Prophet Armed, 1879-1921* (London, 1954), Chapter 11; E. H. Carr, *The Bolshevik Revolution,* Volume 3, Chapter 21.

9. *Chrezvychainoe sobranie upolnomochennykh fabrik i zavodov g. Petrograda; Perepiska sekretariata,* Volume 3, docs.196, 202, 231 and 329; F. Kaplan, *Bolshevik Ideology and the Ethics of Soviet Labour, 1917-1920: The Formative Years* (London, 1968), Chapters 5-8; E. H. Carr, *The Bolshevik Revolution,* Volume 2, Chapter 16.

10. S. G. Strumilin, *Vserossiiskaya perepis' chlenov RKP(b); Partiinaya Zhizn',* no.19, October 1967, p.10.

11. *Sed'moi (ekstrennii) s"ezd,* pp.115-16; *Vos'moi s"ezd RKP(b): mart 1919 goda; protokoly* (Moscow, 1959), p.280.

12. F. I. Goloshchekin, *Ural'skii Rabochii* (Ekaterinburg), no.3, 5 January 1918.

13. On October Communists see T. H. Rigby, *Communist Party Membership,* pp.63-9.

14. On Ivanovo:*Shestoi s"ezd* (p.333) and *Rabochii Krai* (Ivanovo), no.56/141, 16 May 1918; on the Urals: *Ural'skii Rabochii* (Ekaterinburg), no.69/166, 13 April 1918.

15. The ballast metaphor is used in *Ural'skii Rabochii* (Ekaterinburg), no.69/166, 13 April 1918.

16. See this Chapter, note 9.

17. *Perepiska sekretariata,* Volume 2, docs.250 and 275.

18. Y. M. Sverdlov, *Sed'moi (ekstrennii) s"ezd,* pp.3-4.

19. The drive to establish a rural organisational network was seriously begun only later in the year: Chapter 4, pp.96-7.

20. *Rabochii Krai* (Ivanovo), no.49/134, 3 May 1918; *Ural'skii Rabochii* (Ekaterinburg), no.3, 5 January 1918; *Otchet severnoi oblastnoi konferentsii, s 3-go po 6-go aprelya* (St Petersburg, 1918; *Perepiska sekretariata,* Volume 2, docs,314, 325, 329, 373, 382, 392, 396, 401, 432, 479 and Volume 3, docs.205, 285, 318, 319, 420. The Secretariat recognised what was happening:*Perepiska sekretariata,* Volume 2, docs.127, 161, 234 and 275.

21. *Petrogradskaya Pravda,* no.65/291, 3 April 1918; *Ural'skii Rabochii* (Ekaterinburg), no.3, 5 January 1918 and no.69/166, 12 April 1918; *Protokoly tret'ei moskovskoi oblastnoi konferentsii RSDRP(b) 1917 goda* in *Proletarskaya Revolyutsisya,* 1930, no.10/105, pp.98-120; *Perepiska sekretariata,* Volume 3, doc. 251; *Bor'ba za vlast' sovetov v tobol'skoi (tyumenskoi) gubernii, 1917-1920 gg.: sbornik dokumental'nykh materialov* (Sverdlovsk, 1967), doc.102.

22. On chairmen see E. V. Bosh, *God bor'by* (Moscow-Leningrad, 1925), pp.88-92

and *Perepiska sekretariata*, Volume 3, doc. 176; on secretaries see *Perepiska sekretariata*, Volume 3, doc.251.

23. On the Brest-Litovsk controversy see this Chapter, pp.79–83.

24. M. I. Minkov, *Vyatskaya Pravda*, nos.43–7, 23–8 February 1923.

25. On renegacy see G. Lelevich, 'Chetyre mogily: otryvki iz vospominanii', *Proletarskaya Revolutsiya*, 1922, no.6, p.19.

26. According to Provincial Committee candidate S. P. Efremov's memoirs in *Ocherki istorii vologdskoi organizatsii KPSS*, 1895–1968 (Vologda, 1969), pp.203–4.

27. See I. V. Mgeladze's biting comments about the Northern region in *Otchet severnoi oblastnoi konferentsii*, pp.29–30.

28. On Astrakhan: *Ocherki istorii astrakhanskoi organizatsii KPSS* (Volgograd, 1971, pp.178–80); on Penza: *Izvestiya* (Penza), no.56/259, 27 March 1918 and following numbers; on Nikolaev: *Vtoroi s"ezd KP(b)U: protokoly* (Istpart KPbU, 1927), pp.34–7 (where the phenomenon is called 'an epidemic').

29. Examples are to be found in *Vtoroi s'ezd KP(b)U*, pp.31–7; A. Vasilev, 'Pervaya sovetskaya vlast' v Krymu i ee padenie', *Proletarskaya Revolyutsiya*, 1922, no.7, pp.9–10; S. Shreiber, 'K protokolam pervogo vseukrainskogo soveshchaniya bol'shevikov', *Letopis' Revolyutsiya*, 1926, no.5/20, p.62.

30. *Perepiska sekretariata*, Volume 3, doc.303.

31. *Otchet severnoi oblastnoi konferentsii*, p.8; *Sed'moi (ekstrennii) s"ezd*, pp.3–5 and 163.

32. Central Committee minutes for November 1917 through to February 1918 are given in *Protokoly Tsentral'nogo Komiteta*, docs.34–46.

33. Thus, in Sverdlov's absence, the Secretariat was markedly reluctant to give a ruling in the dispute between the Bolshevik military commander Antonov-Ovseenko and the Donbass Regional Committee: *Perepiska sekretariata*, Volume 2, p.151.

34. *Perepiska sekretariata*, Volume 3, doc.9.

35. B. Z. Stankina (who worked in the Secretariat in 1918), 'O rabote Sekretariata TsK RKP(b), aprel'-1918 g—mart 1919 g.', *Istoricheskii Arkhiv*, 1958, no.3, p.161.

36. *Perepiska sekretariata*, Volume 3, doc.36.

37. *Sed'moi (ekstrennii) s"ezd*, p.164.

38. Chapter 4, pp.107–8.

39. R. V. Daniels, *The Conscience of the Revolution*, Chapter 3.

40. See the study by W. E. Mosse, 'Revolution in Saratov: October to November 1917', *Slavonic and East European Review, 1917*, pp.586–602.

41. *Perepiska sekretariata*, Volume 2, docs.314, 325, 329, 373, 382, 401, 432, 440, 467, 479, 480; Volume 3, docs.205, 273, 285, 298.

42. *Perepiska sekretariata*, Volume 3, doc.300. For further examples see the same volume, docs.176, 240, 252 and 272.

43. *Ural'skii Rabochii* (Ekaterinburg), no.63/160, 6 April 1918.

44. *Perepiska sekretariata*, Volume 2, doc.209; *Ocherki istorii astrakhanskoi organizatsii* (Volgograd, 1971), pp. 178–80.

45. P. Voevodin, '20 let raboty v bol'shevistskikh organizatsiyakh i vstrechi s Leninym', *Proletarskaya Revolyutsiya*, 1922, no.6, pp.188–92; *Vtoroi s"ezd KP(b)U*, pp.34–7; E. V. Bosh, *God bor'by*, pp.108–9.

46. Chapter 4, pp.103–6.

47. D. Z. Oznobishin, *Politika partii v period peredyshki 1918 g.* (Moscow, 1973), pp.64–79.

48. R. V. Daniels, *The Conscience Of The Revolution*, pp.76–7 and 98–104.

49. *Bor'ba* (Tsaritsyn), no.59, 21 March (6 March) 1918; *Perepiska sekretariata*, Volume 3, doc.23.

50. Z. N. Berlina and N. T. Gorbunov, 'Brestskii mir i mestnye partiinye organizatsii', *Voprosy Istorii KPSS*, 1963, no.9, p.40 (on Yakovleva).

51. *Protokoly Tsentral'nogo Komiteta*, doc.38.

52. *Bor'ba* (Tsaritsyn), nos.40, 15 February (27 January) 1918 and 47, 19 (6) February 1918.

53. Charles Duval gives a detailed account of the behaviour of Lenin and Sverdlov in March 1918 in *Yakov Mikhailovich Sverdlov: Founder of the Bolshevik Party Machine* in R. C. Elwood (editor), *Reconsiderations on the Russian Revolution* (Slavica, 1976), pp.226-7. Not all the Left Communists' troubles at the Congress, however, stemmed from Sverdlovian machinations. Travel difficulties were also important as regards the Ukraine, the Volga and the Transcaucasus. Lenin's supporters too suffered as a result. Thus, for example, the Tsaritsyn Bolsheviks (who are discussed in this Chapter, p.81) failed to get their delegation to the Congress: *Sed'moi (ekstrennii) s"ezd*, pp.200-6.

54. *Rabochii Krai* (Ivanovo), no.11/96, 19 March 1918.

55. *Ural'skii Rabochii* (Ekaterinburg), nos.24/121, 15 February 1918 and 47/144, 19 (6) March 1918.

56. See the remarks of P. Baturin, director of the local soviet executive committee's military department, *Rabochii Krai* (Ivanovo), no.44/129, 26 April 1918.

57. *Protokoly Tsentral'nogo Komiteta*, doc. 38.

58. See the criticisms of Chicherin's conduct of foreign policy in *Ural'skii Rabochii* (Ekaterinburg), nos.87/184, 11 May 1918 and 91/188, 16 May 1918.

59. See Left Communist G. Safarov's explanation in *Ural'skii Rabochii* (Ekaterinburg), no.81/178, 28 April 1918.

Chapter 4

1. I. Deutscher, *Trotsky: The Prophet Armed*, Chapter 12; J. Erickson, *The Soviet High Command* (London, 1962), Chapter 3.

2. D. Footman, *Civil War in Russia* (London, 1961); S. F. Naida (editor), *Istoriya grazhdanskoi voiny v SSSR* (Moscow, 1959); R. H. Ullman, *Anglo-Soviet Relations, 1917-1921* (Princeton, 1968).

3. E. H. Carr, *The Bolshevik Revolution, 1917-1923*, Volume 1 (London, 1950), Chapters 7-9; K. G. Federov, *VTsIK v pervye gody sovetskoi vlasti*.

4. D. J. Male, *Russian Peasant Organisation*, pp.1-12; A. Nove, *An Economic History of the USSR* (London, 1960), Chapter 3; Y. Taniuchi, *The Village Gathering in Russia*, pp.14-20.

5. E. V. Gimpel'son, *Sovetskii rabochii klass*.

6. L. B. Schapiro, *The Origins of the Communist Autocracy* (Massachussetts, 1955); A. J. Mayer, *The Politics and Diplomacy of Peacemaking: Containment and Counter-revolution at Versailles, 1918-1919* (London, 1968), Chapters 10 and 13-6.

7. G. E. Zinoviev, *Vos'moi s"ezd*, p. 280; S. G. Strumilin, *Vserossiiskaya perepis' chlenov RKP(b)*.

8. *Pravda*, 22 May 1918.

9. G. E. Zinoviev, *Vos'moi s"ezd*, p.294.

10. S. G. Strumilin, *Vserossiiskaya perepis' chlenov RKP(b)*; V. P. Antonov-Saratovski, 'Otbleski besed s Il'ichem', *Proletarskaya Revolyutsiya*, 1924, no.3/26, pp.188-9.

11. *Perepiska sekretariata*, Volume 3, doc.381; *Pravda*, no.29, 8 February 1919.

12. *Petrogradskaya Pravda*, 123/349, 14 June 1918; *Kommuna* (Samara), no.78, 15 March 1918.
13. See this Chapter, note 7.
14. *Vos'moi s"ezd*, pp.457-74; Y. P. Petrov, *Partiinoe stroitel'stvo v sovetskoi armii i flote: deyatel'nost' KPSS po sozdaniyu i ukrepleniyu politorganov, partiinykh i komsomol'skikh organizatsii v vooruzhennykh silakh, 1918-1961 gg.* (Moscow, 1964), p.69.
15. After all, a considerable number of working-class Red Army soldiers in 1918 were volunteers: see this Chapter, p.87.
16. *Pravda*, no.124, 26 June 1918; *Perepiska sekretariata*, Volume 3, docs.144 and 157.
17. *Izvestiya* (Penza), no.5/388, 7 January 1919; *Perepiska sekretariata*, Volume 5, docs.297 and 304 and Volume 6, docs.50, 185, 240 and 269.
18. Naturally, however, party life was still a long, long way from being as highly disciplined as it became by the mid-1920s: see Chapter 7.
19. S. Milnichuk's memoirs in *Proletarskaya Revolyutsiya*, 1922, no.11, pp.146-60.
20. *Perepiska sekretariata*, Volume 4, doc.111 (25 October 1918).
21. *Kommunisticheskaya partiya Sovetskogo Soyuza v rezolyutsiyakh i resheniyakh*, Volume 2, pp.114-15; *Pravda*, no.5, 10 January 1919; *Vos'moi s"ezd*, pp.421-3.
22. S. I. Gusev, *Pravda*, 3 January 1919; *Kommunisticheskaya partiya Sovetskogo Soyuza v rezolyutsiyakh i resheniyakh*, Volume 2, pp.11-12.
23. Cited in N. Davies, *White Eagle, Red Star: The Polish-Soviet War, 1919-20* (London, 1972), pp.118-19.
24. *Perepiska sekretariata*, Volume 8, doc.612.
25. *Perepiska sekretariata*, Volume 6, doc.50; F. G. Zaikina, 'Organizatsionnaya perestroika kommunisticheskoi partii', p.56.
26. *Perepiska sekretariata*, Volume 4, docs.5, 8, 13, 21, 22, 59, 70, 75, 100, 101, 106; Volume 6, docs.51, 96, 100, 101, 149.
27. *Izvestiya* (Penza), no.271/374, 20 December 1918; *Rabochii Krai* (Ivanovo), no.197/282, 6 November 1918.
28. *Zvezda* (Novgorod), no.64, 5 March 1919.
29. *Perepiska sekretariata*, Volume 4, doc.437.
30. *Nizhegorodskaya Kommuna* (Nizhni Novgorod), no.56, 12 March 1919.
31. *Perepiska sekretariata*, Volume 6, doc.359.
32. *Vos'moi s"ezd*, p.425.
33. *Materialy i dokumenty pervogo s"ezda kompartii Turkestana*, pp.45-8.
34. Unfortunately, the minutes of most regional party gatherings in this period have not yet been made public.
35. *Perepiska sekretariata*, especially Volume 5; *Pravda*, no.271, 13 December 1918.
36. *Vtoroi s"ezd KP(b)U*, pp.21-33 and 117-39.
37. *Perepiska sekretariata*, Volume 3, docs.318, 319, 327, 360, 420; Volume 4, docs.129, 228, 234, 263, 309, 451, 464, 465; Volume 5, docs.197, 211, 214, 236, 242, 322; Volume 6, docs.179, 184, 188, 190, 192, 205, 208, 247, 254, 260, 266, 279, 293, 294, 302, 309, 316, 332, 348, 354, 358, 369, 472.
38. See this Chapter, pp.000-00.
39. *Perepiska sekretariata*, Volume 6, doc.266.
40. For provincial committees: *Perepiska sekretariata*, Volume 4, doc.437 (Vladimir), Volume 6, docs.293 (Kaluga) and 373 (Vitebsk); for regional committees: *Perepiska sekretariata*, Volume 4, pp.252-3 (Moscow) and Volume 5, pp.126-8 (North).

41. *Nizhegorodskaya Kommuna* (Nizhni Novgorod), no.25, 3 February 1919; *Perepiska sekretariata*, Volume 4, doc.437; *Petrogradskaya Pravda*, no.123/349, 14 June 1918.
42. *Pravda*, no.125, 6 October 1918.
43. V. A. Avanesov, *Vos'moi s"ezd*, p.176.
44. Numerous letters, telegrams and conversations are reprinted in *The Trotsky Papers* (edited by J. Meijer: The Hague, 1964).
45. Nevertheless they caused a certain amount of irritation among several officials such as N. Osinski: *Vos'moi s"ezd*, p.164.
46. S. Liberman, *Dela i lyudi: na sovetskom stroe* (New York, 1945); L. Trotsky, *Stalin: An Appraisal of the Man and His Influence* (London, 1947), Chapter 8.
47. B. Z. Stankina, 'O rabote Sekretariata', pp.165-6; M. Gaisinski, *Yakov Mikhailovich Sverdlov: ego zhizn' i deyatel'nost'* (Moscow-Leningrad, 1929), p.96; *Izvestiya Tsentral'nogo Komiteta*, no.8, 2 December 1919.
48. *Perepiska sekretariata*, Volume 3, pp.92-5; *Izvestiya Tsentral'nogo Komiteta*, no.8, 2 December 1919.
49. *Perepiska sekretariata*, Volume 4, doc.243 and Volume 5, doc.210; *Rabochii Krai* (Ivanovo), no.183/282, 6 November 1918.
50. *Pravda*, no.271, 13 December 1918; V. P. Khmelevski, *Severnoi oblastnoi komitet* (Leningrad, 1972), pp.201-7.
51. *Perepiska sekretariata*, Volume 5, p.61; V. P. Nikolaeva, 'Turkkomissiya kak polnomochnyi organ TsK RKP(b)', *Voprosy Istorii KPSS*, 1958, no.2, pp.73-88; *Vtoroi s"ezd KP(b)U*, p.173.
52. Y. M. Sverdlov, *Izbrannye proizvedeniya* (Moscow, 1976), p.250.
53. V. I. Lenin, *Vos'moi s"ezd*, p.24.
54. B. Z. Stankina, 'O rabote Sekretariata', p.162.
55. *Stenograficheskii otchet pyatoi nizhegorodskoi gubernskoi konferentsii RKP (bol'shevikov)* (Nizhni Novgorod, 1918), p.67; *Nizhegorodskaya Kommuna*, no.27, 6 February 1919 and no.32, 12 February 1919.
56. N. A. Petrovichev, *Partiinoe stroitel'stvo: uchebnoe posobie* (Moscow, 1970), p.141; *Perepiska sekretariata*, Volume 6, doc.114.
57. *Perepiska sekretariata*, Volume 6, doc.128.
58. *Pravda*, no.155, 12 March 1919.
59. *Proletarii* (Simbirsk), nos.51 (2 February 1919), 73 (28 February 1919) and 74 (1 March 1919).
60. *Pravda*, no.55, 12 March 1919; *Vos'moi s"ezd*, pp.30-1. Other calls of a similar kind are given in *Zvezda* (Novgorod), no.57, 25 February 1919 and in *Bor'ba za vlast' sovetov v astrakhanskom krae*, pp.130-1.
61. See Chapter 8.
62. G. E. Zinoviev, *Vos'moi s"ezd*, pp.160-2, 219-25, 277-95; Lenin, *Vos'moi s"ezd*, pp.11-26.
63. *Vos'moi s"ezd*, pp.178-80.
64. Osinski, *Vos'moi s"ezd*, pp.27-8, 164-7, 182-4, 187-97, 216-18, 303-14, 319-22; Sapronov, *Vos'moi s"ezd*, pp.169-70, 201-3, 314-15.
65. See this Chapter, note 62.

Chapter 5
1. E. H. Carr, *The Bolshevik Revolution*, Volume 3, Chapters 24-5; A. J. Mayer, *The Politics And Diplomacy Of Peacemaking*, Chapters 13-16.

2. E. H. Carr, *The Bolshevik Revolution*, Volume 2, Chapter 17; M. Y. Latsis, *Dva goda bor'by na vnutrennom fronte* (Moscow, 1920), pp.75-6.

3. E. V. Gimpel'son, *Sovetskii rabochii klass*, pp.76-7.

4. A. Varentsova, 'O partiinoi rabote za 1920 god', *Ivanovo-Voznesenskii gubernskii ezhegodnik (kalendar'-spravochnik) na 1921 god* (Ivanovo, 1921), pp.74-6; *Perepiska sekretariata*, Volume 8. docs.412 and 612; A. Berkman, *The Bolshevik Myth (Diary 1920-1922)* (London, 1925), pp.32-41.

5. *Pravda*, no.86, 24 April 1919; *Izvestiya Tsentral'nogo Komiteta*, no.15, 24 March 1920.

6. *Roslavl'skii Kommunist*, no.89/199, 13 September 1919.

7. *Izvestiya Tsentral'nogo Komiteta*, no.15, 24 March 1920.

8. S. G. Strumilin, *Vserossiiskaya perepis' chlenov RKP(b)*.

9. *Izvestiya Tsentral'nogo Komiteta*, no.15, 24 March 1920 (though this report must be treated with caution since the Yaroslavl figure was contradicted in the previous number of the same journal).

10. *Izvestiya Tsentral'nogo Komiteta*, no.15, 24 March 1920. And it was said that merely 4 per cent of Petrograd Bolsheviks in January 1920 had joined before the February Revolution: V. Vasilevski, *Petrogradskaya Pravda*, no.65, 24 March 1920.

11. As we shall see in Chapter 6, however, this is not to say that the old rank-and-filers were permanently reconciled to submission to higher party authority.

12. *Petrogradskaya Pravda*, no.62, 20 March 1920.

13. *The Smolensk Archives*, WKP 6 (9 January 1920).

14. *Kommunar* (Tula), no.3/449, 4 January 1920.

15. A. Berkman, *The Bolshevik Myth*, pp.36-7.

16. V. Shulgin, *Tysyacha devyat'sot dvadtsatyi god* (Sofia, 1922), p.83.

17. This theme is taken up again in Chapter 6, pp.141-57.

18. A. Berkman, *The Bolshevik Myth*, pp.36-7; *Devyataya konferentsiya RKP(b): sentyabr' 1920 goda; protokoly* (Moscow, 1972), pp.280-1.

19. I. V. Mgeladze, *Vos'maya konferentsiya RKP(b): dekabr' 1919 goda; protokoly* (Moscow, 1961), p.33; S. Milnichuk in *Proletarskaya Revolyutsiya*, 1922, no.11, pp.146-60.

20. *Perepiska sekretariata*, Volume 7, doc.436.

21. *Kommunist* (Kiev), no.28, 24 January 1920.

22. *Izvestiya* (Penza), no.180/563, 14 August 1919; *Petrogradskaya Pravda*, no.62, 20 March 1920.

23. *Perepiska sekretariata*, Volume 8, doc.604; *The Smolensk Archives*, WKP6.

24. *Izvestiya* (Penza), no.84/467, 16 April 1919; *Zvezda* (Novgorod), no.283, 30 November 1919.

25. *The Smolensk Archives*, WKP6, 8 January 1920 (Provincial Committee meeting).

26. *Kommunar* (Tula), no.155/304, 15 July 1919.

27. *Perepiska sekretariata*, Volume 7, docs.377, 387, 485, 486, 499, 501, 518.

28. V. Shklovski, *Santimental'noe puteshestvie: vospominaniya, 1917-1922* (Moscow, 1923).

29. See F. I. Goloshchekin's letter in *Perepiska sekretariata*, Volume 8, doc.517.

30. *Perepiska sekretariata*, Volume 6, doc.439.

31. *Izvestiya Tsentral'nogo Komiteta*, no.8, 2 December 1919.

32. *Izvestiya Tsentral'nogo Komiteta*, no.16, 28 March 1920.

33. Examples are discoverable in V. I. Lenin, *Polnoe Sobranie Sochinenii*, Volume 51,

pp.22, 30, 33, 42, 44, 45 and in *The Trotsky Papers*, Volume 1, pp.360–2, 406,468, 636.
34. *The Trotsky Papers*, Volume 1, p.726.
35. V. I. Lenin, *Polnoe Sobranie Sochinenii*, Volume 51, pp.69, 114, 207.
36. *Izvestiya Tsentral'nogo Komiteta*, no.8, 2 December 1919 and no.16, March 1920.
37. V. I. Lenin, *Polnoe Sobranie Sochinenii*, Volume 50, doc.601 and Volume 51, doc.168; V. I. Lenin, *Devyatyi s"ezd RKP(b): mart-aprel' 1920 goda; protokoly* (Moscow, 1960), pp.13 and 86–7.
38. *Izvestiya Tsentral'nogo Komiteta*, no.16, 28 March 1920.
39. *Izvestiya Tsentral'nogo Komiteta*, no.15, 24 March 1920 and no.16, 28 March 1920.
40. A good example is to be found in *Perepiska sekretariata*, Volume 7, doc.51.
41. *Vos'maya konferentsiya*, p.31.
42. See Chapter 6, pp.136 and 140.
43. V. I. Lenin, *Polnoe Sobranie Sochinenii*, Volume 51, doc.168.
44. *Kommunist* (Kiev), no.28, 24 January 1910 and no.35, 1 February 1920; *Kommunist* (Kharkov), no.61, 17 March 1920; B. M. Violin, *Iz vospominanii* (Moscow, 1967), pp.9–11.
45. V. I. Lenin, *Polnoe Sobranie Sochinenii*, Volume 51, doc.292; *Kommunist* (Karkov), no.83, 16 April 1920; T. Sapronov, *Vos' maya konferentsiya*, pp.40–2.
46. N. N. Krestinski, *Devyatyi s"ezd*, p.43.
47. *Perepiska sekretariata*, Volume 8, doc.773; *Devyatyi s"ezd*, pp.43–4.
48. See Chapter 7, pp.180–3.
49. Kaganovich, *Nizhegorodskaya Kommuna* (Nizhni Novgorod), no.160, 22 July 1919; Sapronov, *Vos'maya konferentsiya*, pp.40–2.
50. Detailed illustrations are given by I. N. Stukov, *Kommuna* (Samara), no.207, 21 August 1919 and by I. V. Mgeladze, N. K. Kozlov and A. I. Mikoyan, *Vos'maya konferentsiya*, pp.33 and 37–9.
51. *Vos'maya konferentsiya*, pp.31–111.
52. *Devyatyi s"ezd*, pp.48–50, 318–20 and 353.
53. *Devyatyi s"ezd*, p.398; *Izvestiya Tsentral'nogo Komiteta*, no.18, 23 May 1920.
54. Krestinski, *Devyatyi s"ezd*, pp.33–4; Trotski, *Devyatyi s"ezd*, pp.75–7.
55. *Devyatyi s"ezd*, pp.84–5.
56. E. D. Stasova, *Vospominaniya*, (Moscow, 1969), pp.175–6.
57. *Devyatyi s"ezd*, pp.66–9 and 147–50.
58. Chapter 4, pp.109–10.
59. *Vospominaniya*, pp.175–6; *Izvestiya Tsentral'nogo Komiteta*, no.18, 23 May 1920.
60. On Krestinski see Chapter 4, pp.102–3, on Preobrazkenski see this Chapter, p.132 on Serebryakov see *Perepiska sekretariata*, Volume 3, doc.281 and 408.

Chapter 6

1. N. Davies, *White Eagle, Red Star*; I. Deutscher, *Trotsky: The Prophet Armed*, Chapter 14.
2. E. H. Carr, *The Bolshevik Revolution*, Volume 3, Chapter 25; A. S. Lindemann, *The 'Red Years': European Socialism Versus Bolshevism, 1919–1921* (London, 1974), Chapters 6–7.
3. A. A. Matyugin, *Rabochii klass SSSR v gody vosstanovleniya narodnogo khozyaistva* (Moscow, 1962); E. V. Gimpel'son, *Sovestskii rabochii klass*, Chapters 1–2; O. I.

Shkaratan, *Problemy sotsial'noi struktury rabochego klassa SSSR: istoriko-sotsiologicheskoe issledovanie* (Moscow, 1970), pp.251-4.
4. Trotski, *Sochineniya* (Moscow, 1925-6), Volume 15, pp.324-5 and *Pravda*, 16 January 1920; Lenin, *Polnoe Sobranie Sochinenii*, Volume 42, p.147.
5. On Petrograd see E. Goldman, *My Further Disillusionment in Russia* (New York, 1924), pp.38-68; on Tula see *Kommunar* (Tula), nos.120/566 (3 June 1920), 126/572 (10 June 1920) and 128/574 (12 June 1920).
6. O. H. Radkey, *The Unknown Civil War in Soviet Russia: A Study of the Green Movement in the Tambov Region 1920-1921* (Stanford, 1976).
7. P. Avrich, *Kronstadt, 1921* (New Jersey, 1970); E. Mawdsley, 'The Baltic Fleet and the Kronstadt Mutiny', *Soviet Studies*, 1973, no.4, pp.506-21.
8. *Izvestiya Tsentral'nogo Komiteta*, no.18, 23 May 1920; N. N. Krestinski, *Devyataya konferentsiya*, pp.83-4.
9. *Izvestiya Tsentral'nogo Komiteta*, no.28, 5 March 1921.
10. *Deyatyi s"ezd RKP(b): mart 1921 goda; stenograficheskii otchet* (Moscow, 1963), p.51.
11. *Trotsky Papers*, Volume 2, doc.602.
12. *Izvestiya Tsentral'nogo Komiteta*, no.18, 23 May 1920 and no.29, 7 March 1921.
13. See Chapter 8.
14. N. N. Krestinski, *Devyataya konferentsiya*, pp.94-6; *The Smolensk Archives*, WKP6, 16 July, 22 August, 3 September and 17 September 1920 (Provincial Committee meetings).
15. *The Smolensk Archives*, WKP6, 22 August 1920.
16. K. I. Bukov and G. A. Nagapetyan, 'Ideino-organizatsionnoe ukreplenie moskovskoi partiinoi organizatsii v gody grazhdanskoi voiny', *Voprosy Istorii KPSS*, 1959 no.6, p.53.
17. *Kommuna* (Samara), nos.510 (31 August 1920) and 569 (7 November 1920); *Kommunar* (Tula), nos.120/566 (3 June 1920), 124/570 (8 June 1920), 126/572 (10 June 1920) and 128/574 (12 June 1920).
18. See this Chapter, pp.147-8.
19. A general discussion is to be found in the speech by G. E. Zinoviev, *Devyataya konferentsiya*, pp.139-56.
20. A. Varentsova, 'O partiinoi rabote za 1920 god', pp.74-5.
21. *Kommuna* (Samara), nos.510 (31 August 1920), 529 (22 September 1920) and 569 (7 November 1920).
22. *Kommunar* (Tula), nos.120/566 (3 June 1920), 124/570 (8 June 1920), 126/572 (10 June 1920) and 128/574 (12 June 1920).
23. *Izvestiya Tsentral'nogo Komiteta*, no.29, 7 March 1921; *Petrogradskaya Pravda*, nos.10 (15 January 1920) and 207 (17 September 1920).
24. *Devyataya konferentsiya*, pp.1-139.
25. *Devyataya konferentsiya*, pp.139-56.
26. *Devyataya konferentsiya*, pp.156-62 and 171-2.
27. *Devyataya konferentsiya*, pp.163-4 and 186-8.
28. *Devyataya konferentsiya*, pp.276-82.
29. *Devyataya konferentsiya*, pp.172-4.
30. *Devyataya konferentsiya*, pp.188-92.
31. *Kommuna* (Samara), nos.536 (30 September 1920), 538 (2 October 1920), 549 (15 October 1920), 561 (29 October 1920), 569 (7 November 1920), 571 (10 November 1920), no.588 (30 November 1920) and 614 (30 December 1920).

32. *Kommunar* (Tula), nos.263/709 (20 November 1920) and 274/720 (3 December 1920).

33. *Petrogradskaya Pravda*, nos.222 (5 October 1920) and 227 (10 October 1920); *Vyatskaya Pravda*, no.190, 12 December 1920; *Kommunist* (Kharkov), no.219, 1 October 1920.

34. *The Smolensk Archives*, WKP6, 1 October 1920.

35. A. A. Solts, *Desyatyi s"ezd*, pp.57-8.

36. *The Smolensk Archives* (WKP6) again provide an excellent behind-the-scenes glimpse of trends inside party committees.

37. *Izvestiya Tsentral'nogo Komiteta*, no.24 (12 October 1920) and 26 October 1920). I. E. Veitser was thus redesignated, *Vyatskaya Pravda*, no.190, 12 December 1920. The demobilisation of commissars from the Red Army led to the displacement of numerous civilian party chairmen in 1920-1, meaning that redesignation frequently involved a turnover of personnel.

38. *Ocherki istorii ul"yanovskoi organizatsii KPSS* (Ulyanovsk, 1972), Volume 2, pp.8-11. Further examples are given in *Izvestiya Tsentral'nogo Komiteta*, no.32, 6 August 1921, p.8.

39. *Devyatyi s"ezd*, pp.457-74; *Desyatyi s"ezd*, pp.716-45.

40. R. B. Day, *Leon Trotsky and the Politics of Economic Isolation* (Cambridge, 1973), Chapter 3.

41. *Desyatyi s"ezd*, editorial notes on pp.846-7.

42. See, for example, I. S. Chirva, *Bor'ba bol'shevikov za uprochenie sovetskoi vlasti, vosstanovleniya i razvitiya narodnogo khozyaistva Kryma* (Simferopol, 1958), pp.131-2.

43. *Desyatyi s"ezd*, editorial notes on pp.845-6.

44. G. E. Zinoviev, *Pravda*, no.295, 30 December 1920; L. D. Trotsky, *O zadachakh professional'nykh soyuzov: doklad, prochitannyi na sobranii 30 dekabrya 1920 goda* (Moscow, 1921).

45. *Desyatyi s"ezd*, editorial notes on p.868.

46. *Petrogradskaya Pravda*, no.11, 18 January 1921.

47. In none of his various memoirs did Trotsky ever spend many words on the reasons for his defeat. Rather he preferred to contend that the strict labour discipline which he had advocated in 1920 did in fact come to be instituted from 1921 onwards. This, however, was historically incorrect (as we shall see).

48. Trotski recognised this: *Kommuna* (Samara), nos.641-2, 4-5 February 1921.

49. *Desyatyi s"ezd*, editorial notes on p.846.

50. Shlyapnikov's programme, *Desyatyi s"ezd*, pp.819-23.

51. *Petrogradskaya Pravda*, nos.3-4, 5-6 January 1921; *Vyatskaya Pravda*, no.17, 21 January 1921.

52. *Polnoe Sobranie Sochinenii*, Volume 43, pp.366-70.

53. V. I. Lenin, *Desyatyi s"ezd*, pp.21-40.

54. *Desyatyi s"ezd*, pp.40-137.

55. A. I. Mikoyan, *Mysli i vospominaniya o V. I. Lenine* (Moscow, 1970).

56. *Desyatyi s"ezd*, pp.218-334.

57. I. T. Smilga, *Na povorote: zametki k desyatomu s"ezdu partii* (Moscow, 1921) and *Desyatyi s"ezd*, pp.233-4 and 252-9.

58. *Desyatyi s"ezd*, p.402.

59. *Desyatyi s"ezd*, pp.340-92.

60. *Desyatyi s"ezd*, pp.450-517 and 536-9.

61. *Desyatyi s"ezd*, pp.524-6 and 774-8.

62. Shlyapnikov and Medvedev, *Desyatyi s"ezd*, pp.526-35.
63. *Desyatyi s"ezd*, pp.532-4.

Chapter 7
1. E. H. Carr, *The Bolshevik Revolution*, Volume 2, Chapter 19.
2. L. B. Schapiro, *Origins of the Communist Autocracy*, Chapters 16-17.
3. E. H. Carr, *The Interregnum, 1923-1924* (London, 1954), Part 2; R. B. Day, *Leon Trotsky And The Politics Of Economic Isolation*, Chapters 3-4.
4. O. H. Radkey, *The Unknown Civil War*, Chapter 12; Y. Taniuchi, *The Village Gathering in Russia in the Mid-Twenties*, Chapter 4, sections A and B.
5. E. H. Carr, *The Interregnum*, Chapter 2.
6. E. H. Carr, *The Interregnum*, Chapters 1-2; R. B. Day, *Leon Trotsky And The Politics Of Economic Isolation*, Chapter 4; R. Sinigaglia, *Mjasnikov e la rivoluzione russa* (Milan, 1973).
7. *Pravda*, 30 June 1921.
8. *Izvestiya Tsentral'nogo Komiteta*, no.41, April 1922.
9. *The Smolensk Archives*, WKP120.
10. *Izvestiya Tsentral'nogo Komiteta*, no.40, March 1922.
11. A. Mikoyan, *Mysli i vospominaniya o V. I. Lenine*, pp.205-11; *Izvestiya Tsentral'nogo Komiteta*, no.31, 20 May 1921; *Nizhegorodskaya Kommuna* (Nizhni Novgorod), nos.98 (6 May 1921) and 101 (10 May 1921).
12. A. A. Timofeevski (editor), *V. I. Lenin i stroitel'stvo partii v pervye gody sovetskoi vlasti* (Moscow, 1965), pp.229-30.
13. *The Smolensk Archives*, WKP128: Provincial Committee report, probably composed in December 1924.
14. M. P. Tomski, *Nizhegorodskaya Kommuna* (Nizhni Novgorod), no.296, 25 December 1923; *Sotsialisticheskii Vestnik* (Berlin), nos.19/65 (18 October 1923) and 14/84 (6 July 1924).
15. *Odinnatsatyi s"ezd RKP(b): mart-aprel' 1922 goda; stenograficheskii otchet*, p.463; *Kommunisticheskaya partiya Sovetskogo Soyuza v rezolyutsiyakh*, Volume 1, pp.623-4 and 727.
16. A. S. Bubnov, *Bol'shaya Sovetskaya Entsiklopediya*, Volume II, column 533; *Izvestiya Tsentral'nogo Komiteta*, no.5, June 1923.
17. *Kommuna* (Samara), no.1279, 21 March 1923.
18. *Izvestiya Tsentral'nogo Komiteta*, no.5, June 1923.
19. *Petrogradskaya Pravda*, no.273, 1 December 1923. See also Krovitski, *Vyatskaya Pravda*, no.195, 28 August 1923; D. Z. Manuilski, *Odinnadtsatyi s"ezd*, p.438.
20. This, however, was probably the least successfully implemented aspect of recruitment policy: D. J. Male, *Russian Peasant Organisation*, pp.132-6.
21. Women by 1922 had fallen to constituting merely 8 per cent of the entire party: *Izvestiya Tsentral'nogo Komiteta*, no.1, January 1923.
22. See this Chapter, pp.000-00.
23. *Bryanskii Rabochii*, no.4/100 25 August 1922.
24. *Saratovskie Izvestiya*, no.203, 12 December 1923. Other articles along similar lines are found in *Nizhegorodskaya Kommuna* (Nizhni Novgorod), no.269, 23 November 1923; *Kommuna* (Samara), no.1010, 28 April 1922; *Kommunar* (Tula), no.212/1546, 11 September 1923.
25. *Vyatskaya Pravda*, no.284, 11 November 1923.
26. *Nizhegorodskaya Kommuna* (Nizhni Novgorod), no.269, 23 November 1923.

27. *Kommunar* (Tula), no.212/1546, 11 September 1923.
28. Bolshakov, *Petrogradskaya Pravda*, no.68, 27 March 1921; Zinoviev, *Petrogradskaya Pravda*, no.274, 2 December 1923; Kosterin, *Vyatskaya Pravda*, no.155, 13 July 1921; Krovitski, *Vyatskaya pravda*, nos.159-60, 13-14 July 1923.
29. *Petrogradskaya Pravda*, no.273, 1 December 1923.
30. Krovitski, *Vyatskaya Pravda*, nos.159-60, 13-14 July 1923.
31. Kosterin, *Vyatskaya Pravda*, no.155, 13 July 1921.
32. *The Smolensk Archives*, WKP278.
33. *Vyatskaya Pravda*, no.195, 29 August 1923.
34. *Nizhegorodskaya Kommuna* (Nizhni Novgorod), no.269, 23 November 1923.
35. *Kommunar* (Tula), no.67/1411, 28 March 1923.
36. G. E. Zinoviev reported on the entire party in *Petrogradskaya Pravda*, no.283, 13 December 1923.
37. *Kommuna* (Samara), no.1064, 4 July 1922.
38. See the graphic description in *Saratovskie Izvestiya*, no.283, 12 December 1923.
39. *Bryanskii Rabochii*, no.4/100, 25 August 1922.
40. *Sovetskaya Pravda* (Chelyabinsk), nos.16/938 (24 January 1923) and 263/1185 (17 November 1923).
41. *Kommuna* (Samara), 25 December 1922.
42. *The Smolensk Archives* are a rich mine of information here, especially WKP 9, 120, 122, and 123.
43. *Izvestiya Tsentral'nogo Komiteta*, no.32, 6 August 1921; *Ocherki istorii ul'yanovskoi organizatsii KPSS*, Volume 2, pp.8-11.
44. Unfortunately it is difficult to get hold of reliable quantitative data on the party as a whole. All sources, however, agree that a high turnover did in fact occur after (as well as during) the Civil War.
45. *Izvestiya Tsentral'nogo Komiteta*, no.33, October 1921; Molotov, *Odinnadtsatyi s"ezd*, pp.45-59.
46. These twenty-nine officials were the most influential local leaders. They include both the secretaries of all ten major regional committees and the secretaries of nineteen provincial committees in European Russia which were not subject to a regional committee and were given a group 'A' rating (and were thereby considered the most important provincial committees by the central party apparatus) in the staffing lists announced in *Izvestiya Tsentral'nogo Komiteta*, no.37, January 1922.
47. For Kharitonov see P. Kudelli, *Pervyi legal'nyi Petersburgskii Komitet bol'shevikov v 1917 godu: sbornik materialov i protokolov zasedanii* (Moscow-Leningrad, 1927); for Kviring see *Sovetskaya istoricheskaya entsiklopediya* (Moscow, 1970); for Vareikis see *Bol'shaya sovetskaya entsiklopediya* (1st edition) and the newspaper *Proletarii* (Simbirsk), 1918-19; for Zorin see *Who Was Who in the USSR* (New Jersey, 1972).
48. For Os'mov see *Ocherki istorii kaluzhskoi organizatsii KPSS* (2nd revised edition: Yaroslavl, 1972), pp.219-21 and 536.
49. On Meerzon and Zorin in particular see *Who Was Who in the USSR*.
50. This underestimation had its origins in early works by Trotski and the Menshevik historians but it has since become the stock-in-trade of Western historiography in general. Not that Soviet historians have shown greater care in handling the matter; on the contrary, they have been persistently shy about examining the biographies of the local party leadership in the 1920s.

The Trotsky-Menshevik view is much more likely to be applicable to the late 1920s and the early 1930s; but further research is needed to confirm this.

51 *Izvestiya Tsentral'nogo Komiteta*, no.37, January 1922; Zinoviev, *Petrogradskaya Pravda*, no.283, 13 December 1923.

52. Taking the nineteen major provinces of European Russia (see this Chapter, note 46), we find that P. S. Zaslavski was the only provincial committee secretary of mid-1919 who was to hold a similar kind of post in autumn 1923 (though even he had not built his entire career in exclusively secretarial posts). Of course, it is possible to find others outside the list of nineteen, such as I. A. Akulov, M. P. Zhakov and S. A. Bank, who paralleled Zaslavski's case. But not even this trio fit the traditional viewpoint initiated by Trotski and the Mensheviks. Akulov was vociferously disdainful of secretarial work in the Civil War and eventually got himself transferred to soviet administrative work (*Perepiska sekretariata*, Volume 2, pp.353-4 and *Who Was Who in the USSR*); Zhakov was Kazan Provincial Committee secretary only briefly in 1919 and then joined the Red Army as a political commissar (*Bol'sheviki Tatarii v gody inostrannoi interventsii i grazhdanskoi voiny*, pp.68-75 and 191); S. A. Bank joined the Bolsheviks only in 1917 and therefore occupied predictably lowly posts in the Civil War (*Ocherki istorii kaluzhskoi organizatsii KPSS*, p.700).

53. See Chapter 6, pp.147-8.

54. Petrograd Provincial Committee secretary D. Trilisser commented on this in *Petrogradskaya Pravda*, no.66, 25 March 1921.

55. *Vyatskaya Pravda*, no. no.143, 24 June 1923.

56. *Dvenadtsatyi s"ezd RKP(b): stenograficheskii otchet* (Moscow, 1923), p.169.

57. V. I. Lenin, *Polnoe Sobranie Sochinenii*, Volume 53, doc.414.

58. M. Lewin, *Lenin's Last Struggle* (London, 1969).

59. *Stepnaya Pravda* (Semipalatinsk), nos.96/1174 (30 April 1924) and 106/1184 (15 May 1924): here it is indicated that Ezhov's chauvinism raised its head again even after his earlier disgrace.

60. See Chapter 6, pp.153-5.

61. *Polnoe Sobranie Sochinenii*, Volume 52, doc.257 and Volume 53, doc.130.

62. V. P. Nogin (speaking on behalf of the Central Revisory Commission), *Odinnadtsatyi s"ezd*, pp.60-72.

63. *Izvestiya Tsentral'nogo Komiteta*, nos.36-7, December 1921 and January 1922.

64. *Polnoe Sobranie Sochinenii*, Volume 53, doc.481 and Volume 54, docs.212 and 385.

65. *Moya Zhizn'*, Part 2, p.218.

66. *Izvestiya Tsentral'nogo Komiteta* supplied the election details.

67. *Odinnadtsatyi s"ezd*, pp.86-7.

68. *Izvestiya Tsentral'nogo Komiteta*, no.51, March 1923.

69. M. Lewin, *Lenin's Last Struggle*; R. B. Day, *Leon Trotsky And The Politics Of Economic Isolation*, pp.69-92.

70. *Polnoe Sobranie Sochinenii*, Volume 54, pp.345-6.

71. *Kommuna* (Samara), 25 December 1922; A. Rakitin, *V. A. Antonov-Ovseenko: dokumental'nyi biograficheskii ocherk* (Leningrad, 1975), pp.273-89; *Izvestiya Samarskogo Gubkoma RKP(b)*, no.13, 1921; V. M. Molotov, *Odinnadtsatyi s"ezd*, p.54.

72. *Izvestiya Tsentral'nogo Komiteta*, 28 February 1922.

73. *Izvestiya Tsentral'nogo Komiteta*, no.33, October 1921.

74. K. Paustovski, *Povest' o zhizni* (Moscow, 1962), Book 2, Part 4, pp.301-5.

75. See this Chapter, note 71.

76. *Izvestiya Tsentral'nogo Komiteta*, March 1922.

77. A. I. Mikoyan, *Vospominaniya i mysli o V. I. Lenine.*

78. V. M. Molotov, *Odinnadtsatyi s"ezd*, pp.45–59.

79. *Odinnadtsatyi s"ezd*, pp.84–5.

80. *Izvestiya Tsentral'nogo Komiteta*, no.33, October 1921.

81. *Avtonomnaya Yakutiya* (Yakutsk), no.45, 25 September 1922.

82. *Saratovskie Izvestiya*, no.155, 11 July 1922.

83. *The Smolensk Archives*, WKP8, 20 October 1923.

84. I. Silone, *Uscita di Sicurezza* (Florence, 1965), p.84.

Chapter 8

1. E. H. Carr, *The Interregnum*, Chapters 1–2; R. V. Daniels, *The Conscience Of The Revolution*, Chapter 9.

2. *Pravda*, 13 December 1923.

3. *Sotsialisticheskii Vestnik* (Berlin), 28 May 1924 contains lengthy extracts from this document (which to this day has remained unpublished in the USSR).

4. A. G. Titov, 'Bor'ba kommunisticheskoi partii s trotskizmom v period diskussii 1923–4 gg.', *Voprosy Istorii KPSS*, 1965, no.7, pp.42–6.

5. *The Trotsky Archives* (held in the Houghton Library of Harvard University), T80Z.

6. *Sotsialisticheskii Vestnik* (Berlin), 28 May 1924; *The Trotsky Archives*, T802.

7. A. G. Titov, 'Bor'ba kommunisticheskoi partii s trotskizmom', pp.42–6.

8. *Pravda*, 7 November 1923.

9. L. Trotski, *Moya zhizn': opyt avtobiografii* (Berlin, 1932), Chapter 34.

10. *Chetyrnadtsatyi s"ezd VKP(b): stenograficheskii otchet* (Moscow, 1926): speeches by I. V. Stalin, K. E. Voroshilov and G. E. Zinoviev, pp.398–9, 455–6, 484, 950 and 953.

11. L. Trotski, *Novyi kurs*, which has been translated by M. Schachtman in *The New Course* (Ann Arbor, 1965).

12. *Sovetskaya Pravda* (Chelyabinsk), no.263, 17 November 1923.

13. *Nizhegorodskaya Kommuna* (Nizhni Novgorod), no.280, 6 December 1923.

14. See *Saratovskie Izvestiya* and *Stepnaya Pravda* (Semipalatinsk) for November 1923.

15. *Pravda*, 12, 15, 20 and 21 December 1923.

16. Thus E. H. Carr proceeded to call the Moscow mass meeting of 11 December the last occasion of free expression and free voting in Bolshevik history: *The Interregnum*, Chapter 9.

17. *Stepnaya Pravda* (Semipalatinsk), nos.281/1075 (20 December 1923), 3 (4 January 1924) and 4 (5 January 1924).

18. *Bryanskii Rabochii*, no.285, 19 December 1923; *Nizhegorodskaya Kommuna* (Nizhni Novgorod), no.293, 21 December 1923; *Saratovskie Izvestiya*, no.294, 23 December 1923.

19. Kaluga, Penza, Ryazan and Simbirsk are listed by E. H. Carr (*The Interregnum*, Chapter 3) and R. V. Daniels (*The Conscience of the Revolution*, Chapter 9); Kiev, Khabarovsk and Odessa have been added by A. G. Titov ('Bor'ba kommunisticheskoi partii s trotskizmom', pp.47–9). On Chelyabinsk, Cherepovets, Vyatka and the Crimea see *Sovetskaya Pravda* (Chelyabinsk), nos.6/1225-7/1226 (8–9 January 1924; *Petrogradskaya Pravda*, no.15, 18 January 1924; *Vyatskaya Pravda*,

no.11, 13 January 1924; *Krasnyi Krym* (Simferopol), no.107/1025, 13 May 1924. The Vyatka and Crimea cases are complex: the Opposition there criticised Stalin's slander tactics and upheld the need for reform, but refrained from open support of Trotski and Preobrazhenski. For a further discussion of the Opposition's internal divisions see this Chapter, p.198-9.

20. *Petrogradskaya Pravda*, no.11, 13 January 1924.

21. Chelyabinsk, Penza and Vyatka were remarkable in holding out against the 'troika' until some weeks after the Thirteenth Party Conference: *Ural'skii Rabochii* (Ekaterinburg), no.98, 5 May 1924; *Trudovaya Pravda* (Penza), no.36, 1924; *Vyatskaya Pravda*, no.49, 28 February 1924.

22. See the list of delegates in *Trinadtsataya konferentsiya RKP(b): byulleten'* (Moscow, 1924).

23. *Trinadtsataya konferentsiya*, pp.7-62.

24. Some local committees did in fact report Stalin's speech in detail: see *Petrogradskaya Pravda*, no.17, 20 January 1924; but others—and they were probably the majority—avoided mentioning his emphatic reservations about the immediate possibility of introducing democratic reform; see *Nizhegorodskaya Kommuna* (Nizhni Novgorod), no.17, 20 January 1924.

25. *Trinadtsataya konferentsiya*, pp.93-101 and 151-6.

26. *Trinadtsataya konferentsiya*, pp.100-1.

27. *Trinadtsataya konferentsiya*, pp.113-17 and 123-5.

28. *Trinadtsataya konferentsiya*, pp.104-13, 127-33 and 136.

29. *Trinadtsayaya konferentsiya*, pp.158-80.

30. *Trinadtsayaya konferentsiya*, pp.198-204.

31. *Ocherki istorii kaluzhskoi organizatsii KPSS*, p.183; *Vyatskaya Pravda*, no.49, 28 February 1924; *Krasnyi Krym* (Simferopol), no.107/1025, 13 May 1924.

32. *Saratovskie Izvestiya*, no.293, 23 December 1923.

33. *Stalin*, Chapter 12.

34. A. I. Mikoyan, *Vospominaniya i mysli o V. I. Lenine*, pp.232-3.

35. The results of the census are found in *Izvestiya Tsentral'nogo Komiteta*, no.4, 1923.

36. The Menshevik leaders did indeed welcome Trotski's democratising campaign precisely on the grounds that, if successful, it would supply them with a strong indirect means of influencing official Bolshevik policies: N. Valentinov-Volski, *Novaya ekonomicheskaya politika i krizis partii posle smerti Lenina i gody raboty v VSNKh vo vremya NEP: vospominaniya* (California, 1971), pp.78-9.

37. See Chapter 7, p.181.

38. See Chapter 6, pp.144 and 153-7.

39. *The Trotsky Archives*, T802; *The New Course*. It was only later in the 1920s that the Left Opposition paid much attention to the issue of economic egalitarianism.

40. *The Trotsky Archives*, T802.

41. This appears to have been true not only in Moscow but in the provinces too: see, for example, *Rabochii Klich* (Ryazan), no.1616, 8 May 1924; *Krasnyi Krym* (Simferopol), nos.8/926-9/928 (10-11 January 1924).

42. G. S. Agabekov, *GPU: zapiski chekista* (Berlin, 1930), Part 1, p.63.

43. Working-class opinion in late 1923 is a topic deserving special attention in its own right; but an impressionistic survey of contemporary central and local oppositionist speeches and literature produces little sign of an expectation that industrial workers would take very readily to the Opposition's industrialisation drive.

44. *Vyatskaya Pravda*, no.288, 15 December 1923. See also A. I. Mikoyan, *Mysli i vospominaniya o V. I. Lenine*, pp.232–3 and Sarkis's remarks in *Petrogradskaya Pravda*, no.268, 25 November 1923.

45. As if to put the seal on Stalin's victory, it was an ex-member of the Left Opposition, A. S. Bubnov who was given the job of overseeing the propagation of this distorted view of Lenin's pre-revolutionary writings. For an even greater distortion of historical truth see the beginning of the serialisation of L. M. Kaganovich's pamphlet in *Ural'skii Rabochii*, 6 April 1924.

Index

activists, 20-1, 27, 46-9, 92-4, 118-19,
164, 167-9; their social and political
background, 25, 30, 46-9, 173-5; the
numerical shortage of them, 46-7,
72-3, 97, 100-1, 139-40; their attitude to discipline, 52-3, 73-4, 92-3,
120-2
Agitation—Propaganda Department,
see Secretariat
agriculture, 13, 15-17; governmental
policies towards, 28, 38-9, 64, 66-9,
87-8, 113-14, 135-6; annual production of, 135-6, 159-60
Akselrod, P., 24-5
Alexander II, 14, 16
Allies, the, 40, 89, 113, 135, 161
All-Russian Central Executive Committee of the Congress of Soviets, see
VTsIK
Anarchists, 11, 49
Antonov-Ovseenko, V., 78, 181, 196
appointmentism in the party, 104-5,
121-2, 127-9, 138-40, 143-6, 150,
170-2, 180-2, 186-7, 196, 199
Archangel, 85; its Provincial Committee, 98, 180
Astrakhan Town Committee, 73-4
Austro-Hungarian empire, 32, 67, 76,
80
authoritarian methods, see bureau-
cracy
Azerbaidzhan, 11, 15, 75, 159

Baku, 11, 75, 159
Baltic region, 68, 85, 87, see also
Estonia, Latvia, Lithuania
Beloborodov, A., 125

Belorussia, 98
Berkman, A., 120
Bernstein, E., 21
Black Repartition, 14
Bogdanov, A., 25, 29-30
Bosh, E., 72
'bourgeois specialists', 86, 95, 118-19,
144-5, see also Military Opposition,
Workers' Opposition
Breslav, B., 187
Brest-Litovsk, Treaty of, 68, 76-84,
99-100
Bryansk, 192; its Provincial Com-
mittee, 128; its Town Committee,
171
Bubnov, A., 144
Budenny, S., 134
Bukharin, N., 75, 175, 211; as Left
Communist, 68, 76, 80; in the 'trade
union controversy', 149-50, 154; as
supporter of NEP, 161, 179, 189, 191
bureaucracy, debate about, 33-5, 106-
10, 119-23, 126-33, 140-6, 149-57,
162-3, 180-3, 185-99, 201-10
bureaucratisation, bureaucratism, see
bureaucracy

Cadet Party, 28, 46
Caucasus, 68, 112
cells, 19-20, 49-50, 71, 96-7, 118-19,
144, 167-70, 199
Central Asia, 118, 172-3
Central Bureau of Military Organisations, 59
Central Committee, 32, 39, 42, 56-61,
74-83, 94, 101-10, 123-33, 135-6,
138-9, 143, 147, 153-4, 164, 175-9,
186-8

Central Control Commission, 147, 153, 188

centralisation, see bureaucracy, central-local relations, democratic centralism

central-local relations, 19-20, 25, 27, 59-61, 76-9, 94-5, 103-11, 126-33, 138-40, 143-6, 148-57, 180-3, 185-99

Central Powers, see Austro-Hungarian empire, Germany

Chaikovski, N., 14

Cheka, 67, 113-14, 175, 186, 199

Chelyabinsk, 191-2

Cherepovets, 192

circles, 19-20, 49-50

Civil War, 85-9, 112-15, 134-7

class background of party members, see social composition

committee chairmen, 51, 72, 100-1, 121, 147-8

committee secretaries, 51, 72, 100-1, 147-8, 169-75, 186-7, 199

Communist International, 89, 135, 156, 181

Communist Manifesto, 17

Congress of Soviets: First (June 1917), 40-1; Second (October 1917), 42, 63; Third (1918), 68; Eighth (1920), 149-50

Constituent Assembly, 39, 54, 60, 67, 76, 85-6

Constitutional-Democratic Party, see Cadet Party

Council of Peoples' Commissars, see Sovnarkom

Council of Workers' and Peasants' Defence, 87

Crimea, 112, 135, 192, 196

Declaration of the Forty Six, 187, 190, 194, 198-9

democratic centralism, 29, 51-3, 131, 208

Democratic Centralists, 108, 130-1, 138-9, 144-6, 149, 156-7, 181-2, 209

Denikin, 85-6, 112, 116, 135

Directory, the, 86

district committees, 50, 71, 96-7, 121

Donbass, 11, 15-16, 47, 50, 55, 72, 112; its Regional Committee, 55-6, 78; its Coalmining Political Department, 140; its Soviet Republic, 173

Donets Provincial Committee, 140

Drobnis, Y., 156

Drobnis, Y., 156

Dukhovshchina, 183

Duma, 26, 28-30, 37

Dzerzhinski, F., 125, 186

Dzhaparidze, P., 75

Eastern front, 35, 40, 64, 67, 83

economy, see agriculture, foreign trade, industry

Ekaterinburg, 82-3; its Provincial Committee, 150

Ekaterinoslav Town Committee, 56

Engels, F., 11, 18, 169, see Marxism

Erman (of Tsaritsyn), 80

Esperanto, 169

Estonia, 112

Evdokimov, G., 193

Extraordinary Commission, see Cheka

Ezhov, N., 175, 192

Fabians, 21

factory workers, 15-16, 31, 37-8, 65-6, 87-8, 114-15, 136-7, 162-3, 202-3

factory-workshop committees, 41-2, 48, 72-3, 87

Far-East Regional Bureau, 60

February Revolution, 37-42, 203, 205

Files-Assignment Department, see Secretariat

Finland, 87

First World War, 32-6, see also Eastern front, Brest-Litovsk

foreign policy, 64, 67-8, 85, 89, 112-13, 134-5, 161, 195

foreign trade, 30, 32, 64, 89, 113, 135, 159

France, 12, 18, 32, see also the Allies

French Revolution, 23

General Department, see Secretariat

Genoa Conference, 161

Georgia, 175, 186; its Communist Party Central Committee, 179

German Social-Democratic Party (SPD), 18-19, 23, 31, 33-5, 188, 200-1

Germany, 12, 17-18, 32, 112, 195, 204-5, *see also* Brest-Litovsk, Central Powers, Genoa Conference

Gomel Provincial Committee, 171

governmental coalition, 63-4, 67-9

Great Britain, 12, 18, 21, 32, *see also* the Allies

Great Russian chauvinism, 175, 179

Great Terror, 211

Hilferding, R., 34

Hungary, 112-13

Ignatov, E., 151

industrialisation, debate about, 148-56, 159-63, 185-6, 193-6

industry, 15, 21-2, 30-1, 64-6, 114-15, 136, 159, 185-6

Information—Statistics Department, *see* Secretariat

inner-party democracy, debate about, 22-5, 33-5, 77-9, 81-2, 106-10, 129-33, 140-6, 148-57, 163, 185-99, *see also* bureaucracy, democratic centralism

Interdistricters, 39, 47, 49

Italy, 12

Ivanovo-Kineshma, 83

Ivanovo-Voznesensk, 26, 70, 82, 88, 104, 115, 141; its Provincial Committee, 173

Ivanov, S., 139

Jacobins, 23

Japan, 25-6, 87, 183

Jewish Bund, 173

joint social-democratic organisations, 25, 27, 35, 52-3, 56, 60

July Days, 40, 58-60

Kaganovich, L., 99, 101, 105; as proponent of strict centralism, 106-10, 129, 154, 198, 208-9

Kaluga, 192, 196

Kamenev, L., 125, 143, 156, 211; in the months around the October Revolution, 38, 57-9, 63, 74; as proponent of NEP, 163, 179, 186, 189-93

Kamenski, A., 156

Kaminski, G., 142

Kazan, 85-6, 93; its Provincial Committee, 128

Kerenski, A., 40, 42, 63

Khabarovsk, 192

Kharitonov, M., 172

Kharkov, 73, 128, 146

Kherson, 93

Kienthal, 36

Kiev, 93, 120, 134; its City Committee, 56, 60, 172; its City Soviet, 172

Kiselev, A., 76

Kislovodsk, 189

Kolchak, A., 86, 88, 112-14

Kollontai, A., 45, 58, 103, 144, 151, 183

Kolomna Town Committee, 55

Kopylov, N., 141-2

Kornilov, L., 42, 58

Kostroma Provincial Committee, 104

Kraevski (of Nizhni), 105-6

Krasnodar, 85

Krasnoyarsk Town Committee, 52

Kremer, A., 20

Krestinski, N., 102, 142, 151, 175; as leader in the Orgburo and the Secretariat, 124, 129, 131-3, 137-8, 146, 153, 209

Kronstadt, 46, 53; the outbreak of the mutiny, 137, 152-4

Krupskaya, N., 180

Kuban, 86-7

Kuibyshev, V., 177

Kuskova, E., 21

Kutuzov, I., 144

Kviring, E., 172

labour discontent, 14, 16, 20, 25-6, 31-2, 37-8, 40, 68-9, 114-15, 136-7, 163, 185

Land and Freedom, 13-14

Latko (of Smolensk), 146

Latvia, 45, 98

Left Communists, 68, 76-83, 130

Left Opposition, 187-99, 209-10

Left Socialist-Revolutionaries, 63-4, 67-9, 85, 203

Lena goldfields, 31

Lenin, V., 205, 209; as young activist and theorist, 20-3; as factional leader, 24-5, 29-31, 35-6; calls for seizure of power, 39, 42, 57-8, 61, 63; after October Revolution, 63-4, 67-8, 75, 77, 79-82; as wartime leader, 86, 89, 101-3, 109, 125, 128, 131, 136, 143-6; in the 'trade union controversy', 149-56; and the NEP, 159-61, 176-83, 185-6, 196

'Leninism', the exploitation of, 194-5

Liberation of Labour Group, 19

Lithuania, 98

Lloyd-George, D., 113

local committees, relations among, see district, provincial, regional, suburb, town committees

Lominadze, V., 194

Lomov, G., 76

Lunacharski, A., 192

Lutovinov, Y., 119, 141, 144-5, 150, 181

Luxemburg, R., 33-4

Lvov, G., 37-40

Lyakhovski (agricultural official), 164

Maksimovski, V., 108, 130, 181

Martov, Y., 20-1, 23-5

Marx, K., 18, 201, see Marxism

Marxism, early spread of, 17-25, see 'socialist consciousness'

Medvedev, S., 157

Meerzon, E., 173

Mensheviks, 23-5, 27-33, 38, 40-2, 47-8, 56, 63, 68-9, 88-9, 151

Menshevism, 23-5, 27-9, 160-1, 194-5, 205-7

Metalworkers' Union, 119, 150, 180

Mgeladze, I., 120

Michels, R., 34-5, 200-2, 206

middle-class specialists see bourgeois specialists

Mikhailov, V., 175

Mikoyan, A., 165, 181-2, 193, 197

Military Opposition, 86, 95-6

Military-Revolutionary Committee, see Petrograd Soviet

Milnichuk, S., 93-4, 120

Milonov, Y., 141, 146-7, 151, 180

Milyukov, P., 39-40

Milyukov (overworked of Novosil), 101

Milyutin, V., 57

Minin, S., 51, 192

Minkov, I., 142

Minkov, M., 174, 196

Minsk, 20

Molotov, V., 57, 175-7, 182, 193, 209

Morozov, I., 166

Moscow, 11, 26, 46, 87, 117, 135, 190; its Provincial Committee, 55, 149; its Regional Committee and Bureau, 56, 60, 80-1, 99; its City Committee, 56, 60, 175, 187

Muranov, M., 99

Murmansk, 85

narodniki, 13-17

national background of Bolsheviks, see social composition

nationalism, Russian, see Great Russian chauvinism

Nechaev, S., 13-14

New Course, The, 190, 198

New Economic Policy (NEP), 156-63, 185-6, 201

Nicholas II, 26-8, 37

Nikolaev, 73-4; its Provincial Committee, 78-9

Nizhni Novgorod, 106, 115, 120, 150, 182, 192; its Provincial Committee, 74, 98, 101, 105, 121, 165, 191

Nogin, V., 57, 74

Northern Regional Committee, 74, 104, 107

Novonikolaevsk, 85

Novosil District Committee, 101

numerical size of the party, 25, 30, 42-3, 69-70, 89-90, 115-17, 141, 148, 163-6

'October Communists', 69

October Manifesto, 27-8

October Revolution, 42, 63-9

Odessa, 14, 56, 85, 93, 113, 120, 192; its Provincial Committee, 122, 180-1
Omsk, 86
Ordzhonikidze, G., 175, 179, 186
Orel, 109, 112
Organisational Department, see Secretariat
Organisation-Instruction Department, see Secretariat
Orgburo, 107, 123-32, 137-8, 146, 151, 153, 175-9, 189
Orsha Town Committee, 61
Osinski, N., 108, 110, 130, 178, 181
Osmov, N., 173
Ostrovskaya, N., 101, 104

Panfilov (of Vyatka), 199
Panteleev (military commissar), 91, 95
Party Conference: Sixth (1912), 31-2; Seventh (1917), 39, 53-4, 57; Eighth (1919), 129; Ninth (1920), 142-6, 154; Thirteenth (1924), 192-6
Party Congress: First (1898), 21; Second (1903), 24-5; Fourth (1906), 27, 29; Sixth (1917), 43, 48-9, 57-8; Seventh (1918), 68-9, 76, 81-2; Eighth (1919), 86, 88, 95, 109-10; Ninth (1920), 130-3, 138; Tenth (1921), 149, 152-7; Eleventh (1922), 166, 178, 181; Twelfth (1923), 166, 175, 186
party education, 19-20, 46, 118-19, 168-9
'party masses', see rank-and-file members
party-soviet relations, 41, 65, 72, 87, 106, 119-20, 125, 140, 145-6, 151, 169-70, 194
party-trade union relations, 41, 65, 87, 119-20, 148-56, 169-70
peasantry, 13, 28, 38, 40-1, 66-9, 87-8, 113-14, 159-62, 185
Penza, 121, 192; its Town Committee, 73-4; its Provincial Committee, 97, 120-1
Peoples' Commissariat of Agriculture, 66
Peoples' Commissariat of Enlightenment, 107, 192

Peoples' Freedom, 14
Pereslavl-Zalesski Town Committee, 104
Perm, 83, 86, 104-5
Pestun, K., 143
Petersburg, St, see Petrograd
Petrograd, 11, 14, 16, 20, 26, 32, 37-40, 63, 112, 136; Petrograd Soviet, 38, 40, 63, 65; Petersburg or Petrograd Committee, 50-2, 59, 91, 120, 172; Vyborg Suburb Committee, 51-2, 57; the Soviet's Military-Revolutionary Committee, 63; Petrograd Provincial Committee, 146
Pilsudski, J., 134
Plekhanov, G., 17-21, 24-5
Polish-Soviet war, 134-5, 143
Politburo, 107, 110, 123-30, 134-9, 142, 146-7, 159-62, 175-8, 180-3, 184, 189, 197, 203
political commissars, 86, 94-6, 136, 143-6, 148-9, 172
political departments, see political commissars
populism, populists, see narodniki
Potemkin, battleship, 26
Prague Conference, see Party Conference, Sixth
Pravda, 55-6, 58-9, 61, 92, 115, 163, 191
Preobrazhenski, E., 175, 182, 209; as Left Communist, 77-8, 82; as leader in the Orgburo and the Secretariat, 132-3, 137-9, 142, 145-7; in the 'trade union controversy', 149-51; in the disputes of 1922-3, 162-3, 187-91, 193-4, 196-7
prerevolutionary Bolshevik theories, 21-3, 28-35, 205-6
Prokopovich, S., 21
provincial committees, 54-5, 74, 78-9, 96-8, 120-2, 139-40, 147-8, 170-2
Province-Inspection Department, see Secretariat
Provisional Government, 36-42, 63
Pskov, 192

Radek, K., 157, 195
Railwaymen's Trade Union, 63

Railway Suburb Committee, see Saratov

Rakovski, K., 125

rank-and-file members, 25, 27, 42–6, 69–71, 89–92, 115–19, 140–1, 148, 163–9, 199

Raskolnikov, F., 151

Red Army, 85–9, 91–6, 112–14, 134–6, 173–4

Red Cavalry, 95–6, 134

Red Guard, 85

Red Navy, 96, 104

regional committees, 55–6, 72, 80–1, 98–101, 150, 170–2

Revolutionary Tribunal, 160–1

revolutionary war, see Brest-Litovsk and Polish-Soviet war

Right Opposition, 210

Roslavl Town Committee, 115

Rostov-upon-Don, 197

rural discontent, 17, 22, 26, 38, 41, 68, 113–14, 137, 161–2, 185

Russian Bureau, 57

Ryazan, 56, 192; its Provincial Committee, 172

St Petersburg League of Struggle for the Liberation of the Working Class, 20

Samara, 85, 93, 165, 180; its Provincial Committee, 91, 93, 141, 146, 152, 166, 171, 180

Sapronov, T., 42–3, 45; as a Democratic Centralist, 108, 110, 127–31, 138, 144, 150, 181; as Left Opposition leader, 185, 190–1, 196, 198, 209–10

Saratov, 46, 93, 101, 137, 191–2, 196; Railway Suburb Committee, 52; Town Committee, 52; Town Soviet, 77; Provincial Committee, 128, 183

Sarkis (of Petrograd), 166–7

Schmoller, G., 34

Secretariat, 58–61, 71, 75, 92, 103–5, 107–10, 115–17, 123, 125–6, 130, 133, 137–9, 151, 153, 164, 175–8, 189, 196, 209; Women's Department, 103; Organisation-Instruction Department, 125; Files-Assignment Department, 125, 130, 176, 178; General Department, 126; Special Department, 126; Information-Statistics Department, 126; Agitation-Propaganda Department, 126, 137–8, 176–7; Province-Inspection Department, 126, 138; Organisation Department, 176

Semipalatinsk Provincial Committee, 191–2

Serebryakov, L., 125, 132–3, 137–8, 149–51, 175, 187

Serno-Solovevich, V., 13

Severo-Dvinsk Provincial Committee, 98

sexual composition of the party, see social composition

Shaumyan, S., 75

Shelavin, K., 118, 121

Shklovski, V., 122

Shlikhter, A., 78

Shlyapnikov, A., 57, 119, 141, 144–5, 150–7, 165, 181, 184, 198, 210

Siberia, 78, 85, 112; the Siberian Bureau, 104–5

Simbirsk, 93, 120, 192; its Provincial Committee, 108, 147–8, 171–2

single-party government, 68–9, 88–9, 137, 160–1

Skvortsov-Stepanov, I., 153

Smilga, I., 154–5, 209

Smolensk, 164; its Provincial Committee, 118, 121–2, 139, 146, 169; its Soviet Provincial Executive Committee, 139

Smolyaninov, V., 139

social composition of the party: class background, 25, 30, 43–5, 70–1, 90, 116, 141, 148, 165–7; sexual composition, 45, 116–17, 167; national background, 45, 167

'socialist consciousness', 22–3, 45, 118–19, 146, 168–9

Socialist-Revolutionaries, 17, 22, 26, 33, 39–42, 46, 48–9, 62–3, 67, 76, 84–5, 88, 115, 151, 160–1

soldiers, 26, 38, 66, 86–7, 95–6, 134–7

Solts, A., 153

Sominskaya, F., 118–19

South-west Regional Committee, 56, 72

soviets, 26, 41-2, 64-5, 87, *see also* party-soviet relations

Sovnarkom, 63-8, 75-6, 78-9, 81, 85, 87-8, 94, 122, 161, 178

Spain, 12

Special Department, *see* Secretariat

Stalin, I., 38, 209-11; in the months around the October Revolution, 57-9; in the Civil War, 86, 102, 123-5; in the Polish-Soviet war and in the 'trade union controversy', 134, 143, 155; as organisational leader under NEP, 161, 163, 175-80, 182, 186; in the struggle of 1923 with the Left Opposition, 189-99

Stasova, E., 58, 75, 77, 103, 123, 125, 132-3, 137, 209

State Duma, *see* Duma

Stockholm, 27

Stolypin, P., 28, 66-7, 199

strikes, *see* labour unrest

suburb committees, 51-2, 74, 96, 170

Sverdlova, K., 103, 108-9, 125

Sverdlov, Y., 43; before the October Revolution, 58, 60-1; helps to form Soviet government, 69, 74-5, 77-8, 81-2; in the Civil War, 102-3, 105-6, 109, 209

Sviyazhk, 86

Switzerland, 17, 19, 21, 27, 35

Taganrog, 79-80

Tambov Provincial Committee, 171

Tambov revolt, 137, 161

Tashkent, 71

Tersy, 77

Tomski, M., 175

town committees, 50-4, 70, 72-4, 91, 96-8, 104, 170-1

'trade union controversy', 148-57, 175, 181, 188

Transcaucasus, 64, 167

Treaty of Brest-Litovsk, *see* Brest-Litovsk

'troika', the, 179, 187-99, 210

Trotski, L., 209-10; before the October Revolution, 23, 39, 58; in the Brest-Litovsk dispute, 67, 74; in the Civil War, 85-6, 91, 124-5, 127, 131; in the Polish-Soviet war, 134-7, 140, 143; in the 'trade union controversy', 148-55; as opponent of NEP, 161-3, 175-6, 179-82; leads the struggle of 1923 against the 'troika', 185-99

Trusov (of Astrakhan), 73-4

Tsaritsyn, 80, 172; its Town Committee, 51, 81

Tula, 96, 115, 118, 137, 140, 146, 150, 168, 170; its District Committee, 122; its Provincial Committee, 142

Turkestan, 98; its Central Committee, 99, 105; its Turkkomissia, 105

Turkey, 40

Tver Provincial Committee, 171

Ufa, 132

Ufimtsev, N., 186

Ukraine, 56, 64, 68, 78-9, 83, 85-6, 112, 131, 134-5, 137, 144, 148, 167; its Central Committee, 100, 105, 127-8

United Opposition, 210

United States of America, 85, 102, 161, 202, *see also* the Allies

Urals, 11, 69, 78, 85-6, 105, 112, 172; its Regional Committee, 56, 70, 79, 104-5, 150; its Urals-Siberian Bureau, 123

Vareikis, I., 108-9, 127, 172-3

Vasilev, M., 77

Vladimir, 173

Vladivostok, 85

Volga, 55, 85-6, 93

Vologda, 73

Volunteer Army, 85, *see* Denikin, Wrangel

Voronezh Provincial Committee, 128

Vrachev, S., 195

VTsIK, 65, 75-6, 103

Vyatka, 146, 152, 168, 174, 192, 199

Vyborg Suburb Committee, *see* Petrograd

wage differentials, 115, 118-19, 140-2, 144-5, 149-51, 162-3

War Communism, 85–9, 112–15, 134–7
war-industrial committees, 33
Warsaw, 134
Weber, M., 34, 200–2
White occupation, Bolshevik organisation under, 122–3
Workers' and Peasants' Red Army, *see* Red Army
Workers' and Peasants' Socialist Party, 163, 165
Workers' Group, 163, 165
Workers' Opposition, 133, 141–2, 144–6, 149–57, 163–5, 167, 180–2, 198, 209–10
Workers' Truth, 163, 165
working class, urban, 14, 16, 22, 26, 31, 37–8, 40–2, 65–9, 87–8, 114–15, 136–7, 162–3, 185, 202–3
Wrangel, 135

Yakovleva, V., 81

Yaroslavl, 81, 85; its Provincial Committee, 117
Yaroslavski, E., 153, 175–6, 194
Yudenich, G., 112, 115–16, 121
Yukhnov District Committee, 139

Zalutski, P., 57
Zavyalova, K., 143
Zimmerwald, 36
Zinoviev, G., 31, 35, 210–11; before the October Revolution, 57–8; demands broad coalition, 63–4, 74–5; in the Civil War, 89, 109–10, 124, 135; as 'reformer' in the disputes of 1920–1, 142–6, 149–51, 155–6; as proponent of NEP, 163, 175, 179, 181, 186; in the struggle of 1923 with the Left Opposition, 188–93, 195
Zorin, S., 146, 172–3
Zubov, V., 170

This is no ordinary book about the Bolsheviks. It eschews the temptation to focus exclusively upon the lives and opinions of a few leading figures such as Lenin, Stalin and Trotski.

Its theme is the party's bureaucratisation. Robert Service directs our eyes to every link in the organisational chain stretching from the central party apparatus at the apex, through the many local levels of authority down to the party cells and rank and file members at the base. He draws upon a wide array of previously unexamined sources. His aim is to show us how the anarchistic, democratic features of party life in 1917 came to be thrown over by the rigid authoritarianism of 1923. His conclusion is that the change did not proceed simply from the designs of hardline central leaders. Just as important, as Robert Service shows, was the reaction of the great mass of Bolshevik officialdom to the immensity of the economic, political and administrative problems facing the October Revolution from its very first day. There are no true heroes in his narrative (though he helps us to understand the bewildering complexity of the officials' dilemmas at local as well as central levels). The victims, he argues, were those thousands of working-class members joining the party in 1917 with unbounded hopes of redressing all the wrongs suffered by them in past decades.

This highly readable book will be welcomed by historians, sociologists and political scientists alike. Throughout its pages it maintains a fine balance between the various economic, social, political and ideological factors at work inside the party. In addition it refers us to a wider world of ideas about mass organisations than has previously been applied to Bolshevik history.

Robert Service is Lecturer in Russian Stu the University of Keele. He was educated Northampton Grammar School and King' College, Cambridge, where he took a degr Russian and Ancient Greek literature. He for his M.A. in Soviet government and po at the University of Essex before complet Ph.D., which involved several months' stu Leningrad State University.